AF597497

MICROCOMPUTER APPLICATIONS DEVELOPMENT
TECHNIQUES FOR EVALUATION AND IMPLEMENTATION

Michael Simon Bodner, Ph.D. and
Pamela Kay Hutchins

TAB Professional and Reference Books

Division of TAB BOOKS Inc.
P.O. Box 40, Blue Ridge Summit, PA 17214

This work is dedicated to the spirit of Dagney Taggart

FIRST EDITION

FIRST PRINTING

Printed in the United States of America

Library of Congress Cataloging in Publication Data

Bodner, Michael Simon.
Microcomputer applications development.

Includes index.
1. Computer networks. 2. Local area networks
(Computer networks) I. Hutchins, Pamela Kay. II. Title.
TK5105.5.B6 1987 004.6 86-30008
ISBN 0-8306-2840-1

Contents

Trademark Recognitions

1-2-3 is a registered trademark of Lotus Development Corp.
3COM+, Ethershare, and Etherprint are registered trademarks of 3COM Corp.
APPLE II and Macintosh are registered trademarks of Apple Computer, Inc.
Better Basic is a registered trademark of Summit Software Technology, Inc.
Business BASIC and Open Systems are registered trademarks of Open Systems, Inc.
Business BASIC Extended is a registered trademark of Basis Inc.
C-TERP is a registered trademark of Gimpel Software.
C86 is a registered trademark of Computer Innovations, Inc.
Clipper is a registered trademark of Nantucket, Inc.
Colossus is a registered trademark of IBIS Research Labs, Inc.
CP/M is a registered trademark of Digital Research, Inc.
Crosstalk and Transporter are registered trademarks of Microstuff, Inc.
DAC-EASY is a registered trademark of DAC Software, Inc.
Dan Bricklin's Demo Program is a registered trademark of Software Garden, Inc.
Data Based Advisor is a registered trademark of Data Based Solutions, Inc.
DataEase is a registered trademark of Software Solutions, Inc.
DataFlex is a registered trademark of Data Access Corp.
Datatower is a registered trademark of Priam Corporation.
DB-MAN is a registered trademark of Versasoft Corp.
dBASE II, dBASE III PLUS, and Multimate are registered trademarks of Ashton-Tate.
DBIII Compiler and DBXL are registered trademarks of Wordtech Systems, Inc.
dFlow is a registered trademark of Wallsoft Systems, Inc.
Flash-up and Flashcode are registered trademarks of The Software Bottling Company of NY, Inc.
Genifer is a registered trademark of Bytel Corp.
IBM,IBM-PC/XT/AT, PC-DOS, BASICA, TOPVIEW, IBM BASIC Compiler, and DisplayWrite are registered trademarks of International Business Machines Corp.

IRMA is a registered trademark of Digital Communications Associates, Inc.
Knowledgeman is a registered trademark of Micro Data Base Systems, Inc.
Lattice C and Sidetalk are registered trademarks of Lattice, Inc.
M.B.S.I Accounting is a registered trademark of Realworld Corp.
MEGABASIC is a registered trademark of American Planning Corp.
MS-DOS, Windows, MS-Word, Gwbasic, Quickbasic, Microsoft C, and Multiplan are registered trademarks of Microsoft Corp.
Netware and Advanced Netware are registered trademarks of Novell, Inc.
Norton Utilities is a registered trademark of Peter Norton Computing Company.
Paradox is a registered trademark of ANSA Software.
pfs:file and pfs:write are registered trademarks of Software Publishing Corp.
Pro Search Window is a registered trademark of Bodner, Hutchins & Assoc., Inc.
Professional Basic is a registered trademark of Morgan Computing Co., Inc.
Quickcode, Quickindex, and Quickreport are registered trademarks of Fox & Geller, Inc.
R:base 5000 is a registered trademark of Microrim, Inc.
Six Pack Plus is a registered trademark of AST Research, Inc.
Superkey, Turbo Pascal, and Sidekick are registered trademarks of Borland International, Inc.
Tiara Multilink is a registered trademark of Tiara Computer Systems, Inc.
Timeslips is a registered trademark of North Edge Software Corp.
TRUE BASIC is a registered trademark of TRUE BASIC, Inc.
UCSD Pascal is a registered trademark of Softech, Inc.
UNIX and C are registered trademarks of AT&T Bell Labs.
WATCOM BASIC is a registered trademark of Watcom Products, Inc.
Wordfinder is a registered trademark of Writing Consultants, a Division of Microlytics.
WordStar is a registered trademark of Micropro International Corp.

Acknowledgments

The preparation of a manuscript is a task far more difficult than one who has never done it can imagine. This is our first book and we wish to thank several parties who have helped us.

First, we offer thanks to Ron Powers of TAB BOOKS, Inc. for having enough faith in two first-time authors to give them a chance. The book was accepted from two chapters and an outline, and we were both surprised and delighted. Ron has been helpful, encouraging, and professional.

Second, we would like to thank each other. We have worked hard, and coauthoring is a little like gladitorial conflict mixed with partnership. We hope that enough of each of us is in the book to give you a clear sense of our orientations and opinions.

Third, we recognize our families, friends, and dear ones who had to be so patient with us as the pressures, panics, and euphoria came and went. You are the reason that we do such things. To my sons, Sacha and Zachary Bodner, I thank you for living.

Finally, thank you to all of the software vendors who provided assistance on products to evaluate for inclusion in this book. We hope that the readers will find our reviews informative and helpful, and will buy thousands of copies of their products.

Introduction

This book is a combination of the two authors' different approaches to a single set of problems. Subjects are covered from the technical orientation of one author and the business, organizational and management approach of the other. There is no assumption as to the reader's expertise in either area. Some of the information is historical, some reads like a cookbook, and other parts convey our experiences.

Our industry is going through either a major readjustment or a minor correction, depending on your point of view. Computers are rapidly becoming a permanent fixture of corporate and institutional life. The software industry is rich with a variety of development tools and a diverse set of standard application systems such as spreadsheets, database management systems, and word processors. Hardware grows more powerful and less expensive daily. Opportunities are emerging for consultants and application developers.

This book is an outgrowth of an article originally titled "Application Programming—Planning, Development, and Execution" and ultimately published as "Plan Before You Plunge" in the March, 1986, issue of *Data Based Advisor*. The response to the article and a number of discussions with our colleagues in the software and application development industry led to the belief that a book of this type would be of interest.

We are part of an emerging sub-industry that is attracting a great many highly creative people with very strong technical skills but little or no business and project-management training. The only way to be successful in this highly competitive arena is to have a good mix of technical and business skills. However, many consulting companies are one- or two-person operations, thinly capitalized, and poorly planned. Many developers do not understand even the most fundamental concepts of business, law or project management, and thus are doomed to failure even though they are technically adept. While every developer imagines that they will create the next Lotus, the reality is often much more harsh.

We have brought to this work our own experience, knowledge, and opinions. To this we have added information that we hope will help as you become successful application developers and consultants.

Chapter 1

The New Environment for Application Development

The microcomputer industry has grown in the last decade from an infancy characterized by kits, games, and hackers to a middle age characterized by the actual incorporation of microcomputers into the institutional fabric of corporate America. The rapid growth of the industry is due to two major factors: the ever-increasing power of the hardware and software, and the linear decrease in the cost of the systems.

HISTORY

The earliest microcomputers were 8-bit "kit" systems such as Altair, IMSAI, and Polymorphics. Based on the Intel 8080 chip, with memory available in the 4K to 16K range, these machines were little more than elaborate high-tech toys for hard-core "techno-kids." Building a kit was a major undertaking, both economically and temporally. The finished product could flash binary lights, punch paper tape, and in some cases, read primitive BASIC from a cassette tape so that the game of NIM could be played. Even as hundreds of "kitters" were showing off their home-made electronic wonders, the dreamers of the corporate world (Yes, there are dreamers there!) were beginning to wonder about the possible applications of these curiosities.

The Intel 8080 was actually quite a good microprocessor. It

could address 64K of memory, had strong input/output capability and was going into mass production. A defacto standard operating system, CP/M, was developed, and low-cost, relatively high-speed magnetic storage was introduced. The floppy disk, system "bootstrap" software, and true languages opened the microcomputer to serious, if still elementary, applications. The Apple II, the first appliance computer, was developed around this time. The term "appliance" is used because the Apple was sold as a ready-to-use microcomputer, without the kit-building requirement. With an Apple, a user could purchase an entire system, take it home, plug it in, attach a TV, and play StarTrek or Breakout. Apple even included Integer BASIC on Read Only Memory (ROM), so that the user could begin to program immediately. Its creators, Steven Wozniak and Steven Jobs, who supposedly prototyped their first version on an apple crate, became the embodiment of the American Dream, coming from a garage to a multi-billion dollar Fortune 500 company.

The early days of the industry were full of hype. "Home Computers for all!" "A computer in every kitchen!" Tandy, ATARI, Commodore and others rushed into the market. Tens of thousands of computers were purchased in this early frenzy. Tens of thousands of these computers now reside in attics and at the bottom of closets. The hype was in fact just that. The home computer market was a bubble waiting to burst—which it did, taking hundreds of millions of dollars with it.

Meanwhile, deep in the workings of the most conservative corporate computer company, planners proposed that there might be a market for small office machines based on a new microprocessor, the Intel 8088. This was a 16-bit chip, allowing for more memory, higher speed, and thus more business applications. IBM put a group of innovators together in far-away Boca Raton, Florida and in record time for a giant company (less than two years) the IBM PC was born. The three little letters on the faceplate brought corporate America running.

As a side note it is interesting to look at one of the compromises made in the design of the IBM PC. The 8088 chip was a version of the 8086 chip that allowed for the use of 8-bit memory on the 16-bit chip. This meant that 16-bit data needed to be passed to the bus in two 8-bit chunks, effectively cutting the processor speed in half. Yet, at that time 8-bit memory chips were more available, thus less expensive than the 16-bit Random Access Memory (RAM) chips. IBM thus decided on the less efficient processor. The most remarkable aspect of this machine was that it had an open architecture that enabled third-party hardware and software vendors to jump on the bus. There was 16K, a cassette port, and BASIC on

Read Only Memory (ROM), ideas borrowed from Apple.

IBM made an agreement with Microsoft to provide a new operating system, PC-DOS, for the PC. Analysts were aghast because the entire industry at that time had adopted the CP/M standard and there were simply no applications written in DOS. Nevertheless, within the first year PC-DOS grew revisions, and added path names, pipes, and a number of UNIX-like appendages. Microsoft's DOS was adapted by many other manufacturers jumping on the 8088 bandwagon. MS-DOS, the non-IBM PC-DOS, grew. Applications that did not specifically use calls to machine-specific Read Only Memory BASIC Input/Output System (ROM BIOS) programs could run on all MS-DOS and PC-DOS machines. Hardware manufacturers conforming to the IBM bus structure could make use of the variety of third-party, add-on boards and peripherals.

This resulted in the development of a defacto standard for what had been an immature and erratic industry. The standard might not have been the best technology available, but it was a standard. Hundreds of thousands of PCs were sold. In those early days small companies producing PC compatible add-on cards popped up everywhere, each assured of an exponentially growing market. One small group, manufacturing memory combinations cards, supplied up to 512K (then 640K) with clocks, serial ports, and such. It was run by three really bright and hardworking guys named Albert, Safi, and Tom. Today users are probably familiar with their company name of AST Research, Inc.

It is important to note that these third-party vendors pushed the PC far beyond where IBM wanted it to go. Big Blue was selling 16K memory expansion cards and single-sided low-density drives, while companies like AST Research were selling 512K memory cards and Davong was selling 10 megabyte hard disk subsystems. While IBM was selling a noisy, slow Epson printer, dozens of vendors introduced high-speed matrix and letter-quality printers.

Software developers are also motivated by profits. Millions of users with standard systems means astronomical revenue from the potential market share of a successful software product. Lotus 1-2-3, the first superstar of the PC revolution, is an example. It was reviewed in the *Wall Street Journal* months before its release and presold in hundreds of computer stores. The company came from nowhere, took on VisiCalc, the industry standard, (credited with giving the 8-bit microcomputers a reason to be accepted by business) and rapidly became a publicly traded corporation with profits in the tens of millions.

Visicorp, which owned VisiCalc, faded. There were other failures as well. Programs that failed to adapt to the strengths of

MS-DOS and the PC environment did not make it. The cold realities of the corporate world struck the industry hard; there are only a few windows of the type that Lotus used. The mid-eighties saw a trimming of the computer industry. The standards became firmly entrenched. The "easy" sales were over. Computer retail stores which needed high profit margins to underwrite the level of user support required in the pre-standard days lost business to discounters and mail-order houses. The microcomputers and the software had become commodities. Asian PC clones that were entirely acceptable to users at a much lower price flooded the market. In some cities today a user can purchase a PC clone with 640K RAM, two drives, and a monochrome display for less than $700. The lower cost makes systems viable to an ever-increasing number of users.

CURRENT STATE OF THE INDUSTRY

Software standards have emerged as well. Lotus has over 90 percent of the spreadsheet market, Ashton-Tate dominates the database management world, and WordStar, Multimate, and DisplayWrite share the word-processing scene. Several accounting systems, such as Open Systems, Real World, BPI and DAC, dominate the market. There is also an extremely rich language environment in this industry. Compilers exist for C, Pascal, Fortran, COBOL, BASIC, Modula, and even Ada. Programming languages are included with dBASE, R:base, and a number of other database management systems. In some cases, full compilers are available for these procedural languages. An example is Nantucket's Clipper for dBASE III.

Application developers have written a large number of vertical market packages using the PC and DOS—from medical office systems to geophysical data logging. Many of these applications rival systems running on the minicomputer systems of a decade ago. In fact, the environment has been pushed to the very limits of the technology itself. Some systems, such as Microsoft Windows, which introduce very high-resolution, bit-mapped graphics and multi-tasking to this environment, actually go beyond the limit of the lowly 8088. But fear not! The 80286—a faster, more capable chip—has arrived. With the 80286, multi-tasking is supported using a true memory management module on the chip. While the current versions of DOS do not yet address the true computing power of the chip, it is only a matter of time before this power will be unleashed to a power-hungry world.

Intel, Microsoft, and others are committed to the upward standardization of software and hardware, but the time is coming when evolution will give rise to new species. Soon applications will be written that may not run on the older machines, because they may use aspects of the advanced chips that cannot be emulated on the older chips. This may be a rude awakening for some and a hard pill to swallow for the industry at large, but it is necessary. Developers were told at a recent seminar that Microsoft will guarantee that programs written in the Windows environment will port to the advanced machines without change. This is quite an inducement to write in Windows, but also implies a broad incompatibility for all other applications when the 80286 advanced features are added.

An industry based on evolution must of course continue to evolve, and the future is bright. Even more powerful chips, such as the 32-bit Intel 80386, will begin to appear in machines in 1987. Such chips blur the distinction between the microcomputers and the minicomputers, causing radical changes in the corporate world. Communications systems will link PCs into Local Area Networks and, through gateways, into mainframe-based systems. This will give the user a level of system integration never before considered—from the desktop PC workstation to the corporate mainframe and back.

These developments will place great pressure on application programmers, driven by an ever more hungry user community that can buy more and more computing power for less and less money. Users who now say "What do I need a computer for?" will soon be saying "How could I have lived without one!" and the ever-popular "Wouldn't it be nice if it could . . ."

Music to the developer's ears.

Chapter 2

Marketing in the New Environment

Silicon technology has a built-in economic cycle that loads research and development costs into early product shipments, leading to an ever-declining cost as the products are shipped in larger volumes. This is most noticeable in products such as microcomputers and their peripherals.

As user demands grew, memory-expansion cards, double-sided and double-density floppy disks, hard disks, tape backup systems and more were introduced. When the IBM PC came out it supported only 64K, five slots for expansion cards, a 63-watt power supply and a cassette port. This positioned it squarely against the Apple II+, making little use of its 16-bit processor and larger address space. Apparently, even IBM was not sure where the PC was going because it offered small, single-function, memory-expansion cards at prices similar to the multifunction cards offered by Techmar and AST. Although the PC's standard language, BASICA, could only address 64K, and applications could make use of little more, thousands of users bought the memory-expansion cards and stuffed their machines to the maximum.

THE INFLUENCE OF THIRD-PARTY DEVELOPERS

Third-party vendors moved in to expand the memory capability beyond the minimums offered by IBM. While BASIC and most early PC applications could only use 64K of memory, companies like AST were selling cards that could expand the memory far beyond that. AST knew that if more users had more memory, more developers would write code to make use of that memory. As applications demanded 256K or 512K, users would need to buy still more memory cards from AST. The major hurdle was justifying the purchase of the cards before the applications arrived.

In a stroke of innovative genius, AST bundled a set of software programs that made use of the extra memory. One, a print-spooler, allowed the user to print data to memory and return quickly. While the user continued to work on other tasks, the print-spool memory gradually passed the document to the printer. Because the early printers were slow, print-spoolers made sense. Also, the PC is single-tasking, and this Random Access Memory (RAM) print-spooler made it seem to do two things at once.

The second software package that was bundled with the large memory cards was a RAM disk-emulation program, enabling the user to set up a simulated floppy disk in RAM, give it a logical designator, and use it exactly as if he had a third floppy drive. Most PC's had one or two floppy drives at best, and extra drives cost over $500, so this simulated drive had great economic advantage. Its primary advantage, however, was speed. RAM reads and writes are many times faster than those of floppy drives.

It thus became reasonable for an end-user to buy these memory sizes, because these were clear, immediate advantages, and—when new applications arrived—the user would be ready. These methods made it possible for programs like Lotus 1-2-3 to have a wide range of potential customers who already had 512K machines. Similar tactics are being used in the marketing of the new generation of memory cards for the 80286 machines.

Nevertheless, even the maximum memory supported by the PC shows IBM's shortsightedness. Although the 8088 processor can address over one million bytes of memory, IBM set the top of usable memory at 640K. Above this there is a patchwork quilt of memory regions, some defined to screen displays, others to ROM functions. This limit became a major issue, and several other vendors merged forces to produce an enhanced memory specification, using bank selection and other tricks, to expand the user's memory space.

As millions of PCs were delivered, and millions of peripherals followed, the market responded. Everything became less expensive, and many vendors rushed in with "clones" of the standard IBM PC. As the prices dropped, the hardware became more powerful. Memory chips got faster and denser, allowing first 56K and then 640K to be placed on the motherboard of the PC itself. Hard disks went from a "power user" option to becoming nearly standard. For example, several years ago a 10-megabyte disk cost about $1500 with a disk controller card. Today comparable hard disks (with controller cards) can be had for one-fourth of that price. The early disk-driver software needed to be patched into DOS; the later DOS versions took them for granted. Today the disks have dropped in size and power requirements to the point where anyone can purchase a 30-megabyte disk on a card that fits into an expansion slot and automatically configures itself. Similar examples of power going up as price goes down can be made across the microcomputer market spectrum, from printers to telecommunications.

A NEW CLASS OF USERS

Declining hardware and software prices, coupled with increases in raw computing power and capacity, opened the market to a larger number of potential users. The first phase of this process is now coming to an end. There was a retail "boom" in PC sales, generating a near frenzy across the market. Hundreds of computer stores popped up everywhere, and tens of thousands of users lined up to hear the salesman's promises of "the wonders of automation." Competition lowered the prices, the systems became easier to configure, and the products began to lend themselves to the "commodity" style of marketing previously used in mail-order photographic and stereo sales. The sad fact, however, is that computers are not as simple to use as cameras and VCRs. The user is typically a business person of some intelligence, fairly sure that he can bring the system up himself—"It can't be so hard, because Joe did it, and I'm smarter than he is." He purchases his computer, monitor, printer, modem and software, gets it back to his office, and then gets the feeling that he might be in too deep.

The typical microcomputer end-user group lacks data-processing experience. They have purchased the system lured by the claims of easy installation and use: high power with low economic impact. Many of the software packages have simple step-by-step installation procedures—and even on-disk tutorials—but first, the user must bring up the system. This is no small task. If he wanted to lower costs, as is often the case, he will have a number of different components from different vendors.

Hardware needs to be unpacked, configured, and installed. Switches need to be set, configuration files need to be set up, clocks set, cables placed, and a hundred little tasks can "just pop up." As a case in point, the cost of an accounting system on a PC can be as low as $69.95, but the human and organizational costs can be 50 times that, just in setting up. The salesman was truthful when he said "sure it can do that," but it wasn't quite the whole truth. Because these end-users are new to computing and data-processing methods and procedures, the results are often catastrophic. Most end-user companies are too small to support professional data-processing staffs, and in fact do not need such people after the system is up and running. There is thus a large class of users who could make excellent use of professional computer consultants during implementation to set up, train, define and develop applications, and to ease the transition from a manual to an automated system.

CONSULTANTS AS APPLICATION DEVELOPERS

Where there is a need there is often a way. A new type of service company is developing—consultants and application developers for this new class of microcomputer users. Thousands of unsophisticated end-users would be willing to contract professional expertise to aid in the acquisition, installation, and integration of the new technologies into their existing systems. The economics of using such professionals is appealing. The consultant may help avoid costly mistakes, save time by doing the initial setup and system integration, and can act as a training resource until the client's staff comes up to speed.

Above all, the consultant is able to make dBASE III, for example, do exactly what the user wants it to do. Although "the salesman said it could do it," someone has to write the code, and design and implement the application. The businessman does not want to learn how to program. He wants information processed in a way to help him run his business. He wants reports, invoices, forms and such, and he does not have the time or desire to write code. Hiring a consultant should be the shortest path to a finished, debugged system.

With such a large market, and such a clearly defined need, it is not surprising that a large number of professional programmers are getting the entrepreneurial "bug" and forming consulting firms. First, however, there are a series of business decisions to be made.

BUSINESS ISSUES IN COMPANY STARTUPS

Whether you decide to do only programming or to do other microcomputer consulting, the change in work habits can be drastic.

Developers who currently schedule their own time may have a much easier transition than those who come from the 9-to-5 world. To be free from structure sounds very enticing, but consider that now time spent working will directly affect your income. Before leaving a current job, try to save up at least six months' salary to be used as a backup during slow months.

Often no development can be done during business hours, with phones ringing and marketing calls to be made. Large application projects require uninterrupted work to meet the scheduled deadlines, forcing you to work evenings and possibly weekends. In between projects there might be a day or two to relax, but this is still a major effect on your life-style. Sometimes it is hard to separate work from private life, especially if the office is in the home. If it is to be a one-person company, time will be at a premium. Time should be scheduled for correspondence, accounting, marketing and other administrative duties. If there are partners, these responsibilities can be shared, but good administrative and organizational skills are still a must if this is to be your main source of income.

MARKET DEFINITION

Working in the microcomputer environment can be very rewarding both professionally and financially. There are hundreds of directions a developer can go within programming languages, vertical markets, system designs and training alone. If you are familiar with any of these areas, limit yourself to that area first to help establish some income and a client base.

Consider how a developer experienced in dBASE accounting programs for the construction industry might define his market. Because he is familiar with the computing needs of the construction industry he should approach other construction-related companies to offer his services and experience. Most vertical markets have the same computer needs and problems, just varying in size. The developer can approach these companies with the confidence needed to market himself well.

Once comfortable with marketing, the developer can target other vertical markets, establishing a client base along the way. Constant marketing is the key to any company, but is essential to application/consulting firms. Once enough projects are in progress to pay bills and salaries, it will be very easy for any developer to sit back and do what he enjoys the most: application development. But beware—even though a completed program is satisfying, it does not support a bank account for the future months. It's much easier to market when the money isn't crucial.

MARKETING

While defining a primary market, other areas of potential revenue might become apparent. With the constant change in the microcomputer environment, it would be wise to have additional markets to fall back on.

A brochure is a vital marketing piece for any service business, and application development is no exception. It is not prudent to be elaborate or expensive on the first one, because it will probably have to be modified soon. All new businesses have to be flexible, and having five thousand brochures makes that very difficult. A company's first brochure can look professional without costing a fortune. Use an 8 1/2-by-11 inch sheet of paper which, folded into thirds, allows for six sides of information. If six sides can't be filled, reduce the paper to 7 1/2-by-8 inches. Fold it in half and you now have four panels. The front panel should be reserved for the company name, address, and telephone number. Services can be listed on inside panels, with the back panel containing a capsulized biography. The developer will be required to do a rough layout of each one.

Have the brochure typeset and printed by a printer. Printing looks professional and does not have to be expensive if the design is kept simple. A price sheet should be separate and used as an insert. In many cases this will be the first thing that a potential client will see about the business. We have included our brochure as an example in Fig. 2-1.

The objective of marketing is to increase sales. You must convince people that you are an expert in your field and that they must have your services. Everything should be professional, from your appearance to any printed materials, or you might not even get a foot in the door. There are many ways to market, but you must determine which ones best suit your business and personality.

NETWORKING

"Networking" became one of the key words among salespeople in the '80s. It is the most pleasurable and least aggressive of all forms of marketing, because clients are usually approached on a one-to-one basis in a casual atmosphere ranging from breakfast clubs to large association gatherings. Making contacts is vital to any service company, but the cold fact about networking is that only a small market share can be contacted on such a personal basis. The developer may find this arena very valuable for information about small-company startup "how-to's" from people who have already been through it. Also, suppliers can be established for such needs as printers, office supplies, and equipment. Networking is not recommended as a primary marketing approach, but instead as a supplemental strategy.

Fig. 2-1(A). Inside panel for four-sided brochure.

BODNER, HUTCHINS & ASSOCIATES, INC.

BODNER, HUTCHINS & ASSOCIATES, INC.

High Technology Consultants

High Technology Consultants

Recent advances in computer technology have brought to end users remarkable power at affordable cost. Powerful development tools never before available for systems users enable a wide variety of applications using microcomputers. Using professional application development programmers as consultants is often the most efficient method for a non technical user to utilize the economic and performance advantages of this technology.

CUSTOM PROGRAMMING
FOR MICROCOMPUTERS

- dBase (Interpreted and Compiled)
- Lotus
- Basic (Interpreted and Compiled)
- FORTRAN
- PASCAL
- C

DATA COMMUNICATIONS

- Microcomputer/Mainframe Gateways
- Local Area Networks
- Asynchronous Information Systems
- In House Information Distribution Systems

SYSTEM ANALYSIS AND EVALUATION

- Technical Comparisons of Vendor Proposals
- Economic Comparisons of Vendor Proposals
- Custom Designs

TRAINING IN NEW TECHNOLOGIES

- Corporate Seminars
- User Training
- Technical Training

Bodner, Hutchins & Associates clients include major banks, political parties, news and traffic services, hospitals and construction companies.

DIRECT MAIL

In contrast with networking, direct-mail efforts are limited only by the size of a mailing list. With the help of computers, direct mail has now become a major part of many marketing strategies. Most of this mail very rarely gets opened because of the abundance that arrives each day. Because the average acknowledgment rate can be as low as 1 percent, some guidelines are recommended for a higher return.

Mail Lists

A mailing list should be as *qualified* as possible. The source

Fig. 2-1(B). Front panel for four-sided brochure.

BODNER, HUTCHINS & ASSOCIATES, INC.

BODNER, HUTCHINS & ASSOCIATES, INC.

PRINCIPALS

High Technology Consultants

Pamela Kay Hutchins attended Oklahoma State University where she studied Liberal Arts. She then went on to be a flight attendant for United Airlines. After extensive training on the Sabre Computer System and the Lufthansa System she became Manager of the Corporate Accounts Departments for several travel agencies. Ms. Hutchins joined Comnet, a microcomputer local area networking company based in Houston in 1983. For Comnet she developed branch offices in Austin and El Paso, and then went on to become Director of Administrative Operations at Comnet's Corporate center in Houston. Ms. Hutchins is now the President of Bodner, Hutchins & Associates, Inc., and is involved in systems evaluations, quality control, user interfacing and client account relations.

While at Comnet she aided Dr. Bodner in the design and development of an in house Management Information System written in dBase running on a LAN. She also was responsible for the development and implementation of a series of professional seminars given by Dr. Bodner in Houston, Austin and El Paso.

• • • • •

Dr. Michael Simon Bodner received his Ph.D. in Theoretical Physics from St. John's University in 1975. He has been a University Professor, Radio and Television talk show guest, a visiting scientist at NASA, and a microcomputer consultant since 1976. Dr. Bodner has extensive experience in scientific programming, data communications, data base management systems, local area networks, mainframe to microcomputer interfacing and a variety of programming languages. He has spent the last few years in the design and development of microcomputer local area network systems for businesses and institutions, as well as giving seminars on the new technologies. Dr. Bodner has recently been named to Who's Who in the Southwest.

Dr. Bodner and Ms. Hutchins formed Bodner, Hutchins & Associates, Inc., in June 1985 to focus their efforts on high technology consulting, programming and systems evaluations and analysis.

"The known is finite, the unknown infinite; intellectually we stand on an islet in the midst of an illimitable ocean of inexplicabiltiy. Our business in every generation is to reclaim a little more land, to add something to the extent and solidity of our possessions."

Thomas Henry Huxley on the Reception of the "Origin of Species" (1887)

"The eternal mystery of the world is its comprehensibility."

Albert Einstein (1936)

2300 Old Spanish Trail
Suite 2105
Houston, Texas 77054
713-797-0007

of the mailing list is directly related to any response. Many lists may be available for free or for a small processing charge from associations, publications, or a local chamber of commerce, but be advised that in this case quantity is not necessarily better than quality. For example, you can get a list of every business in your immediate zip-code area—about 1,000 names. This may sound wonderful, but with closer examination you may find that most have names like "Joe's Auto Repair" and "Betty's Beauty Parlor." Many small businesses that do not need and cannot afford your services will be found on lists as general as this one. You may decide to use the list for possible local exposure, but it is likely that the mailer will be found in more trash cans than in the hands of potential clients.

As a second example, assume that the developer is familiar with accounting packages for the construction industry. He investigates and finds that there is an association of people who work in the construction industry. Through networking he is probably a member already, making access to a list quite simple. If not, he might have to pay a small fee to purchase the names. This list might have only 250 names, but these are qualified people and therefore potential clients. The developer's flyer can now be directed at this market for more response and less throw-away.

Contact Names

Most direct mail pieces are thrown out because they are addressed to titles such as "Data-Processing Manager." This can be as offensive as receiving "occupant" mail at home. Many secretaries throw this generic mail away without it even touching their bosses' desks. The more a developer can personalize a mailing the better. The qualified list discussed in the previous example might already have contact names because it was based on association membership. Once again, this type of list proves its worth by saving a busy developer some time. If no names are listed, more work is required before anything can be mailed.

Getting a contact name is very simple but does require effort. If the list does not include telephone numbers, a handy local telephone book will suffice. A telephone book would not be practical if the list were not qualified in some way. One call should get the name and title of a contact. Do not be overwhelmed by the number of calls needed for a large list. These types of calls can be spaced out over a period of weeks so daily work is not completely disrupted.

Follow-Up Calls

Personalize the information mailed as much as possible and state that the recipient will be telephoned within the next ten business days to answer any questions. The importance of this follow-up call cannot be over-emphasized.

You now have a company name, a qualified contact within that company, and a reason for calling. You can now get to this person more easily, in regard to literature sent specifically to the contact. Once you verify that the literature was received and answer any questions, qualify the contact to establish the need and set up an appointment. If this company is not interested, perhaps they know of another company that might be. The developer must ask. Turn a lead into another prospect.

This approach of combining direct mail with telemarketing is much more successful and enjoyable than treating each separately. A direct-mail piece will probably not sell a developer's services, but can be used as an entree into an otherwise closed company. However, this approach takes time. The developer must make sure to control the number of follow-up calls.

Financial Considerations

With a possible 1 percent return rate, many small firms cannot afford the high costs that can be associated with direct-mail operations. Printing costs may range from as low as $50 to several hundred dollars depending on the quality of paper stock, inks, or special artwork desired. Bulk-mail permits will help with mailing costs, but can only be considered if at least 200 pieces are mailed each time the permit number is used. The setup cost of a bulk-mail permit is $100, which will enable the developer to pay 12 1/2 cents on each piece mailed. There are some restrictions and guidelines which the post office requires, so a quick telephone call should be made to get the current facts. If the developer uses our approach of mailing a relatively small number at a time, bulk mail cannot be an option.

The final consideration should be the use of billable man hours used for potential revenue. An ideal situation would be to spend a minimal amount of time while generating a large number of qualified leads. It will take time for a new developer to find which form of marketing best suits his style and generates business. Don't be afraid to try different approaches as long as they convey your professionalism and expertise.

TELEMARKETING

Telemarketing has bombarded the workplace and is also affecting everyone at home with calls for such things as magazines and storm windows. Many people find this very annoying and such feelings are applied to similar calls received at work. Secretaries are taught to screen calls, handling a prospect call with courteous but quick refusal. What's the developer to do? He can spout his knowledge and experience, but this secretary has heard all of the pitches and doesn't care what an application developer can do. Using the same contact-name method mentioned earlier in this chapter will be more productive. However, interest might not be enough to trigger a follow-up face-to-face meeting.

Telemarketing is most effective when directed at an existing client base. This is an excellent way to stir up new business and keep a referral list going. Keeping in touch with clients shows that the developer cares. There are times when clients want additional application work, but other things have taken priority over a phone call to the developer. Help define the new task and initiate more work. Establish a relationship with the company, so they know the high quality of your work and attention to deadlines. Many times the developer not only gets approval to schedule a new task, but also the approval to begin work—all over the phone! The task must be written up and signed for your records, but this new business was simply waiting for your phone call.

If no new business is needed, perhaps your contact knows of another company needing your services. The developer must sell himself constantly. The value of a good referral base cannot be underestimated. It is much easier to approach a new client who is already aware of the quality of your work.

ARTICLES AND SEMINARS

Marketing through articles and seminars can give the developer broad exposure with a monetary plus in some instances. Trade publications often accept articles for publication. Calling in advance to get a contact name and writing guidelines is a necessity. What better introduction than to be able to tell prospective clients about published articles confirming your expertise?

PAID ADVERTISING

Paid advertising is an extremely expensive form of marketing and its value is undeterminable in a service-oriented business. While it might be reasonable to take out ads in major periodicals to announce products, spending thousands of dollars to announce a new consulting firm is not prudent from a business point of view. The money would be better spent on direct-mail efforts and telemarketing.

WHAT KIND OF BUSINESS?

It is very important from the beginning to decide what type of business structure the new firm will have. Often this decision dictates how the company will do things, acquire capital, find space and market its services.

Sole Proprietorship

There are three basic types of legal structures that can be chosen for a new entity. The first, the *sole proprietorship,* is the easiest from the legal point of view to start and run. All that is required is for you to go to work, as long as you do the work under your own name. If, however, you opt to do business using a company name, you must file the local equivalent of a "Certificate of Doing Business Under an Assumed Name" with your city or county clerk. There is no need to hire an attorney because there are no special contracts or agreements required. You are doing business as yourself. You must be the source of all of your funding, because in the initial period any new business is going to dip into the red. You have no partners, no bosses, and may keep all the profits when they arrive. You must also do everything yourself, from marketing to accounting, and from code writing to testing. While it is a very rewarding process in theory, it can be taxing.

Speaking of taxes, as far as the IRS is concerned you and your sole proprietorship are one and the same. Thus, if you begin an application development job while keeping your old job, losses on the new venture can offset income from the old job. This can help soothe the startup trauma that can occur while new companies evolve into viable businesses. Although this structure has low startup expenses, little government intervention, and tax sheltering during the startup, beware of the major pitfall. In a sole proprietorship the entire legal liability rests on the owner. All liabilities of the business are also personal liabilities. If the business fails, as many do, there is no protection from these liabilities. Creditors can come directly after the sole proprietor's house, car, or any other assets. Therefore, a person with considerable assets to protect would be well advised to create a corporation rather than a sole proprietorship.

Another pitfall of this type of business is the inherent difficulty in attracting additional capital, should it become necessary, because a bank or venture group would only have you to hold responsible for any debt. The fragility of the human being is directly related to the health of this type of business, and illness or death can suddenly, irreparably disrupt it. Few investors would take odds like that.

We suggest that you select the sole proprietorship only if you have enough money personally to fund the startup, a limited amount of assets to lose if you are forced into bankruptcy by the business failing, and if you will not need infusions of additional capital at some later date.

Partnership

The second standard business structure is known as the *partnership*. This is a group of people known as *general partners* who will form the company, run it, raise the money required, and share in the responsibilities, liabilities and profits. There is also a special class of participants, known as *limited partners*, who make an investment in return for partial ownership. Limited partners do not participate in the running of the entity and are not personally liable for the business debts. The general partners, conversely, are personally liable for the debts of the company.

Creating a partnership is more complex than creating a sole proprietorship, because two or more parties are involved. Shaking hands and drinking a toast might be one method of forming a new company, but there is no substitute for sound, legal agreements. No matter how friendly the partners are, a good agreement that clearly delineates each partner's duties and responsibilities will often avoid future problems. Write it down and sign it, so no partner is in the position to say, "But you said . . . ." The partnership agreement must also include provisions for buying out one of the partners (the rights of one of the partners to sell his part ownership to someone else). The contract should also discuss terms of liquidation, and the rights of limited partners in such a case.

You might want to form a partnership in which you are the technical resource, another general partner is the business and administrative "guru," and a limited partner puts up the money. If so, we suggest that you try to retain at least 51 percent of the company. While this might not be possible, we must point out that failure to do this could result in the total loss of control of the company in the future.

On the bureaucratic side, the partnership must file a certificate-of-conducting-business-as-partners form with the local authorities and an IRS Form 1065 (U.S. Partnership Return of Income). Income is taxed personally on your share of the partnership's income. You must report it on your 1040 along with any other income you might have received in that tax year.

Partnerships spread the responsibilities, liabilities, and tasks among several key figures. The more skills that are brought to the new venture, the more likely it is that it will succeed. It is easier for a partnership to borrow money or attract new capital due to this broader base. The lender knows that the assets and skills of several people are involved, making the loan more secure.

On the negative side, be prepared to disagree or even fight with your partners. All of the general partners are co-directors of the company. If all is well this is usually not a problem. If problems arise, however, friction can occur and possibly become severe. The partners are also legally responsible for the actions of the entity, so that—even if you knew nothing of a partner's action—you would still be legally liable. As in the sole proprietorship, debts and liabilities of the partnership are the personal responsibility of each of the general partners.

Thus, partnerships are good if the partners need each other's skills and resources, and if they feel that they can work well together. A good partnership agreement with provisions for buy/sell situations and clear statements of responsibilities should help this type of structure succeed.

Corporation

The third type of business structure is the *corporation*. It is the only structure that is a legal entity itself. You will need a lawyer to file the appropriate forms and agreements with the secretary of state for the state in which the corporation will exist. The lawyer will also help with certificates of incorporation, naming of directors, stock certificates, minutes, by-laws, and charters.

Because a corporation is an entity, the unlimited liability of the other business structures is reduced. The stockholder's liability is limited by the amount of investment. Personal holdings do not enter into any corporate bankruptcy actions. If the corporation is declared insolvent, the creditors are limited to dividing only the assets of the corporation. Thus, we strongly suggest this structure for the new application developer.

Corporations with a good record (usually two years of operation) can often borrow funds from banks and other venture capital sources. Corporations can also raise money by issuing stock. Any of the principals can sell their stock and leave, leaving potential liabilities behind.

A negative aspect of the corporation is that the principals are each taxed twice on income. The corporation pays tax on its profits and the stockholders pay income tax on their share of those profits. If the principal is also an employee, he must also pay income tax on his salary. Also, incorporation involves the most reporting to the Federal Government. Records must be current to meet quarterly and yearly reporting periods.

The losses of a corporation are not ordinarily deductible to the shareholders. There is a form of incorporation, however, that does allow losses to be passed through to the stockholders during the startup phase. This is known as a *Subchapter "S" Corporation*. Discuss these options with your attorney and accountant.

Corporations must hold stockholders' meetings and board of directors' meetings, keep minutes, maintain by-laws, and so on, in order to protect the corporation in liability cases. These formalities are taken very seriously by state and federal agencies and must be properly maintained. Even so, we believe the corporation is a good choice. It is the form that we chose when we formed our own consulting company.

Chapter 3

Standard End-User Needs

One of the first questions that comes to mind when you first see a brand-new, gee-whiz, state-of-the-art computer is "What can it do for me?" This is not a frivolous question, because it is probably going to cost a great deal of time and money just to begin to find out the answer. Indeed, a developer should be able to tell someone else exactly what computers can and cannot do.

Computers process information, characters, and numbers, according to specific instructions given to them in programs. That is all. They do not "know," or "think." They just follow orders. If the orders are wrong, either structurally or logically, the results will be erroneous. A computer can add thousands of numbers quickly, but humans must explain which numbers go to which sum. The simple fact that the system is made up of high-technology hardware and software tools—under the control of a human programmer—is often overlooked. A successful system is one integrated into a working environment to accomplish the desired goals with less work than before automation was introduced.

WORD PROCESSING

There are really very few types of end-user computing needs. The most simple to understand is the character-oriented type called word processing. In every endeavor it is necessary to communicate using words on paper. Letters, memos, notes, and contracts play a central role in almost every organization. The invention of the typewriter in the last century revolutionized the office, and played a major part in the information flow in the industrial revolution. As the industrial societies grew, advances in the processing of words become necessary, because the need for greater information flow increased. Computers developed from this need for data, and early in the computer age it became apparent that they could help in the area of word processing. Microcomputers, even in their eight-bit incarnations, were ideally suited to the processing of words. The standard ASCII set of characters and punctuation requires only seven bits, so the microprocessor can store, print, and move blocks of text with far less difficulty than the methods available to the typewriters. Even the more advanced, self-correcting models of electric typewriters cannot compete with the cathode-ray-tube (CRT) orientation of a word processor. A user can type a document into the computer, see the words on the screen, correct errors easily, and print the resulting documents at inconceivable speeds (right justified and perfect each time!). Documents can be saved to magnetic storage, retrieved later, changed slightly, and reprinted at will. Shell letters can be merged with mailing lists to produce thousands of "personalized" letters (much to the dismay of all of us who receive "junk" mail). Since word processing is so common and universal, it is often the entry point for a company into the new technologies. It is also the easiest way to "computerize" a corporate staff, because the concept of processing words is much easier to understand than the processing of numbers in formulae.

Thousands of firms did begin to automate by purchasing "dedicated" word processors. Soon, they began to wish that they could total columns, calculate percentages, and, in general, "compute" more things. Microcomputers could word-process, and offered an upward path for "computing," so some of the more adventurous companies chose them instead of the dedicated systems.

An early microcomputer program was WordStar. It has evolved, along with the microcomputer chips themselves, into an industry-wide standard with an estimated four million users. Other popular packages include Multimate (a Wang word processor look-alike), IBM's DisplayWrite, and Microsoft's Word.

Corporate users demand high-quality printed output, and the industry has responded. The dot-matrix printers of a decade ago have been replaced by more exotic technologies such as ink-jets and laser printers. Speed, graphics, and near-typeset letter-quality are now the norm. Again, the technology price/power curve is active, with more power being offered at progressively lower prices.

Electronic word processing is now probably a standard in corporate America, with typewriters existing only for quick, little jobs like single envelopes or labels. In fact, many modern office typewriters are thinly disguised microcomputers with dedicated word-processing programs. Thus, a large number of users who own microcomputer-based word-processing systems are now beginning to want more.

DESKTOP PUBLISHING

A new area of microcomputer usage is developing—desktop publishing. Over the last two years, the laser-printer market has become extremely competitive. As a result, costs have been dropping while the number of features have been increasing. Software has been written by a number of companies to make use of the high-quality printed output of the new laser printers. It is now possible, using microcomputers and these laser devices, to produce "camera ready" art in-house. Thousands of companies are using such systems to do work that had to be sent out to typesetting houses in the past. The primary market of the Apple Macintosh was created by linking it to the laser printer. Now, with high-resolution, bit-mapped graphics programs available for IBM PC-type machines, many people will use this application as a justification to bring microcomputers into their companies. While some may consider desktop publishing an extension of word processing, we feel that the graphics orientation demands a different type of expertise, and thus different opportunities for application developers and consultants.

ELECTRONIC SPREADSHEETS

The other major area of microcomputer usage is the electronic spreadsheet. In the late 1970s Visicalc was invented, giving the microcomputer the applications it needed to be embraced by corporate "number" people. These folks had been using manual spreadsheets for decades to do budgets, planning, and analysis. Visicalc was an excellent answer to "What can it do for me?" and is credited with being the impetus for the microcomputer revolution. Many analysts claim that Visicalc was the reason that Apple was included in the Fortune 500 list in only five years (a record until Compaq beat it), bringing IBM into the microcomputer market to compete with it.

Spreadsheets are a cross between word processors and calculators. A user can label a column, enter a list of numbers, and use a formula for such calculation as the sum, average, or percentage. The complexity of the calculation is limited in most cases to your imagination, because the spreadsheets include extensive mathematical functions. If you later need to change one or two numbers, the sheet can recalculate in seconds, a time saver of immeasurable value on a large sheet. Financial analysts, bankers, real estate people and others found that they can greatly increase their efficiency, and the cost for this increased productivity is miniscule in relation to its value. When the IBM PC arrived, Lotus created the next generation of the spreadsheet, 1-2-3. Combining a more powerful function set with graphics, a database system, and 16-bit capability, 1-2-3 rapidly became the industry standard. With products like 1-2-3, analysis and number-crunching can be done without programming, and high quality reports and graphics can be produced by users without computer backgrounds.

ACCOUNTING

Another major reason for "computerizing" a business is accounting. Computers make excellent number-crunchers, and competition in the mass market has made a large number of "canned" accounting systems available at a reasonable cost, so many small firms have purchased microcomputer systems specifically for this task. In the early days of the microcomputer revolution applications were severely limited by the relatively low precision and memory capabilities of 8-bit chips. In the 16-bit machines, with large memory and a hard disk, accounting becomes an acceptable use for the system. Out of a large number of available products only a few are in wide use. They vary from the inexpensive, totally integrated system like DAC-EASY to the modular Open Systems package. The latter, which is a minicomputer application "downsized" to the PC, runs under its own Business BASIC. These packages are often sold and supported by accounting firms that charge for "setting up" and customizing the package. Since few existing companies can use a canned accounting package as is, the customization business is quite lucrative for developers and accountants with expertise in one of the major systems. Many of these packages contain report writers and are supposed to be easy to install and modify. This, however, is often as misleading as the "of course it can do it" idea expressed by the unscrupulous salesman. Because the most popular systems have nonstandard file and data structures, it is also a nontrivial task to send data to a spreadsheet or any other application. This issue becomes more important as the automation process continues.

DATABASE MANAGEMENT SYSTEMS

The last "standard" type of application, perhaps the broadest and therefore the most important, is the database management system (DBMS). A DBMS makes use of both the character-handling and number-crunching power of the computer to do almost any task. Simple applications might include the maintenance of a customer mailing list, inventory system, or file of telephone numbers. Linking databases through relations allows for the development of large application systems, such as accounting, which are customized by design rather than by modification.

The flagship of the microcomputer DBMS software is dBASE by Ashton-Tate. From its early days (when it was known as Vulcan) dBASE has evolved into its present version, dBASE III PLUS. It has its own procedural language and a much simplified user-friendly interface. Using the dBASE procedural language, application developers have written thousands of systems. Several analysts are now claiming that dBASE is more a language than a database product. With the introduction of compilers, like Nantucket's Clipper, and a host of tools and utilities, dBASE forms a rich development environment. Other contenders in this area include MicroRims's R:base 5000, Paradox by Ansa, and DataEase by Software Solutions Inc. The combination of database functions and procedural language make these products attractive as the basis of application development.

PROGRAMMING

The microcomputer environment also offers the programmer a full compliment of languages, including C, Fortran, Pascal, COBOL, Ada, Modula, and trusty old BASIC. It is unlikely, however, that unsophisticated end-users would make use of these to develop custom applications. It is also unlikely to find a programmer custom-writing a word processor, spreadsheet, or database management system when such industry standards as Wordstar, 1-2-3 and dBASE exist. The use of standard packages keeps development and support costs down, and frees the end-user from a possibly crippling dependence on a single programmer. In the mainframe and minicomputer eras it was not unusual for a company to spend hundreds of thousands of dollars developing codes that later became difficult if not impossible to support or transport to other hardware configurations.

DATA COMMUNICATIONS

Mainframes and minicomputers do, of course, still exist. They are out there, working away, holding billions of bytes of useful data. They coexist, in a sense, with their descendants, the microcomputers. Users may want or need an access path between their microcomputer workstation and the corporate mainframe. Two paths exist: file transfer and terminal emulation. Since PCs are so smart, it is relatively easy for them to emulate dumb terminals. File uploading and downloading is often far more complex. While it may be easy to actually transport the file, the usefulness of the data is not always clear. Communication is complicated by file and data interchangeability as well as protocol compatibility. This is now becoming a major issue in corporate management information systems (MIS) departments.

Many companies find that they have a large number of PCs that have been acquired through nonstandard purchasing channels. In the past, the DP or MIS group was in charge of all computing equipment, and had full responsibility to choose the vendor, system, and software. PCs changed all that. Now the financial analyst can go to a computer store, buy a system, have it installed, and be up and running without the knowledge of the company's MIS group. This in itself is not a problem. However, a number of such users, making demands on MIS people and resources for communication and file interchangeability, programming help, and support in general, is a big problem.

The DP manager is usually of mainframe orientation, tending to favor centralized control of computing staff and resources. The microcomputer proliferation is not part of his training or experience, and can rapidly seem anarchistic, even to an open-minded manager. After all, is it reasonable to assume that a small MIS staff should be able to support six different word processors, three spreadsheets, and five DMBSs, and still run the data processing functions of the company mainframe?

LOCAL AREA NETWORKS

Consultants can provide a solution to this dilemma. They can simplify the process of integrating the PCs into a unified data-processing system. For example, in recent years a localized communication system concept has been developed that allows a number of PCs to be linked together to share data and peripherals. These Local Area Networks (LANs) are a step toward more centralized control and resource sharing. They tend to be less frightening to the MIS people than the image of hundreds of stand-alone PCs springing up uncontrolled on every desk in the company.

LANs can have common program libraries, share things like large hard disks and laser printers, and centralize responsibility for system backup and security. Since LANs are communications subsystems themselves, they lend themselves well to integration into data communications networks using "gateways" and "bridges" to link the LANs to mainframe hosts.

Once the user is comfortable with a set of standard applications on the PC, and host communications needs are met, the major need becomes total system integration. There has been much lip-service paid to this concept, in which a mainframe data set can be manipulated by a microcomputer application, fed to another microcomputer application, and the results returned to the host for final processing. Because such work crosses many boundaries, consultants can usually get involved in some part of this process, filling in the gaps in the technological understanding of the MIS staff.

Many companies, planning to become self-sufficient at a later time, may just need help in project definition and initial development. Again, the consulting service becomes a valuable tool.

The microcomputer environment is rich with tools, but complex in execution. Many new users needing organizational and developmental help find professional consultants to be very valuable.

Chapter 4

Proposals and Contracts

Before any code is written, a good developer spends time studying the user's requests. In order to set up a complete definition of work, the needs, expectations, potential problems, and goals of the project must be defined. An interview with the end-user(s) is essential to outline, as well as possible, exactly what they want. Often, a good inquiry at this point will save hundreds of hours of work later, as well as create a good foundation for the relationship between the developer and the user.

It is important to remember that many users might be completely unaware of what computers can and cannot do. They might not even be able to concisely express what they do. Manual systems that have had years to develop can be convoluted beyond belief. If a manual system exists, study it. Look at the input forms, the manual processes, and the output reports. Do not make the mistake of merely translating the manual system into an automated process. Look at the procedures from a systems point of view. If any inefficiencies exist, this would be a great time to change them. This is the systems analysis phase, and there is value beyond the user's expectation if the analysis can increase productivity through system redesign.

If the user has an automated system in place, evaluate its structure and find out if the users wish to keep or redesign it. They might, for example, be running their accounting through a time-sharing service bureau. Your system analysis might then be overwhelmed by the large number of available input forms and output reports. Find out if the user actually uses all of the reports offered by the service bureau. It would be foolish and wasteful to develop programs on the new system that would not even be used.

It is in this first phase that the developer and the user must come to a written agreement as to what the project will accomplish. The user, therefore, must be educated about how the development process works, what the computer can do, and how much it will cost. The technical evaluation becomes the basis of the business proposal, defining the work, time required, resources needed and milestones expected.

PROPOSALS

The actual design proposal has standard components. To help the end-user evaluate the proposal, have the parts separated in a logical manner. The first section should include a complete list of all hardware required for the project. The list should include the complete description of each component, the retail price, the "street" price, potential vendors, and the reason that the device is required. An example is shown in Fig. 4-1.

Some consulting groups choose to resell hardware, and so would not list other vendors. The "street" price should be included since most users are now aware of the type of market competition in the computer hardware area, and they expect not to pay retail. In some cases it is valuable to offer options to the user within hardware categories. For example, if an uninterruptible power supply is suggested, two or three competing products with a price spread could be offered, allowing the user to choose one. Similar issues arise if cost considerations push the user toward the use of "clones" instead of name brand PCs and cards. This type of proposal would not have a bottom line, but should instead include the cost of a few sample systems. Typically, you should include a minimum-price configuration, a mid-range, and a top-of-the-line, then discuss the relative merits of each choice.

The second major item in the proposal should be software, divided into "off the shelf" and custom-developed packages. The "off the shelf" section should be handled much as the hardware—listing name, prices, vendors, and justification for each package. If dBASE III is going to be used in the application, the client should expect to buy a copy for each central processing unit (CPU), as is required by law. If, however, the code will be written in the procedural language of dBASE, and then compiled (using a product like Clipper) into an executable file that does not require dBASE, it

Fig. 4-1. Sample proposal.

PROPOSAL FOR ABC SPORTSWEAR, INC.

HARDWARE			RETAIL	XYZ	DISCOUNT VENDORS
1 ea.	PC-XT or clone, w/640K,mono monitor monitor,1 floppy DOS 3.1	$	2912.00	*2912.00	** 800.00
1 ea.	30 megabyte internal hard disk with controller		1304.00	1304.00	754.00
1 ea.	AST Advantage 128K for AT w/Sidekick		595.00	595.00	399.00
1 ea.	Modem 2400 baud internal		899.00	899.00	559.00
1 ea.	650 Watt Battery Back-up		1595.00	1595.00	1400.00
1 ea.	Surge protector		30.00	30.00	25.00
2 ea.	Keyboard and monitor extension cables		196.00	196.00	155.00
2 ea.	CPU stand and monitor stands		120.00	120.00	80.00
1 ea.	Texas Instruments model 855 printer w/tractor		799.00	799.00	750.00
	Setup and testing by XYZ			150.00	N/A
	Setup and testing by BHA (Hourly charge estimated)			N/A	375.00
	subtotal			$ 8,600.00	5,297.00

NETWORK				
2 ea.	3Com Ether Link Board	1300.00	1300.00	1300.00
1 ea.	3Com Share Software	650.00	650.00	650.00
1 ea.	Terminator kit	50.00	50.00	50.00
1 ea.	Bus.Basic Interpreter	695.00	695.00	695.00
	Installation and training by XYZ		500.00	N/A
	Installation and training by BHA (Hourly charge estimated)		N/A	1,500.00
	subtotal		$ 3,195.00	4,195.00

SOFTWARE

Colossus			
1 ea. Accts. rec. acct. history	200.00	200.00	200.00
1 ea. Accts. pay. purchase history	150.00	150.00	150.00
1 ea. Sales history w/quantity	150.00	150.00	150.00
Additional software packages			
1 ea. Wordstar Professional	595.00	495.00	329.00
1 ea. Lotus 1-2-3 ver.2.0	495.00	395.00	339.00
1 ea. SideKick	85.00	85.00	55.00
1 ea. Superkey	70.00	70.00	49.00
1 ea. Fixed Disk Organizer	55.00	55.00	49.00
Installation and training by XYZ		150.00	N/A
Installation and training by BHA (Hourly charge estimated)		N/A	1,500.00
subtotal		$ 1,750.00	2,821.00

HARDWARE	$ 8,600.00	5,297.00
NETWORK	3,195.00	4,195.00
SOFTWARE	1,750.00	2,821.00
TOTAL	$ 13,545.00	12,313.00

* all IBM equipment
** IBM compatible
Total does not include sales tax
Prices reflect current market conditions and are not guaranteed

APPLICATION DEVELOPMENT

Task Order Request 1	
Part 1 - Export Accounting Data	1,500.00
Part 2 - Import Accounting Data to DBF format	1,500.00
Part 3 - Custom Database System	4,500.00
subtotal	7,500.00

HARDWARE EQUIPMENT SERVICE

On-site service, four hour response time with

equipment loaners provided (yearly rate) 1,782.00

HARDWARE CONSIDERATIONS:

1. A possible savings of $3,303.00 if hardware is purchased through various discount vendors. This savings does not take into account employee time spent ordering and picking up such equipment. Bodner, Hutchins & Associates is available to do this but could decrease this savings by as much as $1000.00. XYZ Corp. is not open to discounting but is available to fulfill only a portion on the over all system.

2. All sales are final when using discount vendors. Defective merchandise must be exchanged within 10 days of purchase. Only manufacturers warranties apply.

3. Many such clones are currently working on 3COM networks without difficulty making this an economical alternative.

NETWORK CONSIDERATIONS:

1. XYZ Corporation has installed many 3COM networks and is familiar with the accounting package that is currently used by your company. We recommend that they be used for installing and training on the network.

SOFTWARE CONSIDERATIONS:

1. Colossus is an approved modification vendor by Open Systems. They offer a variety of modifications to meet your needs.

2. The additional software packages are not network licenses but instead are single user agreements. As per our conversations, all software packages quoted in this proposal are based on single user licenses and cannot be accessed by more than one user at a time. This will not apply to your present accounting system which will be licensed as a multi-user system when the network portion is installed.

APPLICATION DEVELOPMENT

1. These tasks are discribed in detail in each individual Task Order Request.

should not be included in the proposal. The user should not be asked to pay for development tools that the developer will keep, such as editors and compilers. The pricing of this custom-developed software is covered in the Project Agreements and Task Orders, estimated at an hourly rate or at a total project cost. Provisions should be made to cover over- or underestimating. You might need to stick to the estimate, for better or worse. It is a good idea to plan for problems. If a task should take ten hours, plan for twelve. Murphy's Law is not to be taken lightly.

The proposal should also include time for general consulting, which includes product evaluation, negotiations with vendors, problem definition and resolution, and training. If you suggest a LAN, for example, you should oversee the installation and make sure that the users have been sufficiently trained to operate the system after you leave. Training might be as mundane as showing users how to turn on computers and format floppy disks, or as complex as demonstrating elaborate database queries. Make sure to provide a generous estimate for training time. If this time is inadequate, the entire project will suffer. Rarely does a user get too much training. The user does not want to depend on outside vendors or consultants for the maintenance of a system which may be the lifeblood of the business. If the proposal includes enough technical training to make the user self-sufficient, everyone involved will benefit.

Finally, the proposal should contain provisions for ongoing service and support. Service contracts are available on most of the hardware, from the vendors or from third-party service organizations. Typical costs are from 1 to 1 1/2 percent of the retail cost per month. A contract that provides on-site service, "loaners," or replacements is desired, because these limit down-time. These agreements tend to be relatively expensive, and should be compared in the proposal to the less expensive over-the-counter repair services. Some users may opt not to have the insurance of a contract, but would prefer to pay an hourly, per-instance rate. Since microcomputer equipment has the reputation of being very reliable, more and more users are choosing this approach. Experience shows that the electronics are in fact very reliable; once the solid-state components have passed the "infant mortality" phase they are nearly indestructible.

It is always a good idea to include power-protection devices in a system design. There are two types of devices: surge protectors and Uninterruptible Power Supplies.

Surge protectors, which are usually inexpensive, limit the damage to electronic components caused by sudden rises and drops in voltage in a power line. Unconditioned power can vary suddenly, for example, when an air conditioner or copy machine "kicks" on. Such surges can be devastating to RAM, and even cause disk problems if they occur in the middle of a head-access for a read or a write. We suggest placing surge protectors on all system components containing RAM or disks.

Although surge protection will save the hardware from transient spikes and drops, it is completely useless in the event of total power loss. Since RAM is volatile, it loses its data when it loses power. Hard disks can be severely damaged if the power failure occurs at a specific time in the head-access cycle. Imagine the frustration of a power failure ten hours into a twelve-hour posting operation in an accounting program!

There is a way to protect against such a loss. Devices called Uninterruptible Power Supplies (UPSs) can keep the system running even after a power failure. These devices vary in price and function. A critical evaluation parameter is the time it takes to switch on if it senses a power loss. A switch should have a crossover time low enough to protect RAM data. One kind has the client's electronics connected to batteries, while letting the batteries be charged by the main power line. This acts as both a UPS and a surge protector, since the system is not actually connected to the power line.

Adding these devices to the proposal shows a concern for system reliability that should help convince a client that a strong system is being designed.

Components which are electromechanical in nature, such as hard disks and printers, tend to break at the worst possible time. Hard disks seem to have a built-in sensor that knows when there is critical information that is not backed up. It is only then that they fail. The cost of hardware is miniscule next to the value of the data. The best lesson to teach a user is the need for backup. Service contracts might provide replacements for dead disk drives, but it is the user who must put the data back. Key data should be backed up to tape or floppy disk as a procedural part of the final system.

Provisions should also be made for ongoing support of custom and canned software. Bug-fixing should be covered by contract warrantees, and new requests by new tasks, which form the basis of ongoing business relationships. Often the user will need periodic training or problem resolution. You might be asked to add new modules to an accounting system, or to expand to a multi-user LAN. The proposal should include your general fee structure for this type of ongoing support.

CONTRACTS

It is absolutely essential in any business relationship to have explicit written documents that outline mutual duties and responsibilities. Such contracts are the foundation of successful operations. Figure 4-2 shows a contract that could be used by an application developer. We also include a Task Order Request form in Fig. 4-3. These contracts are to be used as guidelines only and not to be considered complete legal documents. The use of these documents as a basis for the development of own contracts is intended to lower the total legal costs of that process.

Fig. 4-2. Sample project agreement contract.

PROJECT AGREEMENT

AGREEMENT made and entered into this ____ day of ___ , 198_, by and between Bodner, Hutchins & Associates, Inc. a Texas Corporation with principal offices at 2300 Old Spanish Trail #2105, Houston, Texas, 77054, hereinafter referred to as "BHA": and ____________ ________________, a _____ Corporation with principal office at ____________________________, hereinafter referred to as "Client".

WITNESSETH that in consideration of the mutual covenants and conditions herein contained, the parties do hereby agree as follows:

1. During the period of this Project Agreement, BHA will perform systems analysis, programming, and consultation services ("Project Work"). At the option of BHA, the Client agrees to delineate on a Project Order to be furnished by BHA, the precise tasks to be performed. These services will be performed between _________, 198_ and _______, 198_. This schedule is predicated upon normal working conditions and is subject to adjustment at any time in the event of intervening factors beyond the control of BHA. In any event, the time schedule for tasks to be performed pursuant to this Project Agreement may be extended by written agreement between the Client and BHA.

2. BHA shall submit an invoice upon execution of this Agreement for one half of the estimated project total. Said invoice must be paid or satisfactory arrangements made with a BHA officer prior to the Commencement of Project Work. The remaining balance will be invoiced at the end of the Agreement and is due and payable within 15 days after date of invoice. Interest may be charged at the maximum non-usurious rate, but in no event to exceed twenty-five percent (25%) on

amounts over forty-five (45) days old. The estimated cost for the project outlined above is $_____.__. If it becomes apparent during the performance of this Agreement that the cost for completion of the Project will exceed the amount stated above by more than ten percent (10%), BHA shall advise Client as far in advance as reasonably possible so that consideration may be given to other arrangements (e.g., change in task requirements, increase in allowable expenditure).

3. BHA retains all rights to inventions, discoveries, improvements, modifications, changes, and developments arising from projects covered under this Project Agreement. End-user and site licenses for any BHA products may be made available at BHA's sole option to the Client by mutual agreement under separate distribution or license agreements.

All programs, specifications, applications, routines, subroutines, techniques, and ideas (BHA Proprietary Information) for Formulae are and shall remain the sole property of BHA. BHA Proprietary Information shall not be disseminated in any means to any person or firm without the prior express written consent of BHA.

4. All statistical, financial, accounting, and personnel data relating to Client's business, which are confidential and clearly designated as such will be kept in strictest confidence by BHA and its employees. BHA is not obligated to keep confidential any techniques relating to electronic data processing that may be developed either solely by BHA or jointly with the Client during the term of this Project Agreement.

5. Client shall reimburse BHA for reasonable and necessary travel and living expenses incurred by personnel of BHA in connection with work provided that Client has given its approval to said travel.

6. Client shall reimburse BHA for all reasonable disbursements including, but not limited to, long distance telephone calls, supplies, and shipping charges incurred by BHA in performing work for Client.

7. Client shall have the right to cancel without advance notice any Project by advising BHA in writing of such canceliation. BHA shall be entitled to payment under the provisions of paragraphs 2, 5, and 6 above with respect to charges and expenses earned or incurred up to the time of said cancellation. In the event of cancellation, any unused prepaid funds will be refunded to the Client.

8. BHA's liability to the Client for any losses or damages, direct or indirect, arising out of this Project Agreement shall not exceed the total amount billed or billable to the Client for the performance of the particular task which gave rise to the loss or damage. BHA shall not be liable for consequential damages in any event. This clause shall supersede any other clause of this contract that may be deemed inconsistent with it.

BHA EXPRESSLY DISCLAIMS ANY WARRANTY, INCLUDING BUT NOT LIMITED TO EXPRESS OR IMPLIED WARRANTIES OF MERCHANTIBILITY OR FITNESS FOR A PARTICULAR PURPOSE.

9. Services performed under this Project Agreement shall be considered to have been accepted by Client unless written proof of Claim is made to BHA no later than six (6) months after the last day that services were performed pursuant to the project order.

10. No Liability is assumed by BHA for the accuracy of any processed data, except for the corrections of BHA's work.

11. This Project Agreement shall be construed in accordance with the laws of the State of Texas.

12. BHA shall not be liable for the loss, destruction, or damage of Client - supplied materials unless such loss was proximately caused by the negligence of BHA. BHA's liability shall be limited to restoring the lost, destroyed or damaged materials if Client furnishes all source data necessary for such restoration.

13. It is expressly agreed that this Project Agreement embodies the entire contractual agreement of the parties in relation to the subject matter hereof, and that no other agreement or understanding, verbal or otherwise, exists between the parties except as herein expressly set forth. This Project Agreement shall not be amended except by written agreement signed by both parties.

14. BHA reserves the right to subcontract to qualified third persons any part of the services described in any project order hereunder.

15. BHA shall have the right to decline the acceptance of any project order requested of it by Client in the event that such order may come into conflict with another previously scheduled activity of BHA of for any other good and sufficient reason. In such case, BHA shall give Client notice that it declines to accept any such project order within

two weeks of receipt of said project order, but in any case not after the date on which the contemplated order was to begin.

16. Each paragraph and provision of this Contract is severable from the Contract and if one provision or part thereof is declared invalid, the remaining provisions shall nevertheless remain in full force and effect.

17. The prevailing party to any action in State or Federal court, at law or in equity to enforce the provisions of this Project Agreement shall be entitled to court costs and reasonable attorney's fees.

18. Client shall not assign this Project Agreement without the written consent of BHA.

Accepted:

Company: ____________________	BODNER, HUTCHINS & ASSOC. INC.
By: ______________________	By: ______________________
Title: ___________________	Title: __________________
Date of Acceptance: ___________	Date Submitted: ____________

In this contractual structure a client would sign a single Project Agreement and a separate Task Order for each individual task. This partitioning of large projects into small tasks is an excellent way to manage such projects. There is also the provision to receive fifty percent of the task estimate upon signing of the Task Order Request, with the remainder due upon completion and acceptance. This helps with the cash flow during the development process.

To reiterate—plan ahead. Interview the user(s), agree on what is to be done, and formulate a written agreement, including start and stop dates, payment schedules, project milestones, ownership rights, and any other mutual responsibilities. Do not begin the project until all business and technical issues are resolved.

The major difference between a new developer and a seasoned, experienced one is that the new one does not know his lawyer's first name.

Fig. 4-3. Sample task order request form.

TASK ORDER REQUEST

This Project Order/Task Order Request shall be governed by all terms and conditions signed by Bodner, Hutchins & Associates, Inc. and ______________________________. _______, 198_ in the Project Agreement and will remain in full force and effect.

PROJECT NAME: __________________________________
PROJECT NUMBER: ____________
TASK NUMBER: _________
DATE OF ORDER: ____________
REQUESTED START DATE: _________________
ASSIGNED START DATE: _________________
ESTIMATED DUE DATE: _________________

COMPANY REQUESTING TASK: ______________________________
CONTACT: ________________________
ADDRESS: ________________________
CITY,STATE,ZIP: __________________
PHONE: __________________________

RATE: ___________________________
ESTIMATED NUMBER OF HOURS: _______

PROJECT DESCRIPTION (IN DETAIL):

____
____
____
____
____
____
____
____
____
____
____

____

____

____

EQUIPMENT (PROJECT SPECIFIC)

ESTIMATED TRAVEL (LIST DESTINATIONS,DATES,AND APPROX. LENGTHS OF STAY):

SOFTWARE PACKAGES REQUIRED:

DBASE III ___

LOTUS 1-2-3 ___

SYMPHONY ___

FRAMEWORK ___

COMMUNICATIONS ___ NAME ______________

WORD PROCESSING ___ NAME ______________

OTHER ___ NAME ______________

NAME ______________

ADDITIONAL PROJECT EXPENSES:

SUBMITTED BY: ______________ ACCEPTED BY: ______________

COMPANY: ______________ BODNER HUTCHINS & ASSOC. INC.

TITLE: ______________ TITLE: ______________

DATE: ______________ DATE: ______________

Chapter 5

Project Design

Fundamental to all computer applications is the definition of the data upon which the programs will operate. Any collection of information can be considered a database, and nearly all applications are database management functions, coupled with numeric and character processing. This may seem unorthodox, but is borne out by the fact that even such "vertical" applications as accounting systems and manufacturing resource planning programs can be grouped under this broad definition of database processors. This may also explain the popularity among application developers of packages such as dBASE III.

Assuming that the database is the foundation of most applications, you must pay great attention to the definition of the database. Before a single line of code is written, the developer and user must agree on the number and kinds of data to be included in the system design. This may not seem to be the proper time to define database structure, but experienced programmers have horror tales to tell concerning hours and hours spent going back over finished code because an important data field was not included in the original design. It is very difficult to go back through thousands of lines of code to change screen formats, reports, or calculations, just because the database definition has been changed. As much as possible, the developer should carve the database design in stone, with end-user approval. This implies that the preliminary study and user interview process was sufficient to result in a complete database definition.

The definition must be sufficiently detailed to include field widths, and whether they are to be alphanumeric, integers, floating-point variables, or calculated. If fields are to be computed from other data, the procedures and formulae for the computation should be written into the definition document. The user and developer must also agree on which data is to be considered "key," that is, which fields will be used to search, sort, or report data. There should also be an agreement about the range validations of variables, so that error checking can be implemented at the data-entry level. For example, a company might allow data-entry personnel to enter discounts on sales orders, but might wish to limit the discount to prohibit allowing the sale of an item below cost. Such validation should be included in the design.

A complete database definition should also include system security. The user may require passwords and security clearance levels. Some employees might be allowed to enter sales orders but not refunds, for example. Security must be designed into the system, setting clearance levels as part of the system definition.

As a final check of the definition, the developer should make sure that all of the data required in all of the output reports has been included. Incorporating the required reports into the Task Order has already limited your contractual responsibility, but check again before code generation begins. After all, the purpose of written agreements is to limit the "but you said it would . . ." syndrome. At the completion of the database definition phase, the developer should meet with the client again, to gain approval on the design, especially on the interpretation of the user's needs. Once the user "signs off" on the definition, coding can begin. This sign-off can actually be accomplished on a dated printout of the database structure, then added to the client contract file as a supporting document.

THE USER INTERFACE

Because the cost of microcomputer systems is lower than their older minicomputer and mainframe counterparts, tens of thousands of new users with little or no previous computer experience are "cutting their teeth" on the newer technologies. Unsophisticated new users bring fear, confusion and other negative attitudes to their first interaction with automation. The developer should be acutely aware of this resistance to "the computer." Some employees are sure that management is bringing in the new system to replace them. Others, with years of service to the firm, take the position that they are too old to learn, or it is too hard, or that computers hate them. In the old days, when applications were written on large, expensive processors, there was often an MIS staff or a data processing department. Modern systems are delivered to users whose companies may not have anyone on staff with any computer expertise at all. Because a professional developer must be concerned with all aspects of a project, user acceptance and level of comfort must be addressed. Some of the anxiety is abated by involving end-users in the definition of system goals and needs. Going to the "old timers" and finding out what they would find useful in the "new-fangled" computer would help them feel more comfortable with the final product.

In this environment the user interface must be easy. "Friendly" is the fashionable term. There is one rule—assume nothing. Do not assume that the user can learn DOS commands, special program codes, or anything about the hardware. The system must run in a menu-driven environment. A number of "shell" processors exist that completely isolate the user from the DOS level. A menu is merely a list of options, any one of which is executed by picking a letter, number, or code and pressing "enter." The system should not even require the user to set the time. It should be set up so that, just by turning the computer on, the operational environment, operation system drive-paths, and any other startup functions are executed automatically. The user should arrive at the main menu instantly—"just point and shoot." The environment might contain a menu that looks like the screen shown in Fig. 5-1, which is a menu from the IBM Fixed Disk Organizer Program. The MS-DOS machines have batch-file capability that makes this automatic setup relatively straightforward. Upon boot-up, a file called AUTOEXEC.BAT is executed and can accomplish the desired functions.

Menus come in many styles. The most common is a vertical list with an entry prompt, awaiting the choice, at the bottom of the screen. More sophisticated menus have a highlight bar that is moved up and down using arrows. Selection occurs when "enter" is pressed, executing the highlighted option. Several popular packages such as Lotus 1-2-3, Paradox, and dBASE III PLUS have horizontal menus using this highlighter concept. These packages also have keyed "help" to explain each menu option. The type of help changes as the highlight bar moves. These are excellent user interfaces, and should be the basis for any new applications developed in these systems. After the users become oriented to menu interfaces, they will find commands like BASICA ACCOUNTING/F:6 too complex—and they will be right. Fixed Disk Organizer is a good menu shell and one that we highly recommend.

Fig. 5-1. Main system menu using fixed disk organizer.

```
                    Bodner, Hutchins & Associates, Inc.


Date: 05-26-1986                                          Page 1 of 3
Time: 13:59:34                                            Version 1.00


          1. Norton Utilities
          2. Personal Editor II
          3. dBASE III Plus
          4. Crosstalk XVI
          5. DOS Commands
          6. Lotus Version 2.0
          7. DAC Easy Accounting
          8. dFlow
          9. WordStar



+---------------------------+----------------------------------------+
|  up or dn point to option |  F1 Help                               |
|                           |  F7 Quit                               |
|   ENTER select option     |  F9 Menu Maintenance   PgDn Next page  |
+---------------------------+----------------------------------------+
```

Some of the menu shells even allow password security for some option levels, or "personalized" menus keyed to the user's name. The menu-driven user interface makes it possible for almost anyone to navigate through the system options according to the security access level.

ON-LINE HELP

A widely used buzzword phrase in microcomputer software is "context specific on-line help." Although hundreds of thousands of dollars are spent producing slick packaging and documentation, users are much more impressed if the program acts as its own documentation. A common user interface for help is the F1 function key. At any point the user can press F1, and get a "help" message related to the function in the program at the moment of the help call. This is what is meant by context specific. Lotus 1-2-3 pioneered the concept, placing reams of information normally found in manuals on the disk, with a keyed recovery program. Many users hate manuals, do not know how to use them, or might not know where they are when they need them. On-line help is a more realistic method of keeping users informed. It is the sign of a good application developer to build this type of help into a program. Users are already learning to expect F1-key help, so new applications that use the method will be easier for them to accept.

The Clipper compiler for dBASE III has built-in help functions that use the F1 key and pass the name of the calling program and the name of the pending variable to the help program. Context specificity is thus determined by simple logic. For example, if the calling program is an ADD routine, display the help screen for ADD. Because the pending variable is also known, it is possible to display a message specifically for that variable, such as the valid range.

There is a limited useful life to most help. Early on the learning curve its value is undeniable, but as the user gets more accomplished and confident, help is used less and less. It could be argued that it is a waste of code after the initial period. Many users, if given the option, would eventually choose to scrap the help in favor of the slight increase in processing speed from shrinking the amount of code. The user might also question the value of paying the developer to write help code that makes itself obsolete. That, however, is exactly the point. The better the help, the sooner it becomes obsolete, and the obsolescence of help means that employees are using the system efficiently. Although the economics are hard to demonstrate, the logic of this argument should suffice as a justification to include the cost of help-code development in the project.

ERROR TRAPPING

On-line help code is optional, but strongly recommended. A systematic error-control procedure, however, is absolutely required for a professional system. The process of building error traps into the code has two phases: theoretical and practical.

The code writers, using the system specification database definitions, and their own experience, create a "theoretical" set of expectations of possible errors that can be encountered during data entry. Code that makes sure that only numbers are placed in numeric fields, and upper case characters in other fields, exemplifies this type of trap. As every experienced programmer knows, however, users can be very creative.

There is, thus, a set of error traps that can be called practical or "real-world sensitive," involving reasoning beyond that imaginable by the programmer. Terms like "idiot-proof" and "bullet-proof" represent this latter class of trapping. These possibilities usually appear only in Alpha and Beta testing, discussed in Chapter 8, and might, in fact, represent the majority of the work done in the late Beta-test fix-up stage. The new developer should be very broad in projections of how a user might crash his code. In time, the "old pro" writes code that shows the burn marks and scars of earlier bouts with idiot-proofing. Type validations, range checking, and computational derivations are all tools that come into play in the error trapping process. Good code is bullet-proof, and the harder it is to crash the better the developer looks. This is good business, and makes the developer seem more professional.

DOCUMENTATION

Care should be taken to follow documentation standards for the implementation of comments internal to the code. In the following code fragment a typical program header is shown. There are a number of important pieces of information in this fragment, shown in Fig. 5-2.

Note that the creation date and author are identified, as well as modification dates, the names of the modifiers, and a comment about what was done. Each individual procedure is clearly marked with a set of block markers denoting beginning and end. The liberal use of comments should make clear what each procedure does, what the variable names mean, what is input, and what is output. This code is dBASE, but similar internal documentation could be used in C (Fig. 5-3), BASICA (Fig. 5-4), and Assembly (Fig. 5-5).

Make note of the conceptual style. Leave nothing unexplained. Although source code is rarely given out to the end-user, clear, easy-to-support code will make future bug-fixes or upgrades straightforward, enhancing profitability as well as supportability.

Internal documentation also leads to more structured coding. Much has been written about the value of structured code. Pascal and C have become popular in the educational community because structural coding is considered the best style to teach. The benefit of this type of code, compared to the potential rat's nests of loops and subroutines in a nonstructured language such as BASIC, is apparent to anyone who has had to go into code written by someone else. Notice that in the BASIC code fragment shown above, however, the documentation gives structure. Treat the internal documentation as if it has to survive the writer and stand on its own. Self-supporting code is its own reward.

A number of products exist that will automatically document code. One that is particularly noteworthy is dFlow by Wallsoft. It takes dBASE code, documents it, indents and marks control loops, builds variable concordance and module cross reference tables, and

Fig. 5-2. Program header and procedure code fragment.

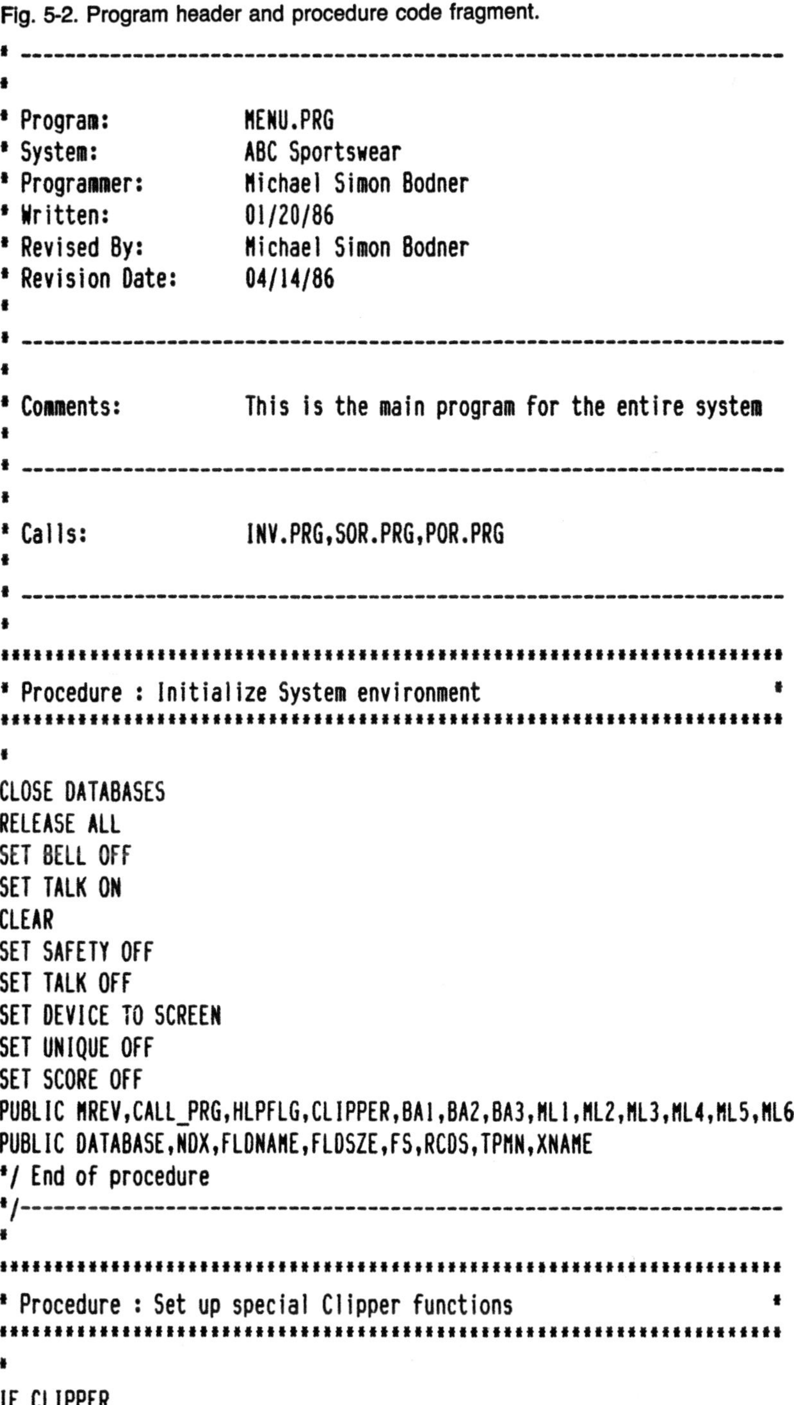

```
* ----------------------------------------------------------------
*
* Program:           MENU.PRG
* System:            ABC Sportswear
* Programmer:        Michael Simon Bodner
* Written:           01/20/86
* Revised By:        Michael Simon Bodner
* Revision Date:     04/14/86
*
* ----------------------------------------------------------------
*
* Comments:          This is the main program for the entire system
*
* ----------------------------------------------------------------
*
* Calls:             INV.PRG,SOR.PRG,POR.PRG
*
* ----------------------------------------------------------------
*
******************************************************************
* Procedure : Initialize System environment                      *
******************************************************************
*
CLOSE DATABASES
RELEASE ALL
SET BELL OFF
SET TALK ON
CLEAR
SET SAFETY OFF
SET TALK OFF
SET DEVICE TO SCREEN
SET UNIQUE OFF
SET SCORE OFF
PUBLIC MREV,CALL_PRG,HLPFLG,CLIPPER,BA1,BA2,BA3,ML1,ML2,ML3,ML4,ML5,ML6
PUBLIC DATABASE,NDX,FLDNAME,FLDSZE,FS,RCDS,TPMN,XNAME
*/ End of procedure
*/---------------------------------------------------------------
*
******************************************************************
* Procedure : Set up special Clipper functions                   *
******************************************************************
*
IF CLIPPER
```

```
  EXTERNAL ISCOLOR,ISPRINTER
  IF ISCOLOR() .AND. CLIPPER
     SET COLOR to GR+/B,R+/
  ELSE
     SET COLOR to W/ , /W
  ENDIF ISCOLOR
ENDIF CLIPPER
*/ End of procedure
*/-------------------------------------------------------------------
*
**********************************************************************
* Procedure : Set up special Clipper or dBase index environment      *
**********************************************************************
*
IF .NOT. CLIPPER
  STORE file('SOR.NTX') TO MQDX
  IF MQDX
   !ERASE *.NTX
  ENDIF
ELSE
  STORE file('SOR.NDX') TO MQDX
  IF MQDX
   !ERASE *.NDX
  ENDIF
ENDIF
IF .NOT. MQDX
  SELECT 1
  USE SALESORDER
  @ 23,10 SAY 'Sales Order Database is now being indexed......       '
  DO SORGO
  CLEAR
ENDIF
*/ End of procedure
*/-------------------------------------------------------------------
```

even creates a diagram of program flow. These types of utilities even check for errors in logic such as unclosed loops or bad syntax. They are valuable tools in the development process.

After the discussion of on-line help earlier in the chapter, you might assume that we dismiss the need for written documentation. Although good help might limit the need for a user to refer to a user manual, it still might be necessary to create one. Depending on the complexity of the system, the developer might have to pre-

Fig. 5-3. Code fragment from C language.

```
main(argc, argv, envp)
        int argc;
        char **argv;
        char **envp;

        {
        register char **p;

        /* print out the argument list for this program */

        for (p = argv; argc > 0; argc--,p++) {
                printf("%s\n", *p);
                }

        /* print out the current environment settings.  Note that
         * the environment table is terminated by a NULL entry
         */

        for (p = envp; *p; p++) {
                printf("%s\n", *p);
                }

        exit(0);
        }
```

Fig. 5-4. Code fragment from BASICA language.

```
200 REM *                                                                  *
210 REM *  COPYRIGHT 1986, BODNER, HUTCHINS & ASSOCIATES, INC. HOUSTON, TX *
220 REM *                                                                  *
230 REM ********************************************************************
240 COLOR 10,1:COUNT=0
250 REM ****************************************************
260 REM *  SET UP SCREEN INFORMATION DISPLAY                *
270 REM ****************************************************
280 LOCATE 11,16:PRINT"Converting Open System ITEMS to dBase III format"
290 LOCATE 17,16:PRINT"Copyright 1986, Bodner, Hutchins & Assoc., Inc. "
300 LOCATE 13,12
305 PRINT"+----------------+--------------+------------------------+"
310 LOCATE 14,12
315 PRINT"| Order #        |Date          |Company                 |"
320 LOCATE 15,12
325 PRINT"+----------------+--------------+------------------------+"
330 WIDTH "LPT1:",132
```

```
340 REM ******************************************************
350 REM * OPEN FILES, INITIALIZE VARIABLES                   *
360 REM ******************************************************
370 OPEN "O",#2,"ITM.APP"
380 DIM A$(13),B$(13),M$(13),O$(13)
390 M$(1)="ORDERNO    "
400 M$(2)="QTY        "
410 M$(3)="CATEGORY   "
420 M$(4)="INVENUMBER "
430 M$(5)="FIGURENUMB "
440 M$(6)="AVGCOST    "
450 M$(7)="UNITPRICE  "
460 M$(8)="AMOUNT     "
470 M$(9)="ORDERDATE  "
480 M$(10)="CONAME     "
490 OPEN "I",#1,"ITEMS.OUT"
500 IF EOF(1) THEN CLOSE #1:CLOSE #2:END
```

pare both a user manual and a technical reference (or system manager) document.

The user manual should make it possible for the user to follow a step-by-step description of how to run the system. It might include instructions about how to turn on the computer, copy the application on to the hard disk, initialize it, and get to work. This might be inappropriate for a large, customized, very complex application. In that case the developer usually brings the system up, and is responsible for installation, initialization, configuration and integration. If the application is to be mailed to a number of branch offices, however, the user document must allow a user to do all of these things without the need to consult the programmer. User manuals must be simple, easy to read, and make no assumptions about the level of computer knowledge of the reader. Although it may seem wasteful to tell a user how to format a disk and copy files from one drive to another, such information is essential to the novice user and will be disregarded by those users who do not need it. Figure 5-6 shows a sample of a user document installation section.

Some applications require the production of technical reference manuals. These documents contain details required by high-level technical staff members to accomplish such things as database support, file interchange, file maintenance, system backup, and security password maintenance. For example, if the application is a compiled dBASE, the user might still wish to use interpreted dBASE's Report Writer to prepare query outputs. In this case, a technical reference manual should include the file structure, index names and keys, and relationships between databases, thus giving a dBASE user all the information necessary to use the data for other purposes.

Fig. 5-5. Public domain Assembly language program.

```
;----------------------------------------------------------------------
; Filename: EXTENDA.ASM
; Program.: Clipper Extended Library
; Authors.: Tom Rettig, Brian Russell
; Date....: November 1, 1985
; Notice..: Placed in the public domain by Tom Rettig Associates.
;           Clipper is a trademark of Nantucket.
;           dBASE and dBASE III are trademarks of Ashton-Tate.
; Notes...: User-defined dBASE functions in 8086 assembly for Clipper.
;
;   dBASE III functions:
;      ISCOLOR()   ::= True if the computer has an active color card.
;
;   Functions not in dBASE III or Clipper:
;      ISPRINTER() ::= True if the printer is online and ready.
;

   NAME   EXTENDA

   PUBLIC ISCOLOR
   PUBLIC ISPRINTER


; Clipper return value calls
   EXTRN    _RETC:FAR     ; return character string
   EXTRN    _RETDS:FAR    ; return date type from date string "YYYYMMDD"
   EXTRN    _RETL:FAR     ; return logical true or false
   EXTRN    _RETNI:FAR    ; return word as numeric
   EXTRN    _RETNL:FAR    ; return double word as numeric
   EXTRN    _RETND:FAR    ; return floating point as numeric

_PROG SEGMENT

         ASSUME CS:_PROG
```

Backup procedures are an essential part of system maintenance. The technical document should identify the files to be backed up, the actual backup procedure, and a rotation schedule for the backups themselves. Again, assume nothing.

In the rare cases when the developer has agreed to supply the source code to the end-user, it can be included as a part of the technical reference documents. Remember that the issue of code ownership and copyrights must be covered in all contracts and that a

Fig. 5-6. Sample installation documentation.

INSTALLATION

Floppy Disk System

If you have a two drive floppy disk system place a DOS diskette with the program DISKCOPY on it in drive A: and a blank formatted diskette in drive B:. Close both doors. From the DOS A> prompt type;

DISKCOPY A: B: <return>

You will then be prompted to place the source disk in drive A:. Remove DOS, insert the Program system disk in drive A:, close the door, and press return. At the end of this process take the disk in drive B: and mark it with a label as Program Backup. Use this diskette as your working copy.

You will be asked if you wish to make any more copies. Answer N.

To configure the working copy, remove from drive B: and place in Drive A: and do the following.

If you will be using a monochrome display please type:
MONO from the DOS A> prompt and press RETURN.

If you have a color graphics system type:
COLOR from the DOS A> prompt and press RETURN.

Place the master diskette in a safe place and proceed to the next chapter for training lessons.

Hard Disk Systems

If you are going to run the system on a hard disk, from the C> prompt please type:

MD\ACCTRPTS to create the subdirectory, then type:
CD\ACCTRPTS to go to that directory. Then place the working diskette in drive A: and type:

COPY A:*.* C:\ACCTRPTS

If you will be using a monochrome display please type:
MONO from the DOS C> prompt and press RETURN.

```
If you have a color graphics system type:
COLOR  from the DOS C> prompt and press RETURN.

When done, please the master diskette in a safe place and proceed to
the next chapter for training lessons.
```

developer will run the risk of compromising his legal rights to the code and algorithms if the source is given to the user without adequate contractual safeguards.

PROGRAM MODULES

Program code should be designed from the outset to be easily supportable by people other than those programmers who wrote it. You should, therefore, consider modular programming your modus operandi.

A module is a compact segment of code that performs a single function, such as allowing the addition of information to a database. Rather than writing a single ten thousand line program, the coder can create a number of functional modules. Each module has, as part of its internal documentation, a description of what its single function is, a list of its internal variables with descriptions, a complete listing of the modules it calls, and perhaps a record of what modules call it. This programming approach has two benefits. The first one has already been mentioned—the code is supportable. The modular method is structured by conceptual definition, and thus is easy to debug, modify, or upgrade at a later time. The second benefit is that it can help the programmer write more efficient code, because some modules are re-used in the program. There might, for example, be a module that is a display-only screen. It could be coded once, tested and declared bug free, and then called from any later module that needs to use such a function, such as a search operation. This approach gives the coder a library of functional modules, some of which might even be useable in other projects. Because so many applications share common features (such as adding, editing, or deleting), algorithms and computational methodologies developed in modules can be easily adapted to other databases in the future. Modules help develop a coding style, so that menus and data-entry screens begin to have a special "look" that presents a very professional user interface, at a relatively low developmental cost. If the modules themselves are constructed using standard structured programming techniques, such as the module shown in Fig. 5-7, the ongoing support of code is even easier.

The major arguments against this approach are that the

Fig. 5-7. dBASE program module with documentation.

```
;-----------------------------------------------------------------------
;  ISCOLOR()
;  Syntax: ISCOLOR()
;  Return: Logical true if there is an active color card in the computer

ISCOLOR PROC FAR

        MOV     AH,15           ; current video status function
        INT     10H             ; read video status

        XOR     BX,BX           ; false
        CMP     AL,07           ; monochrome 80x25
        JE      RET_ISCOLOR     ; return false if other than above
        MOV     BX,1            ; true

RET_ISCOLOR:
        PUSH    BX              ; put return value on the stack
        CALL    _RETL           ; return logical value to Clipper
        POP     BX              ; restore the stack

        RET

ISCOLOR ENDP


;-----------------------------------------------------------------------
;  ISPRINTER()
;  Syntax: ISPRINTER()
;  Return: Logical true if the printer is online and ready, otherwise false

ISPRINTER PROC FAR

        MOV     AH,2H           ; printer status function
        MOV     DX,0H           ; which printer to check
        INT     17H             ; read printer status

        XOR     BX,BX           ; false
        CMP     AH,90H          ; not busy or selected (90h = 10010000)
        JNE     RET_ISPRINTER   ; return false if other than above
        MOV     BX,1            ; true

RET_ISPRINTER:
        PUSH    BX              ; put return value on the stack
```

```
        CALL      _RETL             ; return logical value to Clipper
        POP       BX                ; restore the stack

        RET

ISPRINTER ENDP

_PROG ENDS

        END

; EOF Extenda.asm -----------------------------------------------------
* -------------------------------------------------------------------------
*
* Program:              SWDBDLB.PRG
* System:               SEARCH WINDOW DATABASE
* Programmer:           Michael Simon Bodner
* Written:              02/09/85
* Revised By:           Michael Simon Bodner
* Revision Date:        02/09/85
*
* -------------------------------------------------------------------------
*
* Comments:             This is the DISK LABEL program for the SWDB system
*
* -------------------------------------------------------------------------
*
* Calls:                NONE
*
* -------------------------------------------------------------------------
*
*********************************************************************
* Procedure : Set up screen and display variables                   *
*********************************************************************
*
CLEAR
@ 1,1  SAY DATE()
@ 1,35 SAY 'Disk Labels'
@ 1,18 SAY MREV
@ 1,70 SAY MDAYNAME
LAB1='+----------------------------------------------------------------+'
LAB2='|     S E A R C H  W I N D O W  Customer Data Base Management System |'
LAB3='+----------------------------------------------------------------+'
LAB4='+----------------------------------------------------------------+'
```

```
LAB5='| Copyright 1985  by Bodner, Hutchins & Assoc. Inc.,  Houston, Texas |'
LAB6='+-----------------------------------------------------------------+'
@ 2,0 GET LAB1
@ 3,0 GET LAB2
@ 4,0 GET LAB3
@ 20,0 GET LAB4
@ 21,0 GET LAB5
@ 22,0 GET LAB6
CLEAR GETS
*/ End of procedure
*/----------------------------------------------------------------
*
******************************************************************
* Procedure : Ask user what serial #, Version #, & how many       *
******************************************************************
*
USE SWDBLST
VERN='2.0'
MSER =VAL(SERLAST)
MNUM=0
@ 10,10 SAY 'Please enter the starting serial number 'GET MSER
@ 11,10 SAY 'Enter the Version Number ' GET VERN PICTURE '9.9'
@ 12,10 SAY 'How many labels do you wish to print ? 'get mnum picture '999'
READ
@ 14,10 SAY SPACE(50)
*/ End of procedure
*/----------------------------------------------------------------
*
******************************************************************
* Procedure : Check label alignment using print mask              *
******************************************************************
*
OK='N'
DO WHILE OK='N'
  SET PRINT ON
  SET CONSOLE OFF
  ? 'XXXXXXXXXXXXXXXXXXXXXXXXXXXXXXXXXXXXXXXXXXXX'
  ? 'XXXXXXXXXXXXXXXXXXXXXXXXXXXXXXXXXXXXXXXXXXXX'
  ? 'XXXXXXXXXXXXXXXXXXXXXXXXXXXXXXXXXXXXXXXXXXXX'
  ? 'XXXXXXXXXXXXXXXXXXXXXXXXXXXXXXXXXXXXXXXXXXXX'
  ? 'XXXXXXXXXXXXXXXXXXXXXXXXXXXXXXXXXXXXXXXXXXXX'
  ? 'XXXXXXXXXXXXXXXXXXXXXXXXXXXXXXXXXXXXXXXXXXXX'
  ? 'XXXXXXXXXXXXXXXXXXXXXXXXXXXXXXXXXXXXXXXXXXXX'
  ? 'XXXXXXXXXXXXXXXXXXXXXXXXXXXXXXXXXXXXXXXXXXXX'
```

```
   ?
   ? 'XXXXXXXXXXXXXXXXXXXXXXXXXXXXXXXXXXXXXXXXXXXXXXX'
   ? 'XXXXXXXXXXXXXXXXXXXXXXXXXXXXXXXXXXXXXXXXXXXXXXX'
   ? 'XXXXXXXXXXXXXXXXXXXXXXXXXXXXXXXXXXXXXXXXXXXXXXX'
   ? 'XXXXXXXXXXXXXXXXXXXXXXXXXXXXXXXXXXXXXXXXXXXXXXX'
   ? 'XXXXXXXXXXXXXXXXXXXXXXXXXXXXXXXXXXXXXXXXXXXXXXX'
   ? 'XXXXXXXXXXXXXXXXXXXXXXXXXXXXXXXXXXXXXXXXXXXXXXX'
   ? 'XXXXXXXXXXXXXXXXXXXXXXXXXXXXXXXXXXXXXXXXXXXXXXX'
   ? 'XXXXXXXXXXXXXXXXXXXXXXXXXXXXXXXXXXXXXXXXXXXXXXX'
   ?
   SET PRINT OFF
   SET CONSOLE ON
   @ 14,10 SAY 'Are the labels lined up ?' GET OK
   READ
   @ 16,10 SAY SPACE(50)
ENDDO OK
*/ End of procedure
*/-------------------------------------------------------------------
*
*********************************************************************
* Procedure : Print labels ,increment counter and serial number     *
*********************************************************************
*
NM=1
SET PRINT ON
SET CONSOLE OFF
DO WHILE NM<=MNUM
 SER=1000000000+MSER
 SERC=STR(SER,10,0)
 ?
 ?
 ?
 ? CHR(27)+CHR(69)+'           S_E_A_R_C_H  W_I_N_D_O_W'+CHR(27)+CHR(70)
 ? ' '
 ?
 ? '        Serial # '+SUBSTR(SERC,2,9)+'    Ver. '+VERN
 ?
 ?
 ?
 NM=NM+1
 MSER=MSER+1
ENDDO
SET CONSOLE ON
SET PRINT OFF
```

```
CLEAR
*/ End of procedure
*/---------------------------------------------------------------
RETURN
```

programmer might have dozens of code modules that become unmanageable, that the directory becomes cluttered, and that the environment is messy. These objections are overcome in compiled and assembled applications, because the modules of source code are ultimately linked into a single executable module. In interpreted dBASE, however, you can lose your mind trying to find a module among dozens of similarly named ones. Naming modules is an art, and the novice should try to avoid names like PRG01.PRG, using instead names that explicitly describe the modules, such as EDIT.PRG or ADD.PRG.

As each module is debugged, it can be put aside. If errors occur in modules that call earlier modules, the debug environment is limited to the subset of modules called, rather than the complete code set. Again, this will be a powerful addition to the supportability and "bullet-proof" nature of the final code. If the end-user wants a screen display altered, the programmer will know exactly where to go, make the change in one place, and be fairly confident that the change would "take" throughout the system.

As an additional consideration, the coder can place special algorithms which are copyrighted, or protected under company trade secret or proprietary information laws, into their own modules. This would make the identification of such code easier in the case of legal disputes or contractual negotiations.

THE DEVELOPMENT ENVIRONMENT

It is just as important to define the environment for the development of a specific application as it is to define the application itself. A wide variety of programming languages and development tools exist in the microcomputer world, and a proper choice at the project definition level is essential.

Interpreters

There are two types of programming environments available to the microcomputer programmer. The first, and most straightforward, is the interpreter type of system. Most microcomputers come with a language called BASIC. On the IBM PC, a major part of BASIC exists on Read Only Memory (ROM) chips on the motherboard. The computer will "fall" into ROM BASIC if the DOS boot process fails. We will, therefore, use BASIC as our sample interpreted environment.

Interpreters actually read every line of code each time the program is executed. The line is "parsed," or broken up into key words that the interpreter understands, such as PRINT, READ, or OPEN. Syntax for the phrase is checked, and if the syntax is valid the line is executed by running machine-level code associated with the recognized operation. A code fragment like:

```
100  FOR I=1 to 100
110  PRINT I
120  NEXT I
```

is interpreted in the following manner.

Line number 100 has the key word FOR. BASIC expects a variable name, in this case I, a starting value, 1, and an ending value, 100. In some BASIC spaces are required between each element, and failure to use them would result in the interpreter returning a syntax error. Line 110 has the statement PRINT I, which tells the interpreter to find the value of I in memory and feed it to the machine language routine that will print it on the screen. The last line, 120, terminates the loop, using the syntax NEXT I. It checks to see if the value of I is equal to the ending value. If not, it increments I by one, and loops back to line 110.

Because this is an interpreted language, the loop must be read, analyzed, and executed 100 times. In a large program with hundreds of loops, conditional statements, and input/output routines, speed is sacrificed as the interpreter slowly does its work. The procedural languages used in dBASE, Rbase, and Paradox are interpreted and suffer from the same lack of efficiency. Why, then, use interpreters? The main reason is that they are simple to use. If the programmer wants to change the BASIC code fragment to print the values of I from 50 to 150, using the line editor, the line would be changed to read:

```
100  FOR I=50 to 150
```

Type RUN, press return, and the change would instantly take effect. There is no other step involved in the process.

Compilers

The other programming language environment makes use of things called compilers, which read the source code, and translate it into object code. This object code can be linked with other object modules and libraries into executable machine code. In such systems, loops are optimized, since the translations are done once for the loop by the compiler. Compiled code is smaller, faster, and more efficient. There is a major trade-off if, for example, the developer just wanted to make a change in the loop range. You would have to edit the line, then run the compiler, then the linker, and then have the executable file. If it is still not right, the process would need to be repeated. Compiled languages include C, Pascal, Fortran, COBOL, Modula, and Ada. Programmers coming to the microcomputer world from traditional mainframe and minicomputer "shops" are very comfortable with the compiler environments.

The quality of the executable code depends directly on the quality of the compiler. Software firms like Microsoft have been improving their compiler products for years, removing "quirks" and minimizing work-arounds, to the point where modern microcomputer implementation of these compiled languages is really quite good.

To use a compiler, a programmer must write the code using a text editor or a word processor. The compiler usually works on flat ASCII text, so if a word processor is to be used the non-document mode should be invoked. Text editors like BRIEF, Personal Editor, or Peter Norton's editor provide powerful features such as split screens, multi-file editing, block moves and copies, and automatic indentation. Word processors like WordStar have been used in non-document modes for years by large numbers of programmers. Editors become a fundamental part of the developer's toolbox, and many people have a near-religious regard for the one that they use. If the developer already knows and feels comfortable with a specific editor, do not bother changing to a new whiz-bang system unless there is a pressing need.

Choose the language that best suits the application. A lower-level language, such as C or Assembler, requires the programmer to build all of the fundamental modules required. This is valuable if speed or code size is crucial, because the developer is in complete control. Applications involving real-time processing, such as communications, might require the use of such low-level software. Higher-level languages, like BASIC and Fortran, do not require the development of fundamental modules, but the programmer is stuck with what the compiler is equipped with.

Because so many applications have database orientations, we will discuss the compilation process using dBASE. Products like Clipper and the dBASE III Compiler turn the interpreter-based dBASE code into a full-blown, compilable, language-development system. The development process is thus composed of writing the source code using a chosen editor, testing the code in dBASE using its interpreter, compiling it using Clipper, linking it with the available libraries, and then running the executable module. Notice that testing is done in the interpreter mode. Choosing a language that can be written and tested in interpreted form and then compiled can offer the developer the best of both worlds. Since IBM and Microsoft offer both an interpreter and a compiler for BASIC, the BASIC programmer can do this. In the C world there is a product called C-Terp by Gimpel Software that gives this option to C programmers.

The evolution of dBASE from a product to a full-blown language is enhanced by recent products that allow developers to link Assembly and C code into applications. Ashton-Tate has released the dBASE Tools for C, adding a number of enhanced features normally found in spreadsheets and array processing to dBASE. The Clipper system includes the ability to use extended libraries of C functions and assembled utilities in the final code. dBASE has spawned a plethora of other enhancements and utilities too numerous to mention. Some companies even offer complete dBASE source listings for accounting systems, project management systems, and other vertical applications. This makes it possible for a developer to purchase a working accounting system, modify the source to the clients' project needs, compile the code, and deliver a complex, customized system in a much shorter amount of time than if it was necessary to start from scratch. Using pre-tested source modules also limits debug time, assuming the modules are well-written, documented, and debugged before the developer begins.

You can use extended libraries to incorporate fast communications, file input/output, printer handlers, or whatever else might be lacking in your language of choice. The combination of editors, languages, compilers, linkers, utilities, and enhanced libraries is often referred to as the programmer's "toolbox" or "bag of tricks." Indeed, they do form the basis of the application development environment of any successful programmer.

Chapter 6

The Developer's Toolbox

One of the most exciting aspects of the modern microcomputer industry is the plethora of high-quality software development tools available to application programmers. In this chapter, a number of each type of tool will be compared and some recommendations will be made. Some categories lend themselves to opinion rather than clear-cut technical differences, and in those groups the preferences will be stated as just that—preferences.

The development process, which is a fairly structured entity, requires a number of distinct operations. These "system components" should be in place before any development begins. The programmer must first learn how to use the development software tools before hoping to become creative and productive. Choosing a dandy new editor to use on a project that has a time-crucial deadline would be both irresponsible and foolish, and would almost certainly guarantee failure. The time to become conversant with the development software is between projects, or at the very beginning, as the business is being formed. As time progresses, programmers begin to feel comfortable with a specific development environment. Usually they develop very strong opinions concerning the merits of one language or editor over another. This comfort is good, eliminating many problems associated with the use of new development tools.

The programmer's toolbox can be defined as consisting of the following objects:

- ☐ Editors.
- ☐ Programming Languages.
- ☐ Database Development Systems.
- ☐ Application Generators.
- ☐ Compilers.
- ☐ Utilities.

The remainder of the chapter will deal with descriptions and comparisons of a number of each type of package. These sections are not intended to include all of the available options—such a listing would be unwieldy at best. The products offered for review are to be considered representative of their category. Each month new whiz-bang products are created and should be evaluated by the developer as they arrive, remembering not to try something brand new during a project.

EDITORS

Editors are used to create program source files in an ASCII text format readable by various interpreted languages and compilers. There are two basic type of editors: line editors, with which the user edits a line of data at a time, and screen editors, with which data can be edited anywhere on the screen. In the old days, when the only input/output device available for the computer programmer was a teletype, line editors were the only ones possible. As CRTs became available, screen editors developed.

A classic line editor is the EDLIN program, which is distributed with PC-DOS. It is a simple-to-use program and is often the first kind of editor that a new PC owner gets to play with. EDLIN generates line numbers for the text file for indentification and manipulative functions. EDLIN is simply invoked from the DOS prompt by typing:

```
EDLIN FILE.TXT <cr>
```

where FILE.TXT is the filename to be edited. Because it is a line editor, the user must type a line number followed by the desired function, for example, 3D, which would delete the data on line three. The screen is displayed in Fig. 6-1.

For a big file, it is necessary to find the line that is to be edited by using the list command, L. There is also a search command to locate a specific character string. Other features include copy, insert, move, replace, write, and transfer. These make EDLIN a fairly

Fig. 6-1. Sample EDLIN screen.

```
<C:\devdb3>edlin sclip.bat
End of input file
*l
     1:*CLIPPER SHIP
     2: PLINK86 FI SHIP FI PSRCH FI C:\EXTENDA FI C:\EXTENDCL LI C:\CLIPPER
     3: SHIP
*
```

full-featured line editor reminiscent of the line editors used in mainframes years ago.

Many programmers begin using EDLIN, but they rapidly become frustrated with the difficulties involved in handling large files. After a change is made in, say, line 85, the programmer must type the line number of the next line to be edited, even if it is 86, rather than just continuing to edit. When the frustration level is high enough, the programmer usually discovers that screen editors are easier to use.

A good, low-cost, yet powerful, screen editor is Personal Editor 2 from IBM. This is a classic screen editor with several added features that make it very useful to programmers. Personal Editor allows the simultaneous editing of several files with windowing. Windowing allows the screen to be carved up into two or four regions, each with a view into a different file or into different parts of the same file. Figure 6-2 shows these windows as they appear on the screen.

Personal Editor also enables blocks of data to be moved, copied and deleted. This block data manipulation is a very useful feature in code writing, because the programmer can easily copy sections of working code from one part of a program to another part of the same program, or into a different program. For example, you can build a graphic character screen mask and copy it into various input and output modules. Block copies are much easier to do than line-by-line copies.

Personal Editor has a point-and-shoot approach. The programmer moves the cursor via the arrow keys to the beginning of the desired block of code, then presses the alternate (ALT) key and the B key simultaneously. Moving to the other end of the block, the programmer presses ALT-B again. The block becomes highlighted or inversed, depending on monitor type. The programmer can then move the cursor elsewhere in the same file, or into another file in another window, and press ALT-Z for an inserting copy or ALT-O for an overlay copy. The entire block is then copied to the new location. ALT-M would move the block from its original place to where the cursor is pointing, a feature that is useful when debugging code. This ease of block data manipulation and ability to handle multiple files lead us to recommend Personal Editor.

Many programmers use word processors to do text editing. This is only possible with word processors that do not include control characters for text formatting or that have a mode that produces flat ASCII text files. One of the most popular word processing programs with a non-document mode is Wordstar. Since its introduction on eight-bit CP/M microcomputers in the late seventies, WordStar, by Micropro International, has maintained a major market share and has been very popular with programmers. In its non-document mode, which is invoked by typing N from the main menu, WordStar acts as a flat ASCII text editor. To someone well versed in WordStar commands, the program allows for block manipulation much in the same way as Personal Editor does. A block is marked at its beginning and end, which then can be moved, copied, or deleted. One advantage of WordStar is that the marked

Fig. 6-2. Personal Editor 2 screen windows.

```
--- Top of file ---                       |--- Top of file ---
10 REM * ---------------------------------|BKS       PRG     3358   4-13-86  11:55p
20 REM *                                  |BKSADD    PRG     2785   2-17-86   4:06p
30 REM * Program:             ITEM.BAS    |BKSED     PRG     1401   3-03-86   8:36p
40 REM * System:              ABC Sports  |BKSFAU    PRG      842   1-29-86  11:43p
50 REM * Programmer:          Michael Si  |BKSGET    PRG     5856   4-14-86   7:10a
60 REM * Written:             01/20/86    |BKSGO     PRG      775   2-11-86   3:42p
70 REM * Revised By:          Michael Si  |BKSIO     PRG     4232   3-11-86   7:25a
80 REM * Revision Date:       04/14/86    |BKSOUT    PRG     1376   1-30-86   2:58p
                                          |
c:\ws\item.bas                            |.dir
                                          |
                                          |
------------------------------------------+---------------------------------------
    2  INVENUMBER  Character    12        |***************************************
    3  FIGURENUMB  Character    25        |* Procedure : Initialize System environ
    4  QTYONHAND   Numeric       4        |***************************************
    5  QTYONORDER  Numeric       4        |*
    6  QTYSOLD     Numeric       4        |CLOSE DATABASES
    7  AVAILTOSEL  Numeric       4        |RELEASE ALL
    8  TARGET      Numeric       4        |SET BELL OFF
    9  LASTCOST    Numeric      11        |SET TALK ON
   10  AVGCOST     Numeric      11        |CLEAR
                                          |
c:\devdb3\ABC.TXT     8    1 Replace|c:\devdb3\chap5.fig
                                          |
                                          |
```

block can be written to the disk as a new file. One major disadvantage is that WordStar can handle only one file at a time. This limits "cutting and pasting" to writes and reads of blocks to and from external text files. Even with this disadvantage, users develop loyalties to WordStar, and become comfortable with it. We would rarely try to discourage a loyal WordStar user into changing editors. However, do not recommend it as a choice for the new developer looking for a first text editor.

PROGRAMMING LANGUAGES

The heart of the development environment is the computer language that the programmer chooses. Although many higher-level languages are available for 16-bit microcomputers, we will discuss only a few: BASIC, C, and Pascal.

BASIC

BASIC has long been the major language in microcomputer development. Early microcomputer systems had BASIC included as a system standard; some even had BASIC in ROM. It was developed as an educational computer language at Dartmouth College over 20 years ago, and is claimed to be the most popular and most widely used language in the microcomputer world today. BASICA, the version shipped by Microsoft with the IBM PC, has become a defacto standard in the industry. Other implementations, like MS-DOS's GWBASIC, differ only in minor aspects.

With millions of copies of BASICA and similar interpreters in the public's machines, it is no wonder that so many developers and software writers have chosen to use BASICA. It is easy to learn, has powerful file handling and input/output statements, allows for excellent output formatting, and can provide direct hardware control as well as calls to lower-level machine language routines. Although BASICA suffers from the severe memory limitation of program and data segments limited to 64K, a number of other vendors are now producing enhanced BASICs for microcomputers. Due to competition with fast, compilable, structural languages, like C and Pascal, some of these new implementations bring these features to BASIC. Some of the new products are:

- ☐ Better BASIC by Summit Software Technology.
- ☐ Business BASIC by BASIS, Inc.
- ☐ MEGABASIC by American Planning Corporation.
- ☐ Professional BASIC by Morgan Computing Company.
- ☐ True BASIC by True Basic, Inc.

☐ Watcom BASIC by Watcom Products.

True BASIC is actually written by the team that developed the original BASIC on the timesharing system at Dartmouth. It adds full structured programming constructs, multi-line conditional statements, and enhanced subprogram support.

Refer to the June, 1986, issue of *PC Tech Journal* for a complete review and comparison of these modern BASIC versions. The article is called "Six New Shapes of Basic," by Ted Mirecki. The result of this analysis might surprise some people: BASICA still holds its own against the upstarts. We share this opinion, and feel that the ubiquitous nature of BASICA will continue to make it the dominant language in microcomputer development.

C Language

The major contender for "champion" language, however, is not BASIC, but a language called C.

C was developed by Brian Kernighan and Dennis Ritchie at Bell Laboratories, and has become very popular with "power" programmers. It is the language of choice when execution speed, code size, and file structure control are crucial. C is a structural programming language in the classic sense; there are no GOTO statements as in BASIC. This minimizes the tangled program flows possible in nonstructured languages. Although C is a compiler-based language, products like C-Terp provide an interpreted version, eliminating the necessity to run the compiler to see the effect of each code change. C is modular, so that program modules can be written, compiled, and tested individually, then linked into the final application.

Pascal and Its Derivatives

There is also considerable development being done in other microcomputer languages. Pascal, a structured language written by Nicolas Wirth to help teach programming, became very popular in the academic community. The University of California at San Diego aggressively marketed their version, UCSD Pascal. It was touted as a universal development language, because the compiler produced machine-independent "P-code" which could be executed on a wide variety of machines using various machine-based interpreters. The P-system, as it was called, never became popular, and the few packages written in UCSD Pascal did not do well, because P-system was not compatible with other disk operating systems. IBM PC users balked at spending nearly $1000 for the UCSD P-system when DOS could be had for $40. A very innovative programmer, Phillipe Kahn, formed a company called Borland International and announced a new version of Pascal, called Turbo Pascal, which ran under PC-DOS and sold, at its introduction, for $29.95. This was a major shock to SofTech, which was marketing the UCSD P-system. Turbo Pascal offered programmers a cheap, fast, powerful, structured programming environment. Many people learned to use editors and compilers using Turbo Pascal. Even as the price rose, the product's popularity continued to rise. Currently, Borland sells a series of developer's tools, graphics libraries, game and text editor programs, and other utilities, for the Turbo Pascal environment.

Recently, the author of the original Pascal released a similar language called MODULA. The defense department has specified another Pascal-derivative language, Ada, as the required language for all programs developed for any branch of the Department of Defense. Thus, Pascal and its offspring will be with us for some time. In universities as a teaching language, and in the public sector as a powerful, evolving, development language.

For the new developer choosing a language to learn, the best choice is C. Several of the superstars of the software world, like dBASE III PLUS, are written in C. Unix, which will probably be the operating system standard for microcomputers in the next few years, was written in C. C gives the code writer the benefits of high-level languages coupled with the power available only in low-level languages like Assemblers. C libraries with hundreds of functional modules are commercially available from companies like Greenleaf. This gives even a new developer access to professionally written and debugged program modules for file input/output, character processing, communications, and so on. With C, modules written in Assembler can be linked into the final executable program file as well. C offers the richest environment for the application developer, and thus should be in the developer's toolbox.

DATABASE DEVELOPMENT SYSTEMS

One of the major uses of computers is the manipulation of large amounts of character and numerical data which are in record formats. Many application developers, therefore, find great utility in using database management systems (DBMSs) in their environments. A number of microcomputer DBMSs have evolved into nearly complete development languages. For example, it is not incorrect to consider the procedural command language enclosed with dBASE III PLUS as a true computer language. A particular application is said to be written in dBASE, even though dBASE is the name of a product and not a language. There are a number of

DBMSs with procedural languages, editors, compilers, and utilities, making them excellent alternatives to the microcomputer development language. We will discuss several of the major available systems, and give examples of the available procedural languages. These languages are structured enough to easily be learned by a programmer trained in Pascal or C. They share common philosophical structures, such as conditional IF-THEN-ELSE and DO-WHILE statements. They have the additional advantage of giving the programmer direct access, using high-level command statements, to database functions like FIND, EDIT, DELETE, and REPLACE. These statements do not have to be constructed in their own modules as they might have to be if the work was being done in a "pure" language like C, Pascal, or BASIC.

Additionally, some of these DBMS procedural languages can call modules written in other languages, separately compiled into object formats. For example, a good C programmer can write fast, tight code for a communication device driver, and then call it from a high-level database application. This is in fact the best of both worlds. In the future some of these procedural languages will probably be considered true development languages, but for now they must be considered in this special category.

dBASE III PLUS

dBASE, by Ashton-Tate, is the top-selling database management system in the microcomputer market. It has evolved, along with the machines themselves, from its early eight-bit, CP/M version, to dBASE II, dBASE III, and dBASE III PLUS in the IBM PC 16-bit environment. Command language was introduced in dBASE II. The user was offered a "dot prompt" on a blank screen, which caused considerable criticism. Eventually, primitive help was made available, but it was not context specific, and so was hard to use. However, the good thing about even the early dBASE products was that the programmer could write a series of commands into an ASCII text file, and then execute them by typing DO and the filename at the dot prompt. This was an elementary form of programming. Programmer's quickly learned that simple applications could be created using this aspect of the program. Although there were more powerful, faster DBMSs competing with dBASE, the programmability implied by its procedural language led to the eventual market dominance of dBASE.

As an example of this programmability, assume that a user wishes to get data from a flat ASCII text file, sort it, and then send it to a report. In dBASE the task might be accomplished by the code fragment displayed in Fig. 6-3.

Fig. 6-3. dBASE III code fragment

```
USE FILE
APPEND FROM OLD.TXT SDF
SORT ON NAME TO NEW
USE NEW
REPORT FORM NEW TO PRINT
```

Although this might seem straightforward, it is certainly not reasonable to assume that an end-user would remember each step, and its syntax, each time this report was needed. The developer could have saved this fragment into a text file called REP, and the user would merely type DO REP to accomplish the desired result. This made the system more usable by the end-user group. As programmers began to make more and more demands, the command language improved. Screen input/output functions, character and numerical manipulations, and conditional statements were added. Although the early dBASE products were limited by the eight-bit environment to having only 32 fields per record and 64K records per file, these problems have been more than compensated for in the modern 16-bit incarnations of dBASE III PLUS. Excellent query and file relationship constructs have been added to make the current product a powerful relational database system.

On the negative side, dBASE is slow, has a clumsy indexing and sorting algorithm, and is interpreted. dBASE III PLUS requires 256K of RAM just for itself, so that the user must really go to the maximum DOS RAM size of 640K to run applications of any size. The standard dBASE III PLUS is, like its predecessors, a single-user system. This limitation flies in the face of the huge capacity of the product. Why would one user need a billion records anyway? The reality of the market puts the need for large databases in the hands of multi-user audiences, typically LAN-based. Recently has Ashton-Tate released multi-user LAN-based versions of dBASE III PLUS, so these issues should take care of themselves. There is some resistance to the use of dBASE III PLUS in LANs, however, due to the relatively high cost of each LAN node license.

Ashton-Tate also has runtime versions of dBASE so that each user in a company (not on a LAN) does not need to own a complete copy of it just to run an application. The cost of these runtime licenses has dropped rapidly during the last year, due to intense competition from "third party" suppliers of add-on products.

The greatest phenomenon about dBASE as a product is the proliferation of these add-on program products. Even in the days of dBASE II, software developers who complained about the slow indexing and sorting capability of dBASE were offered external utilities that did these functions more quickly. Small software houses, like Gryphon Inc., sold things like dFastest. Others marketed dozens of products to help users get better performance out of dBASE. Currently, products like QuickIndex by Fox & Geller, and dFlow by Wallsoft, offer developers rapid indexing and code analysis. These companies have done well by addressing the weaknesses of a product that, in spite of its weaknesses, has become the market leader.

dBASE's editor is relatively weak, and has a code size limit that makes it worthless for any but the smallest programs. Ashton-Tate, realizing that many developers might want to use their own editors, has made it relatively easy to designate the editor to be used. dBASE is told which editor is to be called by the use of a configuration file (CONFIG.DB). This makes the system think that Personal Editor, WordStar, or some other package is an integrated component. Therefore, a developer who opts for dBASE as a main development system should also expect to purchase an editor.

A similar statement can be made about compilers. Ashton-Tate has not, to date, supplied a product that can compile dBASE code into executable machine code, which would not require the end-user to own a copy of dBASE to run the application. Other software vendors have jumped in. The most successful is Clipper by Nantucket (discussed in the section on compilers). Wordtech also markets a dBASE III compiler and a number of others might soon appear. There are even rumors that Ashton-Tate has one on the drawing board.

The dBASE environment itself is quite rich in features. The maximum number of records is one billion, assuming there is enough disk space. However, DOS has a file size limitation of about 32 megabytes per file, so the actual number of records per file is much less than a billion. This billion-record potential is just a function of the addressing capability of dBASE III PLUS.

The current program also allows up to 128 fields per record. This number can be effectively increased by using file relationships so that very large applications can be accommodated. There can be up to ten files open simultaneously, providing a speed increase because files can be left open. Some programmers open all of their files at the beginning of execution and close them at the end. This is not technically incorrect, and can be handled by dBASE's multiple-open file capability. However, it may not be good practice, because some of the data might be kept in RAM buffers during processing and could be lost during a power failure or hardware crash. It is, therefore, a good idea to periodically "flush" the buffers by closing and reopening database files during the program's execution.

dBASE allows for a maximum width of 256 characters for a normal data field. There is also a special data field type, called a memo field, which can store up to 4096 bytes of text data. This memo data cannot, however, be used to find, seek, or sort, so many programmers find its usefulness limited. Although the 256 character limit for a normal data field might not seem to be a problem, be aware that the maximum total size for a record is only 4096 bytes. It may not be possible, then, to get 128 fields in a record if a few of them are 256 bytes long.

With all of these limitations you might wonder why dBASE is the superstar that it is. Surely, its competitors wonder. It is the leader because of the size of its installed base and its product identification. With a number of add-on software packages to make up for its limitations, dBASE is a formidable system indeed. We do a great deal of applications development in dBASE, and feel comfortable in recommending it as the DBMS of choice to the new developer. Choosing a good editor, compiler, and programming utilities enables the programmer to develop a nearly complete "pure" language system. A recent release from Ashton-Tate, dBASE Tools for C, also adds the power of C to the developer's toolbox. With this package, matrix or array processing, financial calculations, and direct C calls can be added to dBASE III PLUS applications.

As a side note, Wordtech is now selling a complete dBASE interpreter package called dBXL. This is a complete "clone" of dBASE III PLUS, supporting all of the standard commands offered by the Ashton-Tate product, as well as adding a few of its own. What makes this product interesting is that its list price is roughly one-fourth of that of dBASE III PLUS, or $169. By the time this book is in print its street price will be less then $100. This is an excellent alternative package to dBASE III PLUS at an excellent price. Because dBASE is changing from being a product to becoming a true language, multi-source interpreters are to be expected and even welcomed. The danger to Ashton-Tate, however, is that entire systems might be developed legally in dBASE without the use of a single product supplied by Ashton-Tate itself.

dBASE III is a powerful tool for the application developer. As part of a development environment that includes an editor of choice, a compiler, a C compiler, and various debugging and reporting utilities, we feel that it is the best of the many options available.

R:base 5000

One of the major competitors in the area of DBMSs is the R:base 5000 package from MicroRim, Inc. Like dBASE, R:base has been through several incarnations since its introduction in the early eighties. Early versions relied on a program interface with Pascal, giving programmers access to a library of database management routines to add to the application. MicroRim released its R:base 4000 product to directly compete with dBASE II. When dBASE III was released, some of its new features seemed to be a result of Ashton-Tates' analysis of competitors like R:base. The 4000 was aimed at users who wanted pure DBMS applications, like the maintaining of a customer file or inventory list. In order to address the wider potential markets of custom applications, R:base 5000 was released and targeted at application developers.

There are several valuable components in the standard R:base 5000 package. First, there is a reasonably good editor, called RBEDIT. It can be used to create text files that can be executed by a run-type command, as well as to modify any code generated by the code generator, called Application Express, which is also included in the package.

Another interesting feature is a kind of a compiler, called RCOMPILE. It is not a true compiler, performing more like Ashton-Tate's runtime system than, say, Clipper. RCOMPILE produces binary files that can be run, but not examined or changed, by the end-user. This accomplishes the code security desired by the application developer, but does not free the end-user from having a full version of R:base 5000 at each computer. MicroRim has plans for a runtime version which will run only the binary files. The compiler does not generate machine code, and thus is incapable of producing a free-standing executable module. It does link many program files into one file, making it unnecessary to clutter the user's disk with hundreds of small files.

One major innovation MicroRim offers in the package is the FILEGATEWAY program. This utility allows for the direct importation of files from many of the popular microcomputer applications, including 1-2-3, dBASE, Multiplan and PFS. This type of feature is invaluablebecause the environment that the application is to eventually reside in may have data in several such diverse formats. A discussion of this issue of inter-application file interchange is presented in Chapter 11.

R:base 5000 has most of the syntactical constructs required by a structured programming languages, like IF-THEN-ELSE-ENDIF and WHILE-ENDWHILE. Conditional structures can be nested up to ten deep, but programs can only be nested six deep. The language should be easy for a dBASE, C, or Pascal programmer to learn, although the MicroRim people use some nonstandard terms. A group of files is called a database, a file is known as a table, a record is called a row, and a field is a column. This is a spreadsheet type structure, which is easy to work with once the user gets comfortable with it. See Fig. 6-4 for an example of what a R:base table looks like where NAME, ADDRESS, and CITY are field names (columns), and each record is a row.

R:base can have 400 fields per record (dBASE has maximum of 128), and can have up to 40 tables open simultaneously. R:base also includes, as standard features, array processing, password security, data dictionary rules, and a language interface. These are available in dBASE only through the use of add-on products. There is an excellent report generator included, allowing for the combination of multiple files into single reports, a feature not available in the dBASE report generator. The form creation is screen-oriented; the user simply "paints" the form on the screen, a method that has become very popular with non-sophisticated users and professional programmers alike. This "what you see is what you get" approach is offered to the dBASE user only via the purchase of add-on report generation programs like Quick Report by Fox & Geller.

R:base 5000 is a well thought-out product, but a number of factors prevent our recommending it as the DBMS of choice. The fact that the editor and compiler are included in the package may be part of the problem. Neither is as strong as it needs to be, and there seems to be no third-party source for add-on software products. This lack of third-party competition is a serious problem. Although R:base is powerful, it is not ubiquitous enough to motivate software developers to provide a true compiler, for example. In the computer section of a bookstore you would find dozens of books

Fig. 6-4. Example of R:base table.

```
            +--------------------------------------------------------+
            |NAME              ADDRESS                CITY           |
            |--------------------------------------------------------|
            |Name 1            Address 1              City 1         |
Record # 2  |Name 2            Address 2              City 2         |
            |Name 3            Address 3              City 3         |
            |                                                        |
            |                                                        |
            |Name N            Address N              City N         |
            +--------------------------------------------------------+
```

on programming in dBASE, and very few addressing the R:base 5000 language. The technical and trade periodicals are nearly devoid of R:base utilities. The momentum generated by a large user base with well-defined needs is missing in R:base 5000. Thus, no products, few books, and relatively few programmers market their skills in the R:base language.

If the application developer inherits a project that has been started in R:base 5000, it might make sense to learn the language and finish the project. However, probably would not choose such a path. There is little to recommend dropping dBASE in favor of R:base, and it would be easier to restart the project in a language that the programmer knew.

Thus, we do not recommend R:base 5000 as the DBMS development system in the developer's toolbox.

Paradox

Paradox, by Ansa, is a highly touted new entry into the DBMS arena. Its name comes from its nature; it is a powerful and complex relational database system that is supposed to be very easy to use. It is believed to be a sign of the future of system software, incorporating advanced concepts from artificial intelligence to help the user run the system. The system is written in C, and is very large. Ansa recommends a minimum of 512K of RAM and two floppy drives, but this is not really acceptable for any real use of the system. Paradox really needs much more memory and a hard disk to even begin to be useable.

The program itself is very powerful. It has a user interface similar to Lotus 1-2-3 in which there is a horizontal menu with the current option highlighted and an explanation of the option on the line below.

The database definitions are similar to those of R:base 5000. Files are called tables, fields are denoted as columns, and records are known as rows. This two-dimensional theme is spreadsheet-like as well and adds to the overall feel of familiarity that you get when you first use Paradox. There is excellent on-screen, context-specific help, and excellent documentation as a backup. Users can construct forms using a very crisp screen painter/report writer routine. In this area Paradox outshines all other competitors. Multiple databases can be linked with multilevel queries into a single form. The query "language" is spreadsheet oriented as well, in which the fields (column headings) are displayed horizontally and the user merely "checks" the desired fields and the query conditions under which they are to be selected. An example is shown in Fig. 6-5.

Fig. 6-5. Paradox query.

CLIENT	CLIENT #	LAST NAME	STREET	CITY	ZIP	AMOUNT DUE
	X	X				>1000

This query would give the client number and last name of all customers who owe more than $1000. The resulting table would look like Fig. 6-6.

This visual, two-dimensional representation of databases, queries, and relationships is easy to use for the "semi-sophisticated" user, but non-computer types would still rely on programmed applications. To this end, there is a Paradox Application Language (PAL) included in the Paradox package. PAL is a high-level structured programming language that is executed from special files called scripts. Scripts can be recorded by turning on that feature from the Paradox menu. Once invoked, all key strokes can be saved to a named file, then played back by "playing" the script. There is also a screen-oriented editor, which is really just a plain text processor. This process is entirely analogous to the building of text files using an editor and DO-ing them in dBASE III PLUS. The design philosophy of PAL is very similar to that of the procedural languages in dBASE and R:base. PAL excels in its mathematical functions, array/matrix processing, character and form manipulations, and in the fact that all of the most powerful query capabilities of Paradox are made available to the programmer. Date-variable and environmental data handling are also much more powerful then those found in other products. The language is the richest of the lot, offering more functions and commands than many programmers will ever need. These functions are, however, there.

In fact, the size and power of PAL is probably its great shortcoming. PAL applications are slow. The ultimate paradox of this product, then, is that it is really very powerful, and yet might not become the new standard-bearer in the DBMS world.

Ansa has also developed an excellent import and export facility, allowing for easy interchange of data between Paradox, 1-2-3, dBASE, Symphony, PFS file, and programs that use ASCII or DIF file formats. This should make it easy to integrate PAL applications into end-user systems. There is no compiler, but Ansa is

Fig. 6-6. Result of Paradox query.

ANSWER	CLIENT #	LAST NAME	AMOUNT DUE
1	1	ADAMS	1234.55
2	9	CARSON	2355.11
3	22	DAWSON	1534.66

providing a very liberal runtime policy so that end-users will be able to run the applications without having to purchase Paradox.

We feel that although Paradox is an excellent product, with capabilities that in many areas exceed those of dBASE III, it still cannot be recommended as the primary DBMS tool for the application developer.

A number of other contenders for dBASE's dominance exist, and they are mentioned for completeness:

- ☐ Dataflex by Data Access Corporation.
- ☐ DataEase by Software Solutions.
- ☐ Knowledgeman by MDBS, Inc.
- ☐ dBMan by Versasoft.

In conclusion, dBASE III PLUS is the DBMS of choice, although a number of competitors of very high quality exist. Until such products as Paradox and R:base 5000 develop large user bases and the support of third-party add-on software companies, we feel that they cannot offer the same power as dBASE. Refer to the June 24, 1986, issue of *PC Magazine* for an in-depth comparison of DBMS packages.

APPLICATION GENERATORS

Programmers have a recurring nightmare. They fear the day when end-users will be able to construct their own applications on their own computer, without the need for programmers. As the cost of computers continues to drop, while the power they contain grows by leaps and bounds, the lure of application generators for end-users may become a force for application developers to contend with.

Some programmers might also be considering the use of application generators to increase productivity, standardize code, and make user support easier. Because many computer software projects share common functions, program generators could be allowed to do the "boring stuff," leaving the customization to the human programmer.

The current microcomputer market is top heavy with spreadsheets; database management systems are still in second place as the major applications. Standards have emerged in both market segments, Lotus 1-2-3 and dBASE III, respectively. Recently, the database market has begun to heat up, with a number of new innovative products trying to topple Ashton-Tate's Goliath. During this same period dBASE appears to be evolving from a database product into an application development language, complete with compilers and C language extentions. As thousands of users develop applications in this environment, either by learning dBASE programming or by hiring programmers, the pressure to examine automated program generators grows.

This section compares several major application generators from the perspective of a professional programmer, with special notice to such issues as look and feel of the finished product. The packages to be analyzed are:

- ☐ dBASE III PLUS APPSGEN.
- ☐ Genifer by Bytel, Inc.
- ☐ R:base 5000 Application EXPRESS by MicroRim, Inc.
- ☐ Paradox Application Generator by ANSA Corporation.

The comparison is based on supplying each product with the same application database, and examining the programs that were generated. Our tests were all run a standard IBM PC with an AST Six Pack Plus and Microscience 20 megabyte hard disk. The database

Fig. 6-7. Application generator test database.

Test Database

Field	Width	Type	Decimal
LASTNAME	25	Char	
FIRSTNAME	15	Char	
ADDRESS	25	Char	
CITY	15	Char	
STATE	2	Char	
ZIPCODE	9	Char	
DATE	8	Date	
ORDERNUMB	5	Numb	0
ITEMNUMB	7	Char	
QUANTITY	4	Numb	0
UNITPRICE	11	Numb	2
EXTENDPRCE	11	Numb	2
UNITCOST	11	Numb	2
EXTENDCOST	11	Numb	2
PREPAID	1	Logic	
CREDITCARD	1	Logic	
CCNUMB	16	Char	
EXPDATE	6	Char	
INVOICE	6	Numb	0
COMMENT	50	Char	

used for the comparison test is shown in Fig. 6-7.

This database has many of the elements of a typical application, including several data types, multiple keys, and calculated fields.

The application to be created should allow for the ADDing, DELETing, EDITing, and REPORTing of this data. The index key field is LASTNAME.

dBASE III PLUS APPSGEN

The application generator program APPSGEN is included in the dBASE III Plus package on its own distribution diskette and with its own manual. Much has been said about the high quality of the new dBASE documentation, and the APPSGEN booklet is part of it. The user is guided step-by-step through the installation (which thankfully does not include copy protect machinations), and is shown how to build a sample application. The manual is well illustrated, well written, and should enable even a near novice to successfully navigate through the process.

APPSGEN is a dBASE program, and is executed from the dot prompt. It uses interactive utilities within dBASE to create the database, screens, reports, and labels. If the user has spent even a small amount of time with the tutorials and documentation there should be little trouble creating a simple application. There appears to be some facility for more advanced applications, but the advanced features of APPSGEN are little more than a way to enter DO commands for modules written outside of the program generator, such as DO REPORTS.

The main (and only) menu produced is shown in Fig. 6-8.

The code fragment in Fig. 6-9 shows a clean, structured style, with good internal documentation.

As can be seen from the menu and the code, the output of APPSGEN is plain, but serviceable, meeting the needs of the most basic database management systems. This program is more like a shell around a series of interactive dBASE III PLUS utilities than a true application program generator.

For example, to find a specific record in the database the user must scroll through the database by pressing the PgUp and PgDn keys rather than doing an index key field search using the dBASE commands FIND and SEEK. This would be unwieldy in a database of any significant size, and would be considered bad programming form in any application.

As a matter of interest, the dBASE code generators were subjected to the Clipper compiler. There were six errors during a compile with the Winter, 1985 version of Clipper. Because the compiler

Fig. 6-8. APPSGEN application main menu.

```
+------------------------------------------------------------------------------+
|                          D B A S E    A P P S G E N                          |
|------------------------------------------------------------------------------|
|                                                                              |
|                                                                              |
|                              1. ADD INFORMATION                              |
|                              2. CHANGE INFORMATION                           |
|                              3. REMOVE INFORMATION                           |
|                              4. REVIEW INFORMATION                           |
|                              5. PRINT REPORT                                 |
|                              6. PRINT LABELS                                 |
|                                                                              |
|                              0. EXIT                                         |
|                                                                              |
+------------------------------- select  0 ------------------------------------+
```

Fig. 6-9. APPSGEN application code fragment.

```
USE DBA INDEX DBA

DO WHILE .T.

   * ---Display menu options, centered on the screen.
   *    draw menu border and print heading
   CLEAR
   @ 2, 0 TO 16,79 DOUBLE
   @ 3,10 SAY [D B A S E   A P P S G E N  ]
   @ 4,1 TO 4,78 DOUBLE
   * ---display detail lines
   @  7,30 SAY [1. ADD INFORMATION]
   @  8,30 SAY [2. CHANGE INFORMATION]
   @  9,30 SAY [3. REMOVE INFORMATION]
   @ 10,30 SAY [4. REVIEW INFORMATION]
   @ 11,30 SAY [5. PRINT REPORT]
   @ 12,30 SAY [6. PRINT LABELS]
   @ 14, 30 SAY '0. EXIT'
   STORE 0 TO selectnum
   @ 16,33 SAY " select     "
   @ 16,42 GET selectnum PICTURE "9" RANGE 0,6
   READ

   DO CASE
      CASE selectnum = 0
         SET BELL ON
```

```
    SET TALK ON
    CLEAR ALL
    RETURN

  CASE selectnum = 1
  *  DO ADD INFORMATION
    APPEND
    SET CONFIRM OFF
    STORE ' ' TO wait_subst
    @ 23,0 SAY 'Press any key to continue...' GET wait_subst
    READ
    SET CONFIRM ON

  CASE selectnum = 2
  *  DO CHANGE INFORMATION
```

does not support interactive dBASE commands such as EDIT, APPEND, and BROWSE, this code is unsuitable as the basis of a compiled application. In addition, DOUBLE and SET STATUS errors in dBASE III PLUS are commands not yet implemented in Clipper.

APPSGEN is thus only applicable to the most elementary applications, and may serve perfectly well for the non-programming user of dBASE III Plus who wishes to 'codify' an application.

Genifer

Genifer, by Bytel, is a new application development system for dBASE III. It is a very complete environment, and therefore more complex than other systems. The documentation is good, and an adequate sample set and tutorial are provided. Since the program is oriented toward the more sophisticated developer, several assumptions are made in the development flow. It is heartwarming to see program authors counseling would-be developers to plan, design, and test their applications.

Genifer lets the programmer do all menu design and screen painting using the text editor of your choice, So no new screen editing commands need to be learned. The environmental setup is straightforward, and we had little trouble creating the menu for the test database. The seasoned code writer has a significant advantage over the novice using Genifer, because the old pro has probably built many screens using text editors before, and Genifer offers only a blank screen in the editor of your choice (with no on screen help!).

This even sent this old master back to his last resort (actually reading the manual), and made him clean off a corner of his desk (knocking his dusty mouse onto the carpet) so that he could refer to the manual often as he built his application. This should not be taken as a direct criticism of the product, but more as a wise (and perhaps cynical) appraisal of user approaches to documentation. Most people have become spoiled by the high quality of on-line context-specific help available with many software tools on the market today, and becoming lazy and overly expectant.

Once Genifer is learned this negative attitude should change, because it is a good product, producing code of such good quality that it is almost frightening. It includes enough structure and internal documentation to make it eminently modifiable, providing the software application developer with a good foundation upon which to build custom systems.

The code fragment in Fig. 6-10 is from the ADD procedure. The creation and definition process was not difficult once mastered.

Fig. 6-10. Genifer application code fragment.

```
* PROCEDURES (listed alphabetically)


procedure add
* Add a new record (if option = 'A') or copy the current
* record (if option = 'C')
    do init_key
    do init_fld
  endif
  * The following "get record" loop can be exited either when a valid
  * record is entered (valid_rec = .T.), or when entry is aborted by
  * (1) blank key, (2) duplicate key (if not allowed), or (3) abort
  * request from the validation procedure (if called).
  abort_rec = .F.
  valid_rec = .F.
  do while .not. (valid_rec .or. abort_rec)
    do get_key
    do get_flds
    read
    comp_key = comp_key&num
    if null_key&num = &comp_key
      * blank key
      abort_rec = .T.
    else
      do chk_dupl
      if dupl_rec
        abort_rec = .T.
```

```
    else
      do val_rec
    endif (dupl_rec)
  endif (null_key = comp_key)
enddo (while .not. (valid_rec .or. abort_rec))
if valid_rec
  do save_rec with .T.
else
  * break out of "Add" if record invalid
    if empty
      option = 'Q'
    else
      option = 'M'
      if .not. dupl_rec
        go record_no
      endif
    endif (empty)
  endif (valid_rec)
return
```

The test application including database definition, menu and screen painting, and report design, took less than an hour (not counting re-reading the documentation a few times to clarify ambiguous points). The process is straightfoward: a data entry screen is painted using the text editor, the data fields are marked using a character like "__" or "-" (this is user definable in the environment definitions), and the program prompts the user to define which database variable goes with which field entry. A sample is shown in Fig. 6-11.

The dotted line for field #3 flashes, and the user types in the field name, in this case INVOICE. Once all of the fields are defined, the program creates a series of layout and screen files for later use in program generation. Again, this provides for very flexible design and development.

Figure 6-12 is what the data entry screen looks like, running in dBASE III PLUS.

There are several problems involved in using this generated code with Clipper, which are discussed in some detail in the Genifer documentation. Most of these require the user to go into the code and rename procedure names and some macro definitions. Because we are unabashedly biased in favor of compilers, and Clipper in particular, we feel that this code compiler incompatibility is a major drawback of Genifer for use by an application developer. In the test application there were 29 errors during Clipper compilation, all requiring recoding.

Fig. 6-11. Genifer data field definition screen.

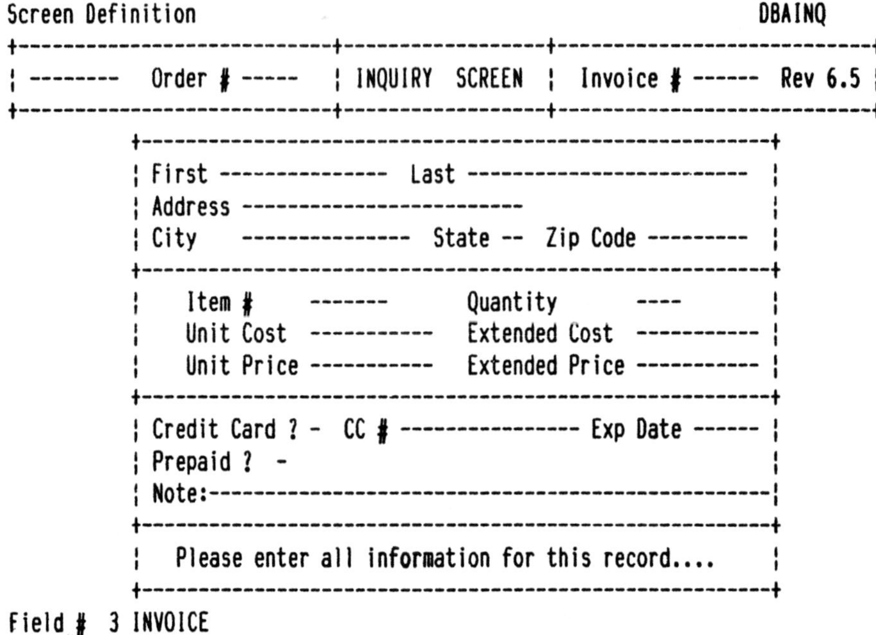

```
Screen Definition                                                DBAINQ
+----------------------------+------------------+----------------------------+
| --------   Order # -----   | INQUIRY  SCREEN  |  Invoice # ------  Rev 6.5 |
+----------------------------+------------------+----------------------------+
           +--------------------------------------------------------+
           | First --------------  Last ------------------------    |
           | Address ------------------------                       |
           | City    ---------------  State --  Zip Code ---------  |
           +--------------------------------------------------------+
           |   Item #     -------      Quantity       ----          |
           |   Unit Cost  -----------  Extended Cost  -----------   |
           |   Unit Price -----------  Extended Price -----------   |
           +--------------------------------------------------------+
           | Credit Card ? -  CC # --------------- Exp Date ------  |
           | Prepaid ?  -                                           |
           | Note:--------------------------------------------------|
           +--------------------------------------------------------+
           |  Please enter all information for this record....      |
           +--------------------------------------------------------+
Field #  3 INVOICE
Enter name of assigned field (Press ESC for options)
```

Fig. 6-12. Genifer application running in dBASE III PLUS.

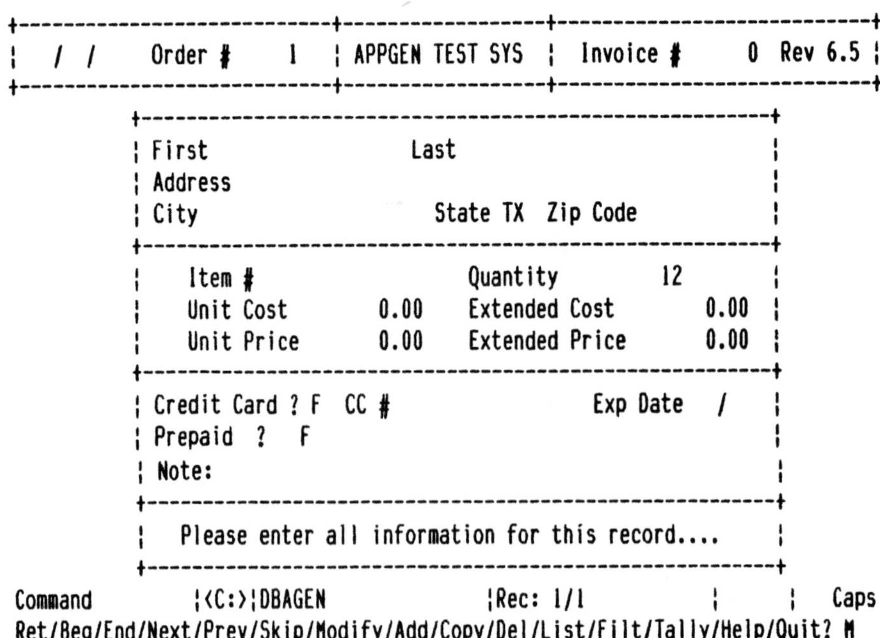

```
+----------------------------+------------------+----------------------------+
|  / /     Order #       1   | APPGEN TEST SYS  |  Invoice #      0  Rev 6.5 |
+----------------------------+------------------+----------------------------+
           +--------------------------------------------------------+
           | First                 Last                             |
           | Address                                                |
           | City                     State TX  Zip Code            |
           +--------------------------------------------------------+
           |   Item #                  Quantity          12         |
           |   Unit Cost        0.00   Extended Cost          0.00  |
           |   Unit Price       0.00   Extended Price         0.00  |
           +--------------------------------------------------------+
           | Credit Card ? F  CC #                 Exp Date    /    |
           | Prepaid  ?   F                                         |
           | Note:                                                  |
           +--------------------------------------------------------+
           |  Please enter all information for this record....      |
           +--------------------------------------------------------+
Command          |<C:>|DBAGEN             |Rec: 1/1          |      |  Caps
Ret/Beg/End/Next/Prev/Skip/Modify/Add/Copy/Del/List/Filt/Tally/Help/Quit? M
```

Genifer is an excellent tool for the developer, producing high quality, easily supported code. It represents the type of product which might well evolve into a fourth generation application development environment, capable of leading even the non-programmer through the development process to produce applications easily.

R:base 5000 Application Express

R:base 5000 is a high power relational database with a procedural language, a good text editor, a built-in compiler, an application generator, and a well thought-out user interface. It is positioned in the market as a competitor to dBASE III PLUS and contains a number of features that exist in dBase III PLUS only as external add-ons, if at all.

The Application Express comes up in a simple menu as shown in Fig. 6-13.

The user is prompted to create a new database by choosing menu option one. There is excellent, context-specific help throughout the process. The actual database creation is graphically guided (Fig. 6-14), again offering help on the way.

A nice feature is the use of data types like REAL, INTEGER, and DOLLAR for many commonly used numerical formats, making it unnecessary to count width and decimal places. There is no logical data type, but a text with width one (checking for Y or N) should work.

After saving the database definition the user goes into option three, the definition of a new application. Menus can be created either in a vertical or horizontal format. A vertical menu is shown in Fig. 6-15.

Fig. 6-13. Application Express menu.

```
                    Application EXPRESS

      Copyright (c) 1985 by Microrim, Inc. (Ver. 1.01 PC-DOS)

+-------------------Select option - [F10] for help-------------------------+
|              (1)  Define a new database                                   |
|              (2)  Change an existing database definition                  |
|              (3)  Define a new application                                |
|              (4)  Change an existing application                          |
|              (5)  Display file directory                                  |
|              (6)  Exit                                                    |
+---------------------------------------------------------------------------+
```

Fig. 6-14. Application Express database creation.

Enter or change the column names - [ESC] when done

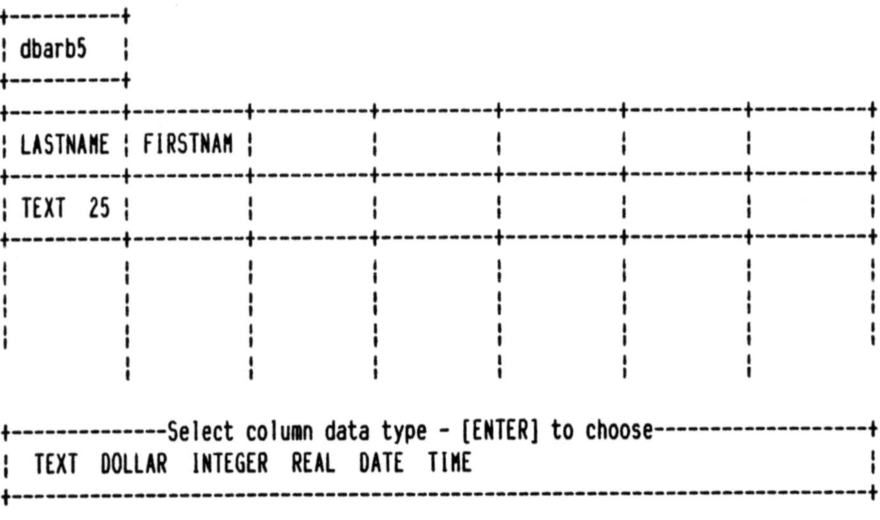

```
+----------+
| dbarb5   |
+----------+
+----------+----------+----------+----------+----------+----------+----------+
| LASTNAME | FIRSTNAM |          |          |          |          |          |
+----------+----------+----------+----------+----------+----------+----------+
| TEXT  25 |          |          |          |          |          |          |
+----------+----------+----------+----------+----------+----------+----------+

+-------------Select column data type - [ENTER] to choose-------------------+
|  TEXT  DOLLAR  INTEGER  REAL  DATE  TIME                                  |
+---------------------------------------------------------------------------+
```

[F1] Insert [F2] Delete [F3] Review [F5] Reset value [F10] Help
Database dbarb5 --- Defining table dbarb5 --- Column 2

Once the menu items are defined, the user is guided, option by option, to describe what each selection should do, i.e., LOAD, EDIT, DELETE, BROWSE, PRINT and so on. The user responds to options as shown in Fig. 6-16.

Fig. 6-15. Application Express application menu.

Enter or change the menu choices - [ESC] when done

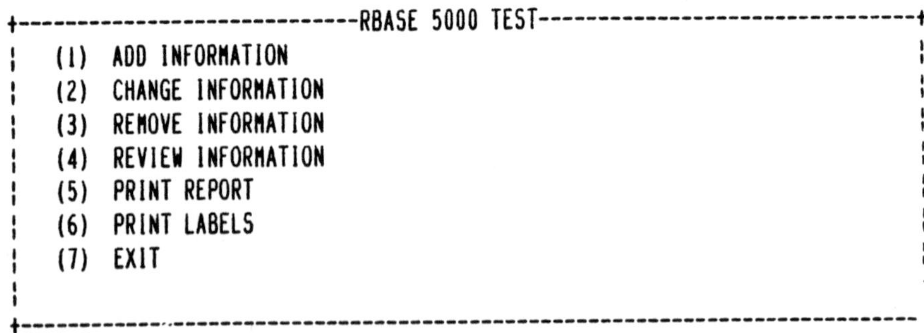

```
+----------------------------RBASE 5000 TEST--------------------------------+
|   (1)  ADD INFORMATION                                                    |
|   (2)  CHANGE INFORMATION                                                 |
|   (3)  REMOVE INFORMATION                                                 |
|   (4)  REVIEW INFORMATION                                                 |
|   (5)  PRINT REPORT                                                       |
|   (6)  PRINT LABELS                                                       |
|   (7)  EXIT                                                               |
|
+--------------------------------------------------------------------------
```

[F1] Insert [F2] Delete [F3] Review [F5] Reset value [F10] Help
Database DBARB5   - Defining Application DBARB5   - Menu MAIN

Fig. 6-16. Application Express menu option definition.

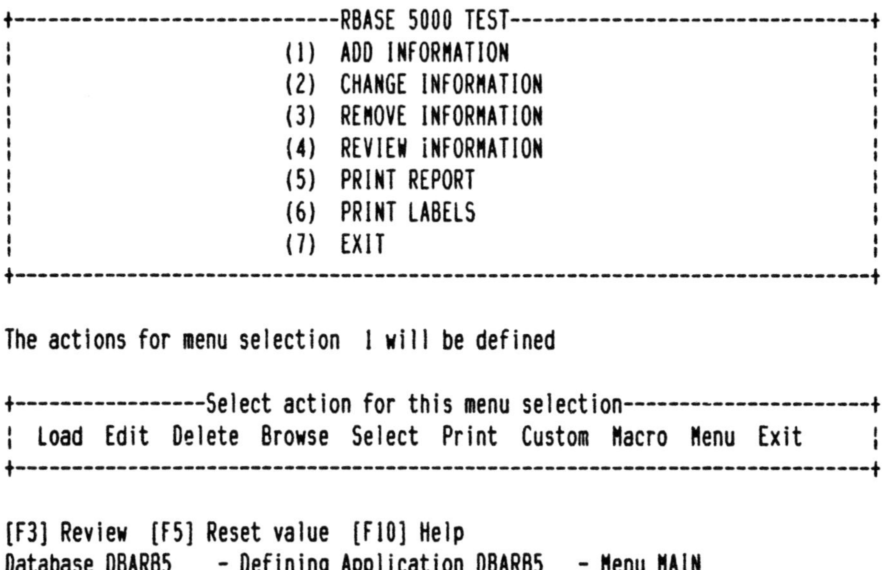

```
+---------------------------RBASE 5000 TEST-------------------------------+
|                      (1)  ADD INFORMATION                                |
|                      (2)  CHANGE INFORMATION                             |
|                      (3)  REMOVE INFORMATION                             |
|                      (4)  REVIEW INFORMATION                             |
|                      (5)  PRINT REPORT                                   |
|                      (6)  PRINT LABELS                                   |
|                      (7)  EXIT                                           |
+-------------------------------------------------------------------------+

The actions for menu selection  1 will be defined

+----------------Select action for this menu selection--------------------+
| Load  Edit  Delete  Browse  Select  Print  Custom  Macro  Menu  Exit    |
+-------------------------------------------------------------------------+

[F3] Review  [F5] Reset value  [F10] Help
Database DBARB5    - Defining Application DBARB5    - Menu MAIN
```

For the more advanced programmer, custom routines can be integrated into the menu. R:base 5000 includes enough standard routines so that even the novice programmer should be able to develop adequate applications in a very short time using Application Express.

In general, the R:base package has excellent documentation and an exceptionally good tutorial system. Included in the system is a text editor called RBEDIT, which enables the user to modify the text files produced by the application generator. A sample of the procedural language is shown in Fig. 6-17.

The language is structured and similar enough conceptually to the dBASE procedural language so that programmers adept in dBASE should have little difficulty programming in this environment.

Thus, we rate the R:base system an acceptable choice to a user not of the dBASE III "religion." It is a very complete and powerful product and allows for novice and professional alike to produce good applications quickly and easily.

Paradox APGEN

Ansa's Paradox is an extremely well-designed relational database system with artificial intelligence characteristics. The new release (1.10) includes an application generator called APGEN.

Fig. 6-17. Application Express code fragment.

```
$COMMAND
DBARB5
SET MESSAGE OFF
OPEN DBARB5
SET ERROR MESSAGE OFF
SET VAR PICK1  INT
LABEL STARTAPP
  NEWPAGE
  CHOOSE PICK1  FROM MAIN     IN DBARB5.APX
  IF PICK1  EQ 0 THEN
    GOTO ENDAPP
  ENDIF
  IF PICK1  EQ           1 THEN
    ENTER dbarb5
    GOTO STARTAPP
  ENDIF
  IF PICK1  EQ           2 THEN
    EDIT USING dbarb5   +
      SORTED BY LASTNAME +
      WHERE LASTNAME EXISTS
```

For those users familiar with Paradox, there will be no need to relearn the interface to use APGEN. For the Lotus or dBASE user, booklets are included to ease the transition into Paradox. Paradox is very user friendly, perhaps the best we have ever seen in this area. The Lotus-style menu bar with explanation lines, coupled with on-line, context-specific help, makes it a real delight to use. Even dBASE III PLUS ASSIST interface pales by comparison.

APGEN is installed from inside of Paradox, but is executed from outside Paradox. This seems strange, but it is a memory requirement. So much of this package is well thought-out, however, that this is only a minor inconvenience.

The documentation is spectacular, guiding the user step-by-step throughout the development process, even through the planning and design process before invoking the generator! All of this good documentation is almost unnecessary, because APGEN uses the bottom of each screen each step of the way to tell the user exactly what is expected, and what to do next. In addition to this information, help is available by pressing the F1 key. There are a full series of default actions like DATAENTRY, EDIT, REPORT, and so on, so that a user can define menu options merely by selecting a standard action. There is a simple facility to include validity

Fig. 6-18. Paradox APGEN menu bar.

```
ADD INFORMATION CHANGE INFORMATION  REMOVE INFORMATION  REVIEW INFORMATION
THIS MENU OPTION ALLOWS YOU TO ADD NEW CUSTOMER DATA
```

and range checks, and a very powerful report generator (one of the strengths of Paradox itself). The user can thus construct a good, user-friendly, application in a Lotus-style menu system (with help) without needing to know any PAL (the Paradox Application Language) commands or programming. A sample menu is shown in Fig. 6-18.

Because Paradox has a built-in script editor, more advanced programmers should have little trouble modifying the APGEN-created code. Note that custom scripts can be linked in at APGEN so that the developer's code can be smoothly linked to the generated code.

If the user selects the standard form for data entry, the application screen looks like Fig. 6-19.

Fig. 6-19. Paradox APGEN application screen.

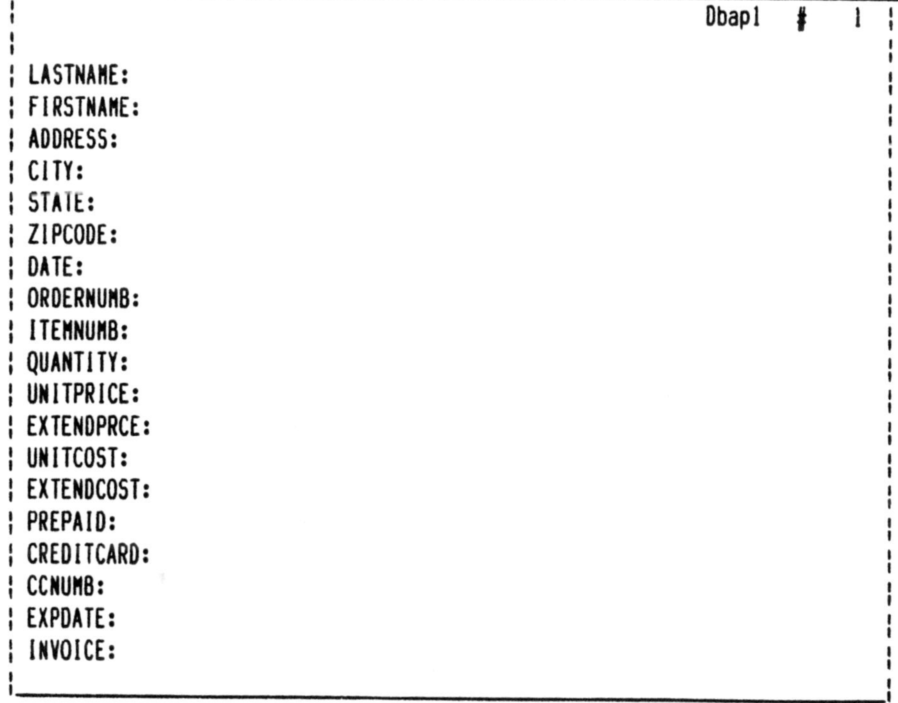

```
[F2] - Data entry completed, Esc - Cancel data entry, Ctrl-U - Undo last change

Dbapl  #  1

LASTNAME:
FIRSTNAME:
ADDRESS:
CITY:
STATE:
ZIPCODE:
DATE:
ORDERNUMB:
ITEMNUMB:
QUANTITY:
UNITPRICE:
EXTENDPRCE:
UNITCOST:
EXTENDCOST:
PREPAID:
CREDITCARD:
CCNUMB:
EXPDATE:
INVOICE:
```

There is no compiler, but Ansa has an excellent runtime policy, so that a developer can give users the application script and get them running without each user needing a copy of Paradox. This is the economic equivalent of compilation.

Before you begin to think that we are in Ansa's employ, fear not—there are flaws in this jewel. The system needs a tremendous amount of memory, so much of the 640K (it requires 600K for itself) that not even Borland's SUPERKEY or the Bricklin Demo Screen capture program can coexist with it. Because many users routinely load such memory-resident software at boot-up, this is a problem. We used the screen capture program to get the other screens into text form for this chapter, but could not for APGEN.

Another problem is the loading speed within the application itself. It took thirty seconds to get into the Data Entry screen, and what seemed like forever to print reports. PAL has never won any speed records, and, although the quality and structure of the generated code is excellent, the performance is seriously inadequate. From our experience with end-users, this would decrease system acceptance, no matter how nice it looks. This should be a consideration in choosing the Paradox APGEN as a development environment.

The Paradox APGEN system is a powerful tool, capable of creating applications with spectacular user interfaces, on-line help, and custom reports. It is useable even by a novice, but advanced programmers can add their own code easily, and modify the generated code with the built-in editor. The package begs for more memory and power, however, and might not be acceptable in the 8088, 640K world. It might easily become the standard in the next generation of PCs, making great use of the raw power and memory addressing capability soon to come. In that environment it might also become the application developer's nightmare: a system so smart that it allows a novice end-user to create applications without the need for programmers.

Summarizing, the products tested all could produce good code, modifiable by a programmer to create high quality applications for end-users. For now, the professional developers do not need to worry about obsolescence—but beware, the time is coming . . .

COMPILERS

Compilers are programs that take source program code and process it into executable machine language form. In machine code, the programs are smaller, faster, and impossible for an end-user to alter. Traditionally-trained programmers are well versed in the care and feeding of compiler-oriented languages. This involves writing the source according to the syntactical rules of a given language, then compiling the file to get a runable program. The coder is at the mercy of the quirks of the compiler.

When using a high level command like PRINT, the compiler builds a routine in machine language to accomplish the task. The way it does this depends on the design of the compiler and the design philosophy of the people who wrote it. There is thus a certain loss of control in using a high-level language. Some programmers prefer to use Assembly code rather than rely on the compiler. Nevertheless, modern compilers are good, efficient, and fast. Your toolbox should contain a number of compilers to cover a wide spectrum of potential application tasks.

C Compilers

Because we have placed such importance on the use of the C language, we shall first discuss a number of C compilers in the microcomputer market place. Some are known as "complete" or "full" implementations, while others are called "subsets" of C. A good rule is to avoid subsets, because Murphy's Law will guarantee that some feature that is absolutely required will be missing in the chosen subset. "Subset" usually means that certain data types are not included, so that coding would need to be restricted.

There are also two memory addressing schemes available: "small" and "large" models. Small models make use of only 64K of code, with another 64K designated for data. Large models can address nearly one megabyte of data. Although some applications would work perfectly under the restrictions of the small model, a compiler that does not provide the option of the large model would be too limiting.

One major 16-bit C compiler for MS-DOS is C86 by Computer Innovations. C86 supports both memory models, has the option of software floating-point arithmetic or hardware arithmetic using the 8087 with coprocessor, and includes an extensive library. C86 is nearly a "full C," but lacks register storage functions, structures, and unions. A C interpreter is also offered for more efficient development.

Another major product is the Lattice C compiler. It too supports both memory models and has a very complete library. A large library makes it less likely that the developer will need to create library modules for specific functions, so the library size should be an important consideration. Several benchmark studies have listed Lattice C very high in performance.

The last C we will discuss is the Microsoft C compiler. This is a full C, supporting both the large and small models. The code it produces is remarkably fast and tight, placing it nearly at the top of every benchmark. Its library is extensive, so much so that we would say it is more than complete. The package has excellent documentation and comes with its own assembler, linker, and library programs. We recommend the Microsoft C compiler because of its advantages in speed, utility, and support by Microsoft. Recent versions include support for the Microsoft Windows environment, which Microsoft claims will allow applications code to be directly transportable to DOS versions yet to come. Microsoft has had a lot of experience in compiler construction (they also market Fortran, Pascal, COBOL and BASIC compilers), and it shows. Although the cost of the package might be higher than Lattice C or C86, we feel that it is the best choice for the application developer's toolbox.

BASIC Compilers

The second major development language is still BASIC. The BASICA shipped with PC-DOS is interpreted, but several good compilers exist to offer the benefits of compiled code to the BASIC programmer. The two best sellers, the IBM Version 2.0 and the Microsoft BASIC Compiler, are both by Microsoft. Ever since Microsoft wrote PC-DOS for IBM, there has been a lot of cross-marketing of products. The new IBM release includes LAN multiuser capabilities, command-line processing and enhanced graphics. The IBM package also includes an extensive Indexed Sequential Access Method (ISAM) program library. For these reasons we suggest choosing the IBM BASIC Compiler (2.0) as the primary tool for development in BASIC. However, this is really a matter of preference, because the Microsoft product is nearly identical.

dBASE Compilers

The DBMS procedural language market is dominated by dBASE III PLUS, which is an interpreted system. There are two major compiler products that take dBASE code and compile it into machine language executable code. The best selling, and most complete, is Clipper, by Nantucket. Its major competitor is the dBASE III Compiler by Wordtech.

Clipper is written in C and has the ability to call other modules written in C or Assembler during execution. This enables the user to create what are called User Defined Functions (UDFs) to add features that are not standard in dBASE. Several modules in the Clipper Extended Library have been written by Tom Rettig, formerly of Ashton-Tate. The potential power of such extensions is unlimited, because each developer can create a personal extended library, adding code written in C or Assembly language, compiled (or assembled) and then linked into the final application. (See the January, 1986, issue of *Data Based Advisor* for Rettig's article on the extended library.)

Clipper has one major shortcoming—its indexing method differs from that of dBASE. Thus, if some functions are handled under dBASE and others under Clipper-compiled code, the user must reindex in each environment or risk messing up the index files. This is not a problem in a pure Clipper application, but since one of the advantages of using dBASE might be to use the dBASE report function, problems can occur. Nantucket claims that they chose a different indexing scheme for speed and efficiency over the method Ashton-Tate used in dBASE III. When dBASE III PLUS was released it had a new indexing scheme, which in some cases is faster than that used by Nantucket. With the primary advantage gone, perhaps Nantucket will support standard dBASE indexing in the future. Clipper should have a multi-user LAN package available soon.

An innovation worth mentioning is Nantucket's method of technical support. They provide a "Nantucket Private Network" on The Source, through which users can get the latest information on bugs, fixes, programs, UDFs and other helpful technical tidbits. There is also a "Post Office" where Clipper users can communicate with Nantucket and each other concerning anything at all. This public information exchange is of great value to a developer, and is something that we would like to see implemented by other software publishers. Recently, Nantucket has also begun to publish a quarterly newsletter.

The major competitor in the dBASE compiler market is the dBASE III Compiler from Wordtech. In its most recent version, it produces true machine code, a vast improvement from the "d-code" of its earlier incarnations. Wordtech chose to use the same index scheme as dBASE uses, which is a great advantage over the Clipper approach. Wordtech also has released a LAN support package that allows direct support for multi-user applications on a wide variety of networks. This product, called Networker, runs on the IBM PC Network, the 3Com 3+ Network, Novell Advanced Netware, TurboDos PC Net, and all other DOS 3.1 compatible networks. This package controls all contention situations, and allows for either file or record locking. A number of additional commands are provided to manage these functions. At $99, this represents a compelling reason to use a compiler over the dBASE III PLUS LAN package for any network application system.

We suggest choosing Clipper as the dBASE compiler because it is very complete, it works, and it is expandable through its easy interface to C and Assembler. Also, many developers have migrated to Clipper over the Wordtech product. This market dominance might change if the new Wordtech product is as good as promised, or if the rumors of an impending release of a compiler by Ashton-Tate are true.

UTILITIES

Utilities are programs that perform useful functions for the programmer, or just make life a little easier. In the C arena, there is a set of very valuable library modules from Greenleaf Software called the Greenleaf functions. The libraries give the program hundreds of functions not included in the standard C libraries, including enhanced string handling, graphics, input/output and communications. Source code is provided so that the programmer can learn how things are done and can modify the modules to individual tastes or needs. The purchase of the Greenleaf functions can save the applications developer a great deal of time and money, and is well worth doing.

For dBASE, we suggest the purchase of a program called dFlow, from Wallsoft, Inc. This remarkable product performs a number of useful functions. dFlow goes through the dBASE III source code, checks it line by line for syntax or logic errors, numbers lines, indents and labels IF-THEN-ELSE and DO WHILE loops, and produces a variable cross reference both within and between all of the programs. The main dFlow menu is shown in Fig. 6-20. It even is capable of creating a diagram of program flow. This product can save a dBASE developer hundreds of hours of time that might be spent hunting down pesky little errors caused by unclosed loops or reused memory variables.

As a standard practice for our dBASE projects, we make a complete dFlow listing with variable concordance, module variable cross references, and program flow diagrams of the final code. To this file copy, we add two copies of the source code on floppy disks, and one backup tape. This package is then taken off-site to our bank vault for permanent storage, as an insurance policy against any catastrophes that might occur. It would be less than pleasant to have to reconstruct an application of any size due to loss of the original source documents.

A wide variety of special software utilities exist for the C and dBASE environments. Windowing, which is fast becoming the "in" thing in software, is available to C programmers using packages like Flash-Up Windows by Software Bottling of New York. In the

Fig. 6-20. dFlow main menu screen.

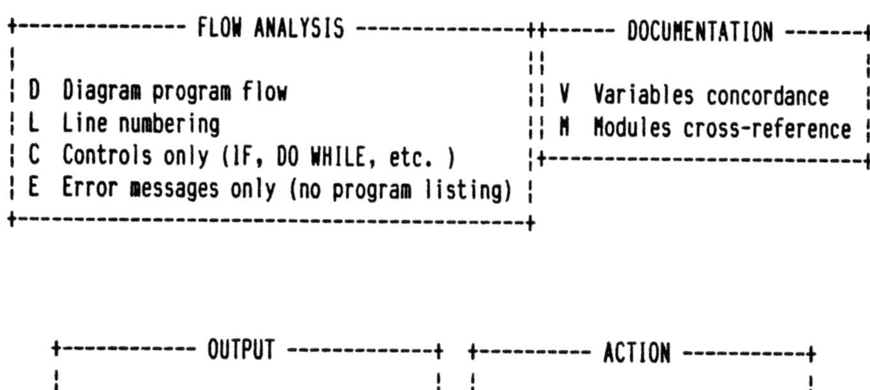

```
                    Your dBASE program file:ABCRPT.PRG

+------------- FLOW ANALYSIS --------------++------ DOCUMENTATION -------+
|                                          ||                            |
| D  Diagram program flow                  || V  Variables concordance   |
| L  Line numbering                        || M  Modules cross-reference |
| C  Controls only (IF, DO WHILE, etc. )   |+----------------------------+
| E  Error messages only (no program listing) |
+------------------------------------------+


   +----------- OUTPUT ------------+  +---------- ACTION -----------+
   |                               |  |                             |
   | S  Screen                     |  |  RETURN when ready          |
   | P  Printer                    |  |  A  Analyze another program |
   | F  File                       |  |  F1 Help                    |
   +-------------------------------+  |  Q  Quit dFLOW              |
                                      +-----------------------------+
```

dBASE world, there is our own Pro Search Window, which opens a window into a database and allows the user to scroll up and down looking for a record using standard arrow and page control keys. There are ISAM and indexing programs, screen painters and report generators. Picking up any copy of *PC Tech Journal* or *Data Based Advisor* would give you more than enough ways to spend your money.

In the application environment, pay special attention to the issues of copyrights and royalties if the final application program incorporates someone else's utility program. This issue arose in our own marketing of Pro Search Window, because it was being sold as an executable file that could be run from within dBASE, as well as an object file that could be linked into the programmer's executable file. As the product gained popularity, particularly with application developers, we were asked what the royalty arrangement would be. After a number of discussions with our attorney and others in the software industry, we arrived at a scheme that seemed to make sense. If a programmer was using our program object file in such a way that it was linked into an application program, and our program, therefore, did not appear on the end-user's directory, we would charge no royalty. If, however, the developed application was to be run under the dBASE III interpreter, and thus our executable file would be given to each end-user, a royalty was due.

This freed some developers from the burden of having to police the number of copies of our program sold as part of a compiled application. Many developers in dBASE ultimately resort to compilation to avoid forcing each end-user to have a copy of dBASE, and so we were imposing no additional hardship. Other utility software vendors will have different schemes. Take care to insure that the incorporation or use of another's code in the developed applications is legal and correct.

A program that deserves special mention is Dan Bricklin's Demo Program. Bricklin was one of the creators of the original VisiCalc electronic spreadsheet. It was a landmark in the infant microcomputer industry and heralded the entry of those "toys" into corporate America. VisiCalc is considered one of the reasons that the microcomputer industry grew, and succeeded as well as it did in those early years. As time went on, competition, in the form of Lotus 1-2-3, undid the fortunes of VisiCalc, and now Bricklin is on his own again. His new product is perhaps one of the neatest tools for programmers that we have ever seen. He calls it a Demo Program because it can be used by a programmer to create a "slide show" demonstration of a program.

Its greatest value is that it can be used to prototype applications. Using this package a developer can design screens that simulate how a finished package will work. You can show this prototype to the end-user during the project definition stage, and giving that user a much better idea of what is going to be developed. Screens, input forms, and diagrams can be simply designed and modified. Self-running demonstrations can be constructed, which are useful in training or marketing. Screens from existing programs can be captured, manipulated as desired, and the "slides" can then be printed to paper or files. The programmer can edit screen data in the files, using a chosen language to actually create program modules for the application. There are many other features, causing the value of Demo Program to grow as the developer learns how to use it. We cannot recommend this product too highly. It is a must for the toolbox.

A number of useful utility programs are not associated with programming tasks themselves. This is one of the exciting areas of entrepreneureal activity in the industry today, where young, small companies are busily dreaming up new, neat, and usually inexpensive things to do with the microcomputers that are already on many desktops.

The "daddy" of all such utilities is Borland International's Sidekick program. Sidekick is a memory-resident utility that combines a number of useful features like a calculator, text editor, automatic telephone dialer, appointment calendar, and an ASCII code table into a series of pop-up overlays available to the user at any time. The user can be using a word processor, need to do a calculation, and just call up the calculator, do what is needed and return to the document without much trouble. The editor allows for "cutting and pasting" screen data between applications. The ASCII table is very useful to developers who need to know ASCII codes while writing application programs.

Sidekick is memory resident; it is always there. Memory resident programs can cause problems with other programs because no standard for managing memory-resident systems exists. Consider this warning: many users have found that weird and potentially destructive things can happen if several such utilities try to coexist in one memory map. With this warning out of the way, we will discuss some other very useful memory-resident programs.

A second truly valuable product is Superkey, also by Borland. Superkey allows the user to build extensive keyboard macros that cause a potentially complicated series of keystrokes to be executed by a single key. For example, you could take a series of commands and keystrokes and "train" them, using Superkey, to be executed each time ALT-A is pressed. This would enable the programmer to "program" keystrokes so that a user would not need to memorize them. Because the keystrokes are played back while a program is running, entire procedures can be easily automated. Other useful features of Superkey include file encryption, screen saver (in which the screen is blanked out if no key has been pressed for a few minutes), and a library of macros for use with the most popular database, spreadsheet, and word processor products. This product is extremely valuable and should be included in most end-user applications.

Some memory-resident utility programs make daily business procedures easier and more efficient. One of the application developer's most important tasks is to keep accurate time and expense records, and then prepare accurate, complete, and timely bills for clients. Many programming and consulting people use date books, calendars, slips of paper, stick-on notes or even the backs of envelopes to keep track of billable time and expenses. Inaccurate recording of activities has direct impact on the bottom line. Because many of the application development and consulting companies in this industry are small, these inaccuracies are very punishing, and can often make the difference between profit and loss. A large number of time and billing systems exist, but we recommend a low-cost memory-resident one called Timeslips, by North Edge Software Corporation. This remarkable utility runs in background, and allows the user to keep an accurate running account of billable and non-billable tasks. It is easy to set up and use, and does an excellent job creating invoices, statements, and a variety of other reports. It has context specific help, and such neat features as an on-screen timer that shows the programmer the dollar amounts as time is billed, as shown in Fig. 6-21.

Timeslips is memory-resident, so it can be called from within any program, and is capable of tracking multiple tasks for several users and clients. A client information form is displayed in Fig. 6-22, showing the amount of detail contained in the database used to generate the invoices and other reports.

Timeslips has the ability to store expense slips and integrate them into the client invoice in a neat, itemized format. Such expenses are often not billed due to sloppy record-keeping, and would be lost revenue without the accuracy of Timeslips. The program is far more powerful and valuable than its $99.95 price would indicate, and can even be offered to end-user companies that might

Fig. 6-21. Timeslips TSTIMER screen.

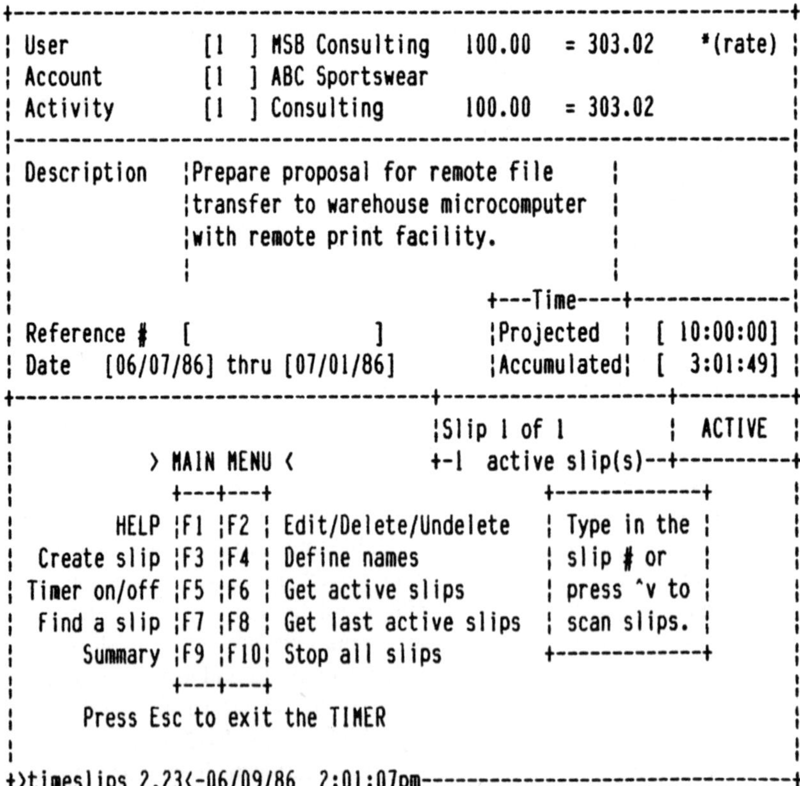

```
+------------------------------------------------------------------+
| User          [1  ] MSB Consulting   100.00   = 303.02   *(rate) |
| Account       [1  ] ABC Sportswear                               |
| Activity      [1  ] Consulting       100.00   = 303.02           |
|------------------------------------------------------------------|
| Description   |Prepare proposal for remote file    |             |
|               |transfer to warehouse microcomputer |             |
|               |with remote print facility.         |             |
|               |                                    |             |
|                                      +---Time----+--------------|
| Reference #   [                 ]    |Projected  |  [ 10:00:00] |
| Date   [06/07/86] thru [07/01/86]    |Accumulated|  [  3:01:49] |
+-----------------------------------+-----------------+-----------+
|                                   |Slip 1 of 1      |  ACTIVE   |
|           > MAIN MENU <           +-1  active slip(s)--+--------+
|              +---+---+                  +------------+          |
|         HELP |F1 |F2 | Edit/Delete/Undelete | Type in the |      |
|  Create slip |F3 |F4 | Define names         | slip # or   |      |
| Timer on/off |F5 |F6 | Get active slips     | press ^v to |      |
|  Find a slip |F7 |F8 | Get last active slips| scan slips. |      |
|      Summary |F9 |F10| Stop all slips       +-------------+      |
|              +---+---+                                           |
|      Press Esc to exit the TIMER                                 |
|                                                                  |
+>timeslips 2.23<-06/09/86  2:01:07pm------------------------------+
```

Fig. 6-22. Timeslips client information screen.

```
+-Client Information for : ABC Sportswear  -+--BALANCES as of LAST BILL        +
¦ Invoice # [                  ]            ¦ 3 MONTH OVERDUE   :[0.00        ]¦
¦ [ABC Sportswear                   ]       ¦ 2 MONTH OVERDUE   :[0.00        ]¦
¦ [2222 Fannin Suite 1202           ]       ¦ 1 MONTH OVERDUE   :[0.00        ]¦
¦ [Houston, TX 77098                ]       ¦ Current Month     :[0.00        ]¦
¦ [                                 ]       ¦ Current  Balance  :[0.00        ]¦
¦ [                                 ]       ¦ Account Balance   :[0.00        ]¦
¦ Phone  [(713) 555-1234    ]               ¦ Retainer Amount   :[0.00        ]¦
+-BILL FORMAT OPTIONS                      -+ Account options   :[No show    ] ¦
¦ General format :[Detail               4] +--INTEREST, TAX and HISTORY       +
¦ Detail time :[Y]es  Detail charges:[Y]es  ¦ Interest rate     :[0.00 ]%[1]  ¦
¦ Detail dates:[Y]es  Initials      :[N]o   ¦ Service Tax       :[0.00 ]%     ¦
¦ Show aging  :[N]o   Double space  :[N]o   ¦ Sales Tax         :[0.00 ]%     ¦
¦ Reference # :[N]o   Show balance  :[Y]es  ¦ Round to minutes  :[  0]        ¦
+-FLAT FEE INFORMATION                     -+ Next Aging        :[  /  /  ]   ¦
¦ Flat fee amount:[0.00        ]            ¦ Last BILL         :[  /  /  ]   ¦
¦ Flat fee type  :[None    ]                ¦ Last PAYMENT date :[  /  /  ]   ¦
¦ Covers         :[Nothing     ]            ¦            amount:[0.00     ]   ¦
+-------------------------------------------+---------------------------------+
  In reference to:[Microcomputer based accounting system on LAN        ]
+-----------------------------------------------------------------------------+
¦ Type in a number to appear on the bill and override automatic invoice       ¦
¦ numbering.                                                                  ¦
¦                                                                             ¦
Use <-->^v PgUpPgDn F2 Default F5 Matters F7 Hist F9 Trans Esc Undo F10 Accept<+
```

need to do time and billing, such as lawyers, accountants, and advertising companies. Another feature that we are very impressed with is that it can export files in ASCII delimited formats that can be easily used by other microcomputer applications. It is also "well behaved" and will coexist comfortably in RAM with Sidekick and Superkey. For those developers who hate the drudgery of the "business" side of the business, Timeslips is the answer.

Another extremely useful memory-resident utility is Wordfinder from Writing Consultants. This remarkable program is actually a fully computerized on-line thesaurus, with up to 220,000 synonyms available with a single keystroke. It is valuable to anyone using a word processor to produce user documentation, contracts, or proposals. All a user must do is point to a word, in a screen window full of synonyms for that word. This selected word replaces the original word in the document, preserving capitalization and grammatical form. Figure 6-23 shows how Wordfinder looks when it finds the word upon which the cursor is placed; we used "powerful" in this case. If Wordfinder fails to find a match, it offers the user a choice of words. An unsuccessful search for "end-user" can be seen in Fig. 6-24.

Wordfinder is fun to use, and makes the finished document more pleasant to read. We have used it in the preparation of this book, and feel that it is a valuable product for application developers.

As a final product in this section, we mention the Norton Utilities. This package is a collection of a number of valuable programs that every user of a microcomputer should own. From the obvious value of the ability to UNERASE a file that has accidentally been lost, to the ability to change disk file bytes directly, this package is needed. The developer can even hide files in user directories, rename disk volumes, and check system performance using the modules included in the package. Norton Utilities has been a best-seller for a long time, and represents a necessary product for the

Fig. 6-23. Wordfinder successful find under WordStar.

```
+----------------------- WORD FINDER/SYNONYM FINDER ----------------------+
| powerful:                                                 MORE: PgDn     |
|  adj concentrated, hearty, heavy-duty, lusty, potent, robust, stalwart,  |
|      stout, strong, sturdy;                                              |
|      forceful, high-handed, important, intense, maximum, utmost;         |
|      invincible, mighty, omnipotent, supreme;                            |
|      aggressive, dominant, durable, firm, forceful, hardy, hearty, mighty, |
|      robust, rugged, stalwart, stout, strong, sturdy, tenacious, tough;  |
|      coercive, compelling, dynamic, energetic, forceful, hardy, lusty,   |
|      mighty, passionate, robust, strong, sturdy, vigorous;               |
|      ardent, decisive, determined, emphatic, extreme, forceful, intense, |
+- Cursor keys: point    Rtrn: replace    Esc: exit    Command key: look up -+

if he has spent ten thousand dollars on the new application, he should

see clear and powerful improvements in the way he is doing business.

The developer can take the wish list, estimate the time and charges

involved in writing the additional code, and present the client with a

new project task agreement. These are usually little tasks like

adding fields to a report, new sorts, changing the width of a data
1HELP  2INDENT 3SET LM 4SET RM 5UNDLIN 6BLDFCE 7BEGBLK 8ENDBLK 9BEGFIL 10ENDFIL
```

Fig. 6-24. Wordfinder screen if no match is found.

```
        C:BOOKCH.10  PAGE 1 LINE 54 COL 36            INSERT ON
L----!----!----!----!----!----!----!----!----!----!----!------------R
project task agreement outlines all of the work to be done in the

task, changes must be handled in subsequent tasks. This is the seed of

additional business. The satisfied end-user now has a working system.

He knows that you can deliver what you say you can and when. Hopefully,

he is aware of the cost/performance benefits of his new system. Even

+--------- The word was not found. Choose another word to look up. ---------+
|         enclosure            encumbered           endorsement             |
|         encode               encumbrance          endow                   |
|         encompass            encyclopedia         endowment               |
|         encore               end                  endurable               |
|         encounter            endeavor             endurance               |
|         encourage            ended                endure                  |
|         encouragement        endemic              enduring                |
|         encouraging          endless              enema                   |
|         encroach             endlessly            enemy                   |
|         encumber             endorse              energetic               |
+- Cursor keys: point     Rtrn: look up    Esc: exit    Command key: look up -+
```

end-user, if only to UNDELETE a file once.

In conclusion, we have tried to outline for the new developer a list of products to be considered for inclusion in the "bag of tricks." Because the industry is constantly producing new wonders, the reader is cautioned to check the current literature for the best choice in each category at a particular time.

Chapter 7

Data Communications and LAN Issues

This chapter is intended to guide the developer in an area that is becoming more and more important to a large community of users—data communications. As the PC becomes more powerful, and more sophisticated applications are developed for these desktop wonders, the issue of moving data between machines becomes more critical. Many corporations have large mainframes with immense databases on them, and many users wish to have access to this data.

METHODS OF DATA INTERCHANGE

There are two basic methods by which this data access can occur:

- ☐ File Transfer—Data files, usually in some ASCII format, are transferred via modem from one computer to another.
- ☐ Terminal Emulation—The microcomputer, using a combination of hardware and software, acts as if it is a terminal that the host recognizes.

There are also two methods of serial communication in the computer world:

- ☐ Synchronous—Data bits are issued in a time synchronous

manner, i.e., each time the clock ticks, a bit is sent. It is up to the protocol to recognize the synchronization characters, start of message and end of message codes, and to do error checking. The most famous of this type of protocol is the IBM 3270 SNA system.

- Asynchronous—This system sends data in bursts at any time. The packets have start and stop bits and can be either seven or eight bits, depending on the protocol. This is the most popular form of communication in dial-up modem environments. The PC RS232 port is of this type.

COMMUNICATIONS SOFTWARE

The developers should have access to a good asynchronous software package that allows for both file transfer and terminal emulation. We also suggest an auto-dial modem in the 1200—2400 baud range that uses the Hayes modem codes. The most popular software package is Crosstalk, by Microstuff. There are also two excellent "freeware" products available, PC-TALK III and PROCOMM. Any of these will serve to enable a developer to upload and download files, and in some cases operate a remote machine. These features are important in running a consulting practice as well, because features like electronic mail can also be supported.

On the synchronous side, things are more complicated. Special communications boards, synchronous modems, and software are needed to arrange a link with a synchronous host. The most popular systems in this area are the IRMA card, by Digital Communications Assoc., the AST 3270 SNA, and the IBM 3270 card. On projects where host communications of this type are required, the developer will probably have to move on-site to be where the host is, because the costs of installing a leased data line for the duration of the project would be prohibitive.

MICROCOMPUTER TO MAINFRAME LINKS

Modern mainframe to microcomputer links can be topologically complex. The user's SNA host has a front-end communications processor that is usually linked to a number of terminal control units either by direct wire or leased lines. These terminal control units are, in turn, linked to a number of synchronous terminals and printers. Microcomputers equipped with IRMA-type SNA cards can be directly connected to the terminal control unit, and, by running a terminal emulation program, can give the user full-terminal functionality on a PC. If the PC is part of a LAN which is equipped with a 3270 SNA Gateway, the Gateway server looks, to the front-end processor, like a terminal control unit. This allows PCs on the LAN to sign-on to the host as if they were terminals connected to a real terminal control unit. Depending on the number of logical units assigned to the emulated terminal control unit, several PCs can have access simultaneously. In some LANs one PC can use more than one logical unit (LU) at a time, allowing multiple host sessions at a single workstation. A typical microcomputer to mainframe communication system including the elements just discussed is depicted in Fig. 7-1.

The design of integrated data communications systems, with several generations of hardware and software technology, is complex enough to require the use of consultants. This offers an excellent opportunity to penetrate into the inner sanctum of the MIS department. Many of the LAN gateway and synchronous communication products for the PC market can assist in the design of these systems.

Both C and BASIC offer direct control of the RS232 asynchronous port, and some third-party utility manufacturers offer modules to help the programmer get on-line quickly. Greenleaf has a special library dedicated to asynchronous communications for C.

Fig. 7-1. Mainframe/microcomputer communication system.

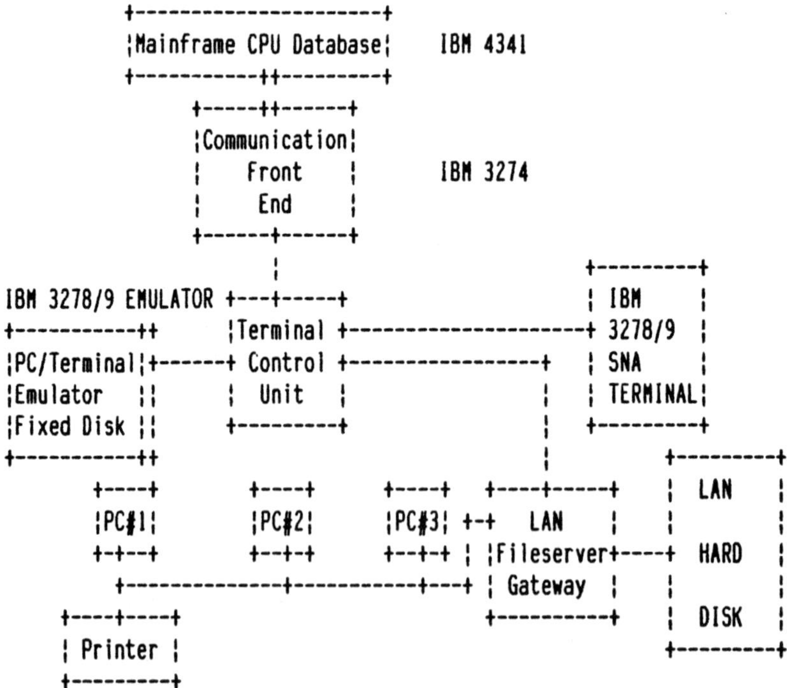

Fig. 7-2. Two computer interconnect topology.

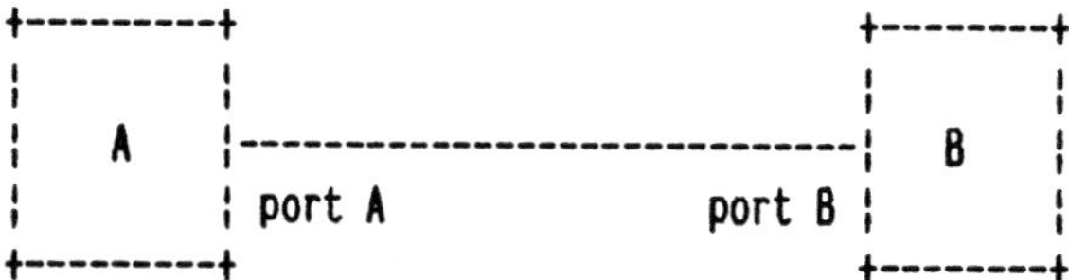

Lattice has also released a program called SideTalk, which is capable of maintaining asynchronous communications in a background mode while another program is running in foreground. This is useful in the single-user machines like the 8088-based PCs, because file transfer and electronic mail can operate unattended while the PC is doing other tasks.

LOCAL AREA NETWORKS

While we are discussing communications, we should mention some problems concerning LANs. LANs are in fact just small, localized, data communication subsystems. The creation of LANs comes from a topological problem of interconnection. If two computers wish to have a data link there is a simple path for communication—just connect one serial port to the other with one cable, as in Fig. 7-2.

If, however, three computers are to be connected using ports, there would need to be three cables and two ports in each computer, as depicted in Fig. 7-3.

The complexity grows for four computers as shown in Fig. 7-4. There are now three ports per machine and six cables. Additionally, software in each machine would need to be provided to check,

Fig. 7-3. Three computer interconnect topology.

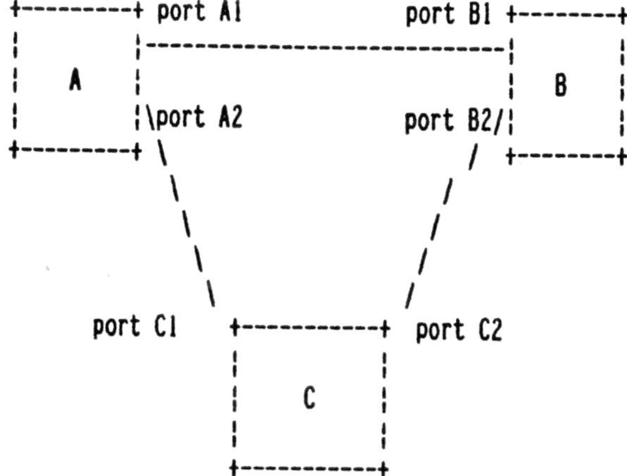

Fig. 7-4. Four computer interconnect topology.

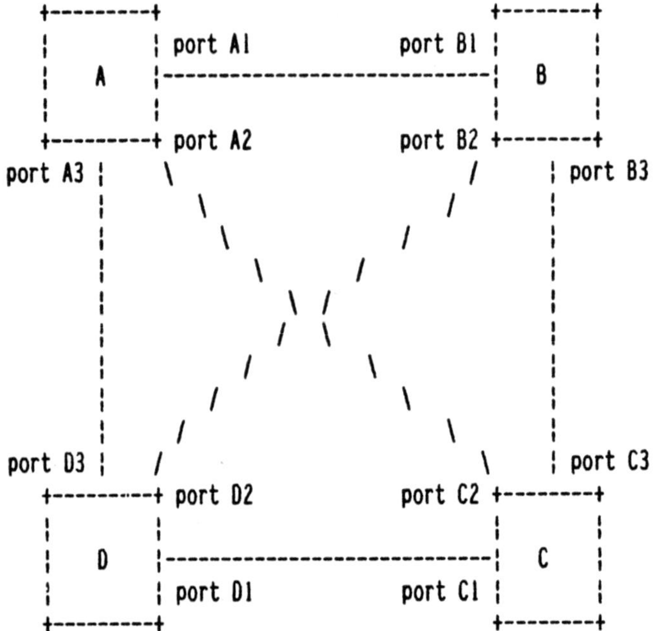

in sequence, whether or not any other machine was sending data. Unwieldy to say the least. Imagine the situation for sixteen machines!

In a large company with, say, 25 PCs that wish to have data communication, such an interconnect scheme would be impossible. The alternative topology is to connect all of the PCs to one cable, and develop a protocol that allows for each to have fair and error-free access. This is how LANs were invented. The question of access rights and procedures is complex, and has led to two major schools of thought.

One believes that each node in the network should be able to talk whenever it needs to. If it crashes into another message, it stops and tries again later. Eventually, it will get its entire message off without collision. This is called the Carrier Sense Multiple Access with Collision Detect (CSMA/CD) method. The most famous network protocol of this type is Ethernet.

The other school proposes a more orderly system, in which each node is given a chance to speak, in a specific sequence. If the node does not have anything to say, it passes the right to speak to the next node on the list. This is called Token Passing, and is the method used by ARCNET and the new IBM Token Ring.

The choice between protocols is not an easy one. If traffic is low, CSMA/CD is faster, since few collisions occur. Token Passing schemes require the token to be passed to everyone on the network even if only one node needs to transmit something. This Token Passing overhead is thus wasted time. If, however, the network traffic increases, the CSMA/CD system gets slower and slower, as multiple retries are required because of the high collision rate. In high traffic systems, the token is more predictable. In fact, a worst-case transmission time can be calculated for Token Passing schemes. No such calculation is possible in CSMA/CD, because it is possible to lock the network if there is too much traffic, giving an infinite worst-case transmission time.

The developer must choose LAN protocol according to the size and nature of the system being created. For example, if the application has a need for real-time processing, CSMA/CD could be disastrous. In factory automation you might use a LAN to link microcomputer-controlled drill presses on an assembly line. A hole is drilled by one computer, then measured optically, and the next computerized drill press decides whether or not to drill deeper. The assembly line moves at a constant rate. If the network is busy, causing collisions and a time delay in data transmission and processing, by the time the component reaches the second computer station the drill might make a new hole rather than drilling the old one deeper. Such problems with the non-predictable nature of CSMA/CD led a major automobile manufacturing firm to choose Token Passing as the basis of its Manufacturing Automation Protocol (MAP). Time-crucial operations like laboratory data acquisition and synchronous data communication also demand Token Passing.

The major LANs in the microcomputer marketplace today are Novell and 3Com. Novell software runs on a variety of hardware and is available in both token and CSMA/CD modes. 3Com is a collision-detect system that only runs on its own hardware. The recent introduction of the IBM Token Ring and the release of a standardized program interface, NETBIOS, has finally stabilized the LAN market. It is for this reason that we make a very conservative recommendation here. We suggest only using the IEEE 802 Token Ring standard. This includes IBM, of course, and Ungermann-Bass at the present time. We feel that the other LAN vendors will conform or perish. The application developer should be aware of the turmoil in this area and should try not to put his client in the unenviable position of having an "orphaned" LAN technology.

The standardization of the LAN software interface should also lead to an increase in the number of multi-user applications that can be constructed. Already dBASE III, R:base, DataFlex, and others are offering multi-user versions to run on the IBM Token Ring using NETBIOS. This should be a very rich market for developers in the near future, and we thus suggest the addition of a NETBIOS system to the developer's toolbox. Technical references are available from IBM.

LAN Application Environmental Issues

As the PC becomes more ubiquitous in the corporate world, applications that may have been designed to run on a stand-alone computer are evolving into multi-user systems as parts of company-wide LANs. The recent release of the IBM Token Ring, an IEEE 802 Standard, and multi-user versions of dBASE III and R:base 5000, drive the application developer in the direction of LAN-compatible upgrades for existing systems.

Some software, such as spreadsheets and word processors, can make the jump to multi-user ability merely by relying on the file-locking capability of the network software. File locking implies that only one user can alter a file at one time. The system may allow read-only access to other users, or deny any access until the file is closed. Databases cannot, however, rely on a global file lock. The entire utility of the database is based on different people accessing different functions and records in the system at the same time. A customer tracking system that would allow only one user to edit only one record in the file would be useless in even a small company. Most LANs include a facility called record locking, which merely locks a specific record. In such systems several people can edit several different records at the same time. dBASE III PLUS has extended such record locking into dBASE itself. The developer should thus be able to create multi-user access systems that rival those on mainframes. Ashton-Tate demonstrated these record locking features, as well as a multilevel security system.

Multi-user systems give rise to an entire new level of potential security problems, and developers will certainly find themselves faced with a new type of requirement. Users will now demand that a system have the ability to give different users different environmental options based on their security levels. "Environmental" means that the menu options, read/write capability, and file and record access might vary from user to user.

For example, one of our clients is running a personnel system we wrote for them in dBASE III, then compiled using Nantucket's Clipper. The development phase has ended. Now the application needs to be moved onto a LAN, and a series of security levels needs to be set up. Some users are to have read-only access to some of the employee data, others are to have full access. Some can generate reports for all employees, others only for employees other than themselves, and so on. The problem is straightforward: How can the developer create a multitiered environment that would encompass an infinite variety of options?

Password security is, of course, the first step, and a wide variety of encryption options exist. In every LAN there should be a System Manager. (If there isn't one now, there will be!) This manager needs to assign LAN access passwords, disk space, printer queues, and, in general, coordinate the user environments. Passwords are a tenuous security measure at best, and can only work if the user population is cooperative in maintaining system security.

Passwords alone cannot solve the multi-environment problem. For example, suppose the system has some users with monochrome displays and others with color graphic systems. The application needs to run differently on the different displays. Advanced database languages have ISCOLOR( )-type variables, but let's use this example to illustrate the concept of a parameter file keyed to each user. The parameter file can contain all the information about a unique user environment, including monitor type, read-only or read/write access, security levels to define access to various functions of the program, and so on. In dBASE a file PARAM.DBF might have the structure in Fig. 7-5.

After the password sign-on session, the record of PARAM.DBF corresponding to that user can be read into public memory variables, so the application can know how to treat the user. Elsewhere on the LAN, another copy of the program is written into another user's CPU and a specific PARAM.DBF record sets up the environment. As a simple example, assume that the ACCESS code is a five character field. Within the main system, a test could be made on a substring of the field to determine if that user should have access to that function. See the code fragment in Fig. 7-6.

This fragment shows that a user whose ACCESS Level is, for example, 'x6xxx' would be able to go to the subprogram EDITREC, but a user with a code of 'x1xxx' would not. Once inside EDITREC, further environmental restrictions can be applied, as can be seen in Fig. 7-7.

Fig. 7-5. Sample parameter database structure.

```
Field  Field Name      Type        Width

    1  USERNUMB        Character   4
    2  TYPEMON         Character   1
    3  ACCESS          Character   5
```

Fig. 7-6. Sample parameter code fragment #1.

```
CASE OPT='G'
  IF SUBSTR (ACCESS,2,1)>'5'
     DO EDITREC
  ELSE
     @10,10 SAY'ACCESS DENIED'
  ENDIF
CASE .........
```

Fig. 7-7. Sample parameter code fragment #2.

```
CLEAR
@10,1 SAY 'NAME :' GET MNAME
@12,1 SAY 'SALARY' GET MSALARY
IF SUBSTR (ACCESS,2,1)>'8'
  READ
  REPLACE NAME WITH MNAME
  REPLACE SALARY WITH MSALARY
ELSE
  CLEAR GETS
  WAIT
ENDIF
```

Fig. 7-8. Sample parameter code fragment #3.

```
CLEAR
@10,1 SAY 'NAME:' GET MNAME
IF SUBSTR (ACCESS,2,1)>'7'
   @11,1 SAY 'SALARY:' GET MSALARY
ENDIF
IF SUBSTR (ACCESS,2,1)>'8'
   READ
   REPLACE SALARY WITH MSALARY
ELSE
   CLEAR GETS
   WAIT
ENDIF
```

In this example, only a user with a '9' in the second position of his ACCESS string can edit the data. Users with a '6,', '7,' or '8' will only be able to view it.

In Fig. 7-8 a further restriction could be placed concerning which records are offered for display. In this example, only users with an '8' or '9' in their codes will even see the salary, and only the '9' will be allowed to edit the data.

The parameter file system can be used together with a security password system to provide a multitiered environment for the new demands of LAN-based multi-user applications.

The area of data communications is one in which the applications developer/consultant will find considerable opportunities and a rich range of problems to be solved. The development of expertise in this area will, thus, be extremely valuable as a business strategy.

Chapter 8

Application Development

Computers, as collections of electronic and mechanical components, do not "know" how to do anything. Complex sets of instructions, called programs or code, are the agents of the magic that most unsophisticated users attribute to the computers themselves. And where does this code come from? People! A "priest class" of technocrats called programmers. They are a varied group, from highly educated scientists to self-taught "bad boys." Some have been described as animals that need to be kept locked up and have raw meat thrown beneath the door at feeding time. Although this might be an exaggerated image, consider the frustration of end-users when they find themselves at the mercy of a temperamental code writer.

Because the actual system operation relies so heavily on the code, you should pay attention to the support and maintenance of it. Even if a "brilliant" programmer develops the system, plans should be made to cover contingencies if the great one leaves, dies, or goes insane. As a rule, most "genius" programmers code rapidly, figure out "neat" algorithms, patch code on the run (responding to every user whim during development), and are guilty of the greatest single sin in applications development—not documenting the code.

In a successful development practice, programmers might work on five to ten new systems a year. The writers assume they will be the one to support their own code, justifying not documenting or commenting it by saying they are too busy, will do it later, or that the code is so good that it explains itself. That is wrong. Professionals will tell you that even six months later some of their own code is undecipherable. If a programming group contains more than one coder, or if it expects to survive the departure of any key programmer, it must develop an internal set of documentation and coding standards. If the code is modular, self-documented, and has comments to tell what each fragment is supposed to do, it is possible, years in the future, to look back and quickly make an improvement or fix a deeply buried bug.

DOCUMENTATION AND CODING STANDARDS

Several companies find it valuable to adopt specific written standards and practices for its programmers. The projects developed under such standards are easier to manage, support, and upgrade. The standards should include the program header, which identifies the project name, program name, creation date, first programmer, all subsequent programmers, and the dates and nature of each modification made. It is also necessary to list all variables, including the label, description, type, and places in other modules where the variable is used. This is a lot of work, but any developer who wants to be able to develop a long-term enterprise will soon find the work worthwhile. When a "prima donna" programmer quits because you won't buy some new toy, your client systems will not be at jeopardy—that is the payoff.

Copious internal comments and documentation are also helpful in the establishment of trade secret company proprietary, and patent and copyright privileges.

THE DEVELOPMENT PROCESS

With all of the contracts signed, specification documents and programming tools in hand, it is time to begin the development process. As the old proverb says, "the longest journey begins with but a single step." So it is with programming.

The classical school of coding suggests that a complete flowchart must be constructed before a single program line is written. This may be good form, but is hardly the way microcomputer programmers work. In the old days, when CPU time was much more expensive than human time, it was extravagant beyond reason to code and test in real time. The old mainframe programmers needed to write flowcharts, code on worksheets, send the code to the punch card room, check the punch cards for typographical errors, and submit the cards in a batch mode to the "guardians of the big brain" in the data processing department. If the code ran (which it rarely did), they would get back output. Normally, however, they would get back the punch cards with a few pages of printout describing the fatal error that brought the job down. Because batch turnaround at that time was in terms of days, development time using multiple runs on the CPU was not practical.

The advent of the microcomputer as a personal workstation changed the philosophical framework of the development process. The complete central processing unit, memory, and disk storage are now on a desktop, at the programmer's beck and call. The once-outrageous cost, in time and money, of developing "on the fly" has become more reasonable. In fact, the microcomputer environment offers interpreted language development systems that almost beg for interactive programming philosophies.

To this end, we will make an outrageous statement. Programmers in the microcomputer application development environment can begin to code without writing a single flowchart! This might shock hundreds of computer science professors and data processing managers, but it will come as no surprise to thousands of programmers who grew up in the microcomputer age.

This is not to say that the developer should not have a plan of attack. Indeed, the design should be well laid out. The system design is dictated by the specifications document, the input and output forms contracted for, and the performance outlined in the project agreement.

STANDARD PROGRAM MODULES

Most, if not all, computer application systems share a number of common features that can be considered the basis of program modules.

Add Data. This is an input module that allows the end-user to add new information into the database. This data is to be validated, have its range checks and error traps performed, and then be consolidated into the system key-index as required. The data must conform exactly to the definitions laid out in the system specification document. If data entry forms are part of the project task, this module should present a blank form as required.

Find Data. This module allows the user to locate a specific record of data within the file. If keyed indices are to be used, the search algorithm is part of this program. It is often valuable to give the user the ability to "scroll" through the records, using a (N)ext or (P)revious feature. After finding a record in the neighborhood of the one that is wanted, (N) and (P) are used to find the exact one.

As an aside, we note that most users cannot remember exact spellings of client names or part numbers in inventory systems. To this end, coupling a non-exacting FIND algorithm with a fine-tuning BROWSE will give the user a more forgiving and thus more useable method of finding the desired record. If the find fails, it is also desirable to offer the user a chance to try again before leaving the module. We consider the FIND module an input program.

Edit Data. The user often wishes to change data in a record that has already been added to the system. Usually, the program uses the FIND to locate the record to be changed, then "opens it up" to allow editing. Security issues are usually incorporated at this point. The end-user may not wish to allow a user to edit any record without proper password clearance, or to allow editing with protected fields, so that the user may not be able to change, or even have displayed, critical or confidential data. EDIT modules also must keep track of changes to index keys, reindexing if necessary. Calculated fields must be recalculated if root fields are changed. In the case of linked databases, if a link key is changed, care must be taken to go to the related files and make the changes required. Editing is extremely important, and must be well thought-out and executed at the code level. If an input form is designated for the ADD module, it is good practice to reuse this form in the EDIT routine, to standardize the user interface for the input routines.

Delete Data. Provisions must be made to allow the user to delete or remove records from the database file. There are two approaches that are generally used. The first is to use the FIND to locate a specific record, then mark it for deletion. The other is to define a class of records using a specific criterion, for example, the end-user might want to delete all paid invoices for the month of May, 1986.

The class-delete action is dangerous, because an error in criterion definition can be catastrophic. As a rule, offer the user at least one "Are you sure?" option for any deletion selected. If possible, offer an "Undelete" option to repair erroneous choices. You might also choose to offer help, or warning messages to suggest backing up the file before the deletes are executed. We suggest, in the case of single deletes, to display the record to be removed using the defined input form while the "Are you sure?" message is being displayed.

Print Data. There should be a facility to display any given record in printed form. The record can be selected using the FIND utility, then the user can be offered the option to print it. It is a good idea to write this module in a way that allows the user a chance to set up the printer, making sure it is on-line, at top of form, and that the right kind of paper is loaded. Good programmers include code to have the program check to see if the printer is on-line before trying to print something. If the printer is off-line, the program should warn the user, rather than allow the system to hang. Little touches like this make the final code look more professional.

Report Modules. These programs take the input from the various database files and present it in a variety of printed or screen formats. Users can define preprinted forms to be used, or design a desirable output report during the project definition phase.

Reports can be as simple as a list of the data, or as complex as a linking of numerous files with computational relationships. As with PRINT DATA, make sure to include printer on-line testing. In the case of preprinted forms or labels, it is valuable to offer a print alignment mask, usually a series of Xs to fill each field. The user can, thus, make sure that the forms are aligned correctly before committing to printing large numbers of forms which would be wasted if the alignment was off. In some system designs it is desirable to use multiple printers, so that pre-printed forms that are going to be used on a regular basis can be aligned once and run at will. Because most microcomputers can address several printers, and the cost of matrix printers is so low, setting up programs so that the print function is routed to printer port two, for example, is often a better alternative than making the user change paper each time a specific form is needed. In the case of accounting systems, where billing is done twice monthly and checks are produced once a week, the single-printer concept might work, but still represents additional headaches to the user.

Many printers have complex microcode to "set them up." The report-printing programs must send codes to set character width, underlining, and so on, to the printer each time the report is invoked. If the reports require special paper or forms, the program should issue a message to the user. If the application environment is going to include multiple-user configurations, with different printers and different set-up microcodes, you must code the program so that the user can select the kind of printer that is going to be used.

For a discussion of a method to cope with hardware environmental variations, such as printers and display cards, please see the LAN section of Chapter Seven.

Computational Routines. The heart of every application is the actual processing of data, whether numeric calculation or character manipulation. Modules of this type would include payroll calculation, invoice charges, and list processing. These programs usually have no user interface, and may be difficult to test without real data. In coding such routines, take care to maintain data type integrity and data precision, and to make sure that the formulae and equations are coded exactly as they should be.

Depending on the language chosen, there is a specific computational hierarchy. An equation must be written so that the operations are performed in the correct order. For example, the equation X = 12*3/2+6 gives two results based on how you choose to evaluate it. If you multiply 12 times 3, divide by 2, then add 6 the answer is 24. If you add 2 and 6 first, then multiply 12 times 3, and divide by the result of the addition, the answer would be 4.5. To avoid this ambiguity make sure that the computer knows exactly which operations it needs to do, in what order. If the desired result is 4.5, the equation should be written as:

```
X = (12*3)/(2+6)
```

Conversely, if the other operation is desired, the equation should read:

```
X = ((12*3)/2) + 6
```

Errors in hierarchical operation logic have caused more than a few grey hairs and ulcers in code writers and end-users alike. Care spent in making sure that each equation is coded correctly will pay off later. We suggest small tests of each equation with known data before including that equation in the code. As you learn the hierarchical rules of a language, you might become overly confident and overlook this test. This is bad. Equation building is enhanced by the requirement to document variables and operations within the code.

It is also essential to make sure that all calculations do not cross the boundaries of the precision that have been defined for the variables that are being used. There are many types of precision available in the microcomputer, but the reasoning is similar from language to language. In BASIC, for instance, there is an integer variable type, which is a whole number (no decimal point) between −32768 and +32767. In IBM BASIC a variable is denoted as an integer by appending a "%" sign. Such variables take two bytes of storage, or 16 bits. If you declare a variable to be an integer type, and an equation yields a value that cannot be expressed in the two byte integer format, there will be a precision-based error. In the case of numbers with decimal points there are two options in BASIC. Single precision is the default numerical type, used to represent seven or fewer digits. The accuracy is guaranteed up to only six digits, and can be made fixed by following the variable name with an exclamation point. For numbers with from eight to 17 digits there is a variable type called double precision, which is denoted by a pound sign. Single precision requires four bytes of storage and double precision, eight.

If you declare a variable like SALES to be a single precision number, and the computation results in a number that is too large to express in six digits, the answer is rounded and accuracy is lost. This is another source of maddening error generation, because the code may be correct, and give erroneous results only when SALES is large enough value to trigger this precision error.

Similar variable types exist in C, Pascal, Fortran, and many other languages. The only way to fix precision is to declare the desired level in the code, so there must be a complete understanding of the needs of each variable as the code is being written. The size and accuracy requirements should be part of the specification document. When in doubt about the precision requirements of a particular computed variable, it is far better to err in the direction of too much precision. You are in the worst case wasting bytes of memory, which is more desirable than losing data integrity by loss of accuracy.

It is this issue of accuracy and precision that made the 16-bit computers more acceptable to the business and scientific communities than the eight-bit microcomputers of the last decade. As new chips evolve, bringing 32-bit architectures to the microcomputer world, larger numbers will be able to be handled at even greater speeds. The accuracy and precision argument is probably the last issue dividing microcomputers from minicomputers and mainframes.

Communications. In some application systems it is necessary to write programs that will perform communication functions, such as data file uploading and downloading, and terminal emulation. Higher-level languages such as BASIC allow the programmer to open a communication port, set up a number of required parameters and read or write data to the port in much the same way as with a file. In C, the programmer could write communications drivers, or use prewritten library functions, such as those offered by Greenleaf. Whatever approach is used, communications routines form a special subset of programs in any application.

There are a large number of variations possible. Some systems are hardwired to other computers, some use dial-up modems, and others run on leased-line modems. In each case there are specific coding requirements. As with all other system needs, the communications procedures must be delineated in the task agreement. If the developer does not have access to a specific communications set-up off-site, it might be necessary to do some of the coding and testing during development on-site. Provisions should be made for temporary passwords or port connections to allow the developer the access needed to accomplish these tasks.

With file uploading or downloading (also called file interchange), the developer must understand the issues of transportability of files, compatibility of data, and the import/export features of various application systems. Although it might be possible to move a file in a binary format using XMODEM or KERMIT protocols, it might be useless to have the data in that format on the target system. Before you promise an end-user that you can download accounting data from the company minicomputer and import it into the dBASE application that is being developed, make sure you understand all of the variables and issues. Otherwise, you might be promising something that is impossible to do. Refer to the communications section of Chapter Seven for a more complete discussion of communication software, hardware, and technologies.

The building of an application should begin from the beginning—the main menu module. This program is the place to initialize all variables, set system environmental parameters, and display the initial menu screen. If you build the application module-by-module, this main menu program could be considered the "root" module, with control always being returned to it. A representation of a modular program tree is shown in Fig. 8-1. A generic menu program structure might look like Fig. 8-2.

The main menu, or root, module can be completely coded and tested even if the programs it calls do not yet exist. The programmer can create dummy programs which are just returns to the calling module, and thus run the root module through its paces. The menu screen can be painted, and features like clocks can be tested. A number of nice touches can be included in menu programs, such

Fig. 8-1. Sample program tree.

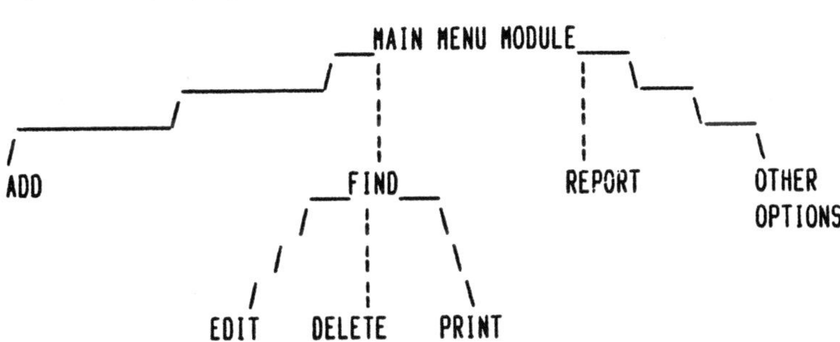

Fig. 8-2. Generic menu program structure.

```
DOCUMENT HEADER

SET UP ENVIRONMENT

INITIALIZE VARIABLE

DISPLAY MENU OPTIONS

LOOP
  OPTION 1
    DO OPTION 1
  OPTION 2
    DO OPTION 2

END LOOP

CLOSE FILES AND QUIT
```

as date, time, and day of week displays. In the case of systems that require user log-ons with passwords, the menu screen can include the name of the logged-on user.

If on-line help is to be included with the system, this is a good time to write a help screen explaining each menu option. The style of help should be consistent throughout the system, so this is also the time to decide whether you will be using full-screen help or "windows." Remember that the program code should be written so that help can be activated by pressing the F1 function key.

The coding method proposed here is one in which the programmer writes the programs module-by-module in the menu path order. If the first menu option is the ADD feature, then it should be written when the menu module is finished. Just code down the menu tree, module-by-module. Debug each module as much as possible as it is being written, and certainly before proceeding to another branch. This method is easy to follow, easy to manage, and shows progress step-by-step.

MODULAR TESTING

If, arriving at the screen format program, you discover that you must redesign the database for some reason, stop. Go back to the specification document, rework the database design, verify the change with the user if necessary, and then go back through the finished modules to make sure that the changes have been implemented throughout the system. Do not, for any reason, leave rework to be done at a later time. At any given point you should be fairly confident of the consistency of the code that has already been written.

This approach is much more organized and easier to manage than having a dozen modules partially written with the plan of linking them all together someday. Also, this method enables the code to survive the loss of specific programmers, and enables several programmers to work on the same system at the same time by giving each group their own tree branch. Internal documentation of each module leads to better supportability. Cross referencing of variables would also help the coders in the case of any changes, since they would know where to look in each module.

It is good form to standardize variable names throughout the system. There is no reason to call salary SAL in one module and SALARY in another. If there are a number of programmers working on a single project, it is often useful to agree on all variable names before coding begins, and then communicate the names assigned by each programmer during intermediate processing. In some programming languages, variables might have to be declared "public" in order to be passed to other programs, while others can be set "private," implying their use is restricted within one module. Public and private declarations should also be closely monitored to prevent confusion in the final system between variable names.

The module-by-module approach also lends itself to project milestone management. We suggest coding all of the input modules first. After the main menu module and the input modules have been coded and tested, it is a good idea to show them to the client. The programmer can get assurance that the required information is all there, that the fields are of correct size and type, and that the screen formats and the visual presentation of the system is acceptable. If problems arise at this point, the rework is restricted to the input modules alone. Once the user has agreed that the input modules are as they should be, the programmer can begin to code the computational and reporting modules. User acceptance at each milestone also minimizes the possibility of any unexpected surprises that might occur if the client does not see the system until all of the work has been done.

OUTPUT DOCUMENT DESIGN

As has been mentioned in the project design section, the output forms should be constructed to emulate existing reports and forms as much as possible. This is extremely important if a client is already using preprinted forms from a previous automated system. This is much more reasonable than to require the user to incur additional costs for the printing of new forms as well as the waste of throwing out the existing forms.

Another good design approach in coding reports is to make the output documents easy to read. Include features like pagination with numbering, time and date stamps, and any identification codes such as branch office names, report revision numbers, and user codes. Professional reports should also include page totals, report totals to page, and report grand totals where applicable. Showing the reports to the client as the report modules are completed again offers a natural milestone and helps catch conceptual design errors. Remember to create only the reports and output forms defined in the project task order. If the user looks at your report, and deems it to be correct, but wants another column or an additional calculation, you should consider these requests as additional tasks. They should be added to the "wish list" that will form the basis of future tasks.

Try at all costs to avoid redesigning a work in progress. This can lead to a number of problems, and will almost certainly guarantee that the project will not flow properly. Once you make the project completion ambiguous, it becomes difficult to finish the task. The contract and design specification completely define the tasks to be performed. The key to successful project management is to stick to the contracted-for tasks, and finish those tasks first, before addressing any of the wishes on the "wish list."

THE USE OF APPLICATION GENERATORS

Using application generators to create the basic modules discussed earlier can save some developers a great deal of time. A number of such generators exist and do provide good code that can act as a foundation for an application. Often, however, the developer will have to extensively modify the generated code to give it the right look and feel, as well as customize the application to the user's needs. Standard input modules such as ADD, EDIT, and FIND are really quite generic, with the screen formats and database key linking.

Some developers build their own library of "standard" modules, and modify these code modules rather than running a program generator each time. Although there are a number of situations that are straightforward enough to make good use of application generators, the amount of customization desired in many cases makes new code more efficient. In any event, the developer should still use the approach discussed here, which necessitates going through each module created by the application generator to learn how it works, add internal documentation, and do testing.

You are going to deliver the final product to the user as a custom-written product. Be very confident, therefore, that the code written by the generator is good and well-documented, and that you understand the generated code as well as if you wrote it. A large application, containing modules from an application generator and modules written by the programmer, without a solid integration plan, could cause problems that could destroy a project. The end-user does not want to have a finger-pointing situation, in which the developer says "That is not my code that is crashing!" The client comes to the developer to get a finished, bug-free product, in the least amount of time. If you choose to use an application generator to build the basic modules of the project, make sure that you still follow the module-by-module concepts discussed above.

As an interesting side issue, consider the copyright issues in a product that you write using some of your own code and some generated code. Bytel's Genifer, for instance, has a copyright statement in each program module that it generates. If you began with this code, modified it extensively, added your own modules to the system, then compiled it, would you have the right to put your own copyright on the executable file? The answer is probably complex enough to require legal counseling, and we expect that even then there would be no clear answer. Thus, if copyright protection is a major issue, as it might be if you expect to mass-market the application, it might be more prudent to avoid application generators. During the development of any application, a programmer might develop algorithms that will be of considerable value in the future, and it is good form not to cloud the issue with other people's code.

Chapter 9

Testing and Evaluation

One of the least understood processes in application development is that of program testing and system evaluation. Because the developer must ultimately interpret the wishes and expectations of the end-users into the system product, there is often a grey area consisting of both errors and misinterpretations. The later set of problems can be minimized by an adequate user interview and the involvement of the user in the development process, as described in Chapter Four.

Errors, however, do crop up. No one is capable of writing perfect code. Even if the specification exactly follows system requirements, there may be errors in logic, arithmetic, output formats, or input screen layouts. When designing a task, include a specific amount of time for the identification of such errors, the recoding to repair these problems, and the testing of the repairs themselves.

Those who come to programming from large engineering or aerospace firms are usually more comfortable with the concept of building test and evaluation costs into the main project budget. Those "large project" corporations also use a check list or "sign-off" approach, developing a series of milestones even within the testing process. Although the actual amount of time spent varies considerably with the size and type of project, it has always been a rule of thumb to add about 20 percent to the project time estimate to allow for the shakedown process. This means that in a project of, say, 100 hours of programming, testing should add 20 hours to the bottom line.

Depending on the nature of the contractual relationship between the developer and the client, it may be possible to merely bill the testing as an hourly fee above the contract price, or offer a refund if the 20 percent overage is not used. In no case, however, should the developer not charge for this work. This could lead to an impossible economic situation, with the inexperienced developer working hundreds of hours with no billable charges, just because of underestimating the amount of time needed during the final project stages.

It is also extremely important to create a clear demarkation of the end of a project. A good contract completely delineates the responsibilities of the programmer regarding what the system must do. If the user wants an additional calculated field on a given report, that request should not be considered an error to be fixed, but rather should be tabled and brought up again as a new task. Build the wish list. Inexperienced programmers make this mistake often. An error is a problem in the code that has been defined in the project task specification. It cannot, and must not, include the results of "wouldn't it be nice if . . . ."

One way to avoid any confusion about this phase of development is to list the stages in the task schedule. There are a number of distinct parts to this process, and they must be sequential. Using big project concepts, treat each step as a milestone and have the appropriate parties "sign off" at each stage. What follows is a series of suggested testing and evaluation stages.

PHASE ONE—INTERNAL (PRE-ALPHA)

Internal testing is often done by the coders themselves. It should be done on a module-by-module basis while the programming is being done. In dBASE applications, for example, menus, data entry screens, computations, and reports can easily be checked as they are written. This is the great value of an interpreted language development system. Using an interpreter, you can code the module, test it, fix problems, test again, and so on until it looks right.

A good philosophical approach is "once you make it, try to break it." In every place where data entry is made, the code writer should try to anticipate every possible type of input, no matter how bizarre. Hopefully, there are enough error traps, range and validation checks, and whatever else is necessary, to keep users from demolishing the system by making a "creative" entry. This pre-Alpha testing can and should be done by the programmers themselves.

Unfortunately, this is sometimes all of the testing that there is. Even if the modules check out individually, the integration of the modules into the final system is not assured. Before the project leaves your hands, go through the system menu item-by-item, use every data entry screen, call every help screen, and print every report. Only when the code writers themselves have successfully navigated the entire system should the "pre-Alpha" test be considered complete. Have the testers sign off, and begin the next phase.

PHASE TWO—INTERNAL (ALPHA)

Phase one should only be considered the first level of testing. There should always be an Alpha test by people other than those who wrote the code. This may be difficult for one person shops, but its value cannot be over-emphasized. The alternative is to let the user do Alpha testing, which must be avoided at all costs. Minor bugs that may turn up in this phase make even a good programmer look sloppy.

Find an Alpha tester who can try to crash the system in the most outrageous ways possible. Everyone knows people like that. They could be nontechnical employees of your own firm, friends, or former clients. The more nàive the Alpha tester the better, so that no preconceived notions or prejudices will be brought to bear. Even if the firm is large enough to be able to give the program to programmers other than the authors of the system, still try to find a novice for the Alpha test.

Printouts, reports, and forms from this testing stage can and should be presented to the user before you deliver the code. In this way the development group still has time to catch any actual design errors in-house.

Once the technical and non-technical Alpha test is complete and has been signed off, there should be no possibility of such things as syntax errors or data type mismatches. The system is now at the stage where Beta testing can begin.

PHASE THREE—EXTERNAL (BETA)

Although the system has been through two stages of internal testing, it would not be prudent to offer it as a completely debugged product to the user. In no case should it go "on-line" or "into production" without a complete Beta test. In large applications, in which there may be a number of end-user sites that will be using the final product, or if the application is in a vertical market and will be mass-marketed, choose a small number of sites as "Beta test sites." Arrange for a set of dummy data to be entered, for a complete set of documentation to be delivered, and let the system do its work.

The best style of Beta test is called the blind test. In this approach, the tester gets the disks, manuals, and whatever written instructions the developer intends to give the end-user. The tester must install, configure, and learn the system without the help of the programmers or the technical staff of development firm. There are some cases where this approach is not appropriate, such as a highly specialized custom application. In such a system the application developer's people will have to set up, configure, and train, and get the Beta test users going. Then they should leave.

Let the Beta testers do what they will with a minimum of interference. They should not be encouraged to call the programmer at the drop of a hat with any question. They must test both the software and the support documentation, whether on-line or in the manual.

An evaluation form would be helpful as a part of the Beta site package. Figure 9-1 shows an excerpt from an evaluation form we have used. Such a form will give your people written comments, problems, and suggestions, some of which may be valid enough to prompt a rework of the program before release. This is a grey area. If the changes requested are not errors, but merely enhance the quality of the final product, the justification for the time and money to do the changes becomes a judgment call, with more business implications than technical ones. This issue is much more crucial in an application that you intend to market to many users. In the customized application world, you should consider the Beta comments and suggestions as things to be discussed when defining future tasks.

If problems arise in the Beta test that require changes in code for whatever reason, it is essential to remember that the testing process must recycle to phase one. It is easy to ignore this protocol, but it could hurt you when you try to deliver final code, claiming it to be fully debugged, and the user finds a fatal error. Depending on the size and nature of the code change, the time to redo phase one and two Alphas can be focused to minimize delays.

Special care should be taken to build a valid set of test data. This "dummy" data should mimic the real data as much as possible, so that you can be sure that the system will handle such things as high precision numbers and wide character columns. A typical programmer's nightmare is that the entire system is written to handle six digit numerical inventory codes, Alpha and Beta testers are told to enter only numbers, error traps are built to prevent any-

Fig. 9-1. Sample Beta test evaluation form excerpt.

BETA TEST SYSTEM EVALUATION FORM

We greatly appreciate your taking time to complete this questionaire. Your evaluations and comments are very important to us, as they help us to improve our products.

COMPANY: ______________________________ DATE: __________

PERSON COMPLETING FORM: __________________ PHONE: _____________

DATE TESTING BEGAN: ___________ DATE TESTING ENDED: ____________

EXCELLENT [E] GOOD [G] AVERAGE [A] FAIR [F] POOR [P]

Please use the scale above to answer the following questions.

CHAPTER 1 - ADDING RECORDS

(Manual)

1. Format [ ]
2. Ease of use [ ]
3. Informative [ ]
4. Organization [ ]

Additional comments: ______________________________________

____

____

EXCELLENT [E] GOOD [G] AVERAGE [A] FAIR [F] POOR [P]

Please use the scale above to answer the following questions.

(Program)

1. Format [ ]
2. Ease of use [ ]
3. Speed [ ]
4. Operator friendly [ ]
5. The contents of the help messages [ ]
6. The use of program error checking [ ]

Do you prefer F1 type help instead of the current on-line? (Y/N) [ ]

Additional comments: ____________________

____

____

Final recommendations and comments ____________________

____

____

____

____

____

____

____

____

____

thing other than numbers from being entered, and then it is discovered that someone in accounting uses dashes or letters. By choosing a valid dummy data set the developer would be spared this embarrassment. This problem should not arise if the user interview process has led to a complete and correct project specification. Sometimes, however, the user might say that 381-091 is a six digit number, when it is in fact a seven character alphanumeric data field. Often in such cases, the developer must swallow hard, and make the corrections at no charge. Again, such costs could be covered in the budget for the testing and debugging phase.

In mass-marketed applications the Beta is the end of the testing line. Some prudent developers would then ship a low number of final products before releasing actual production quantities into distribution channels. This is sometimes considered a second phase Beta test, because any errors caught in this phase could still be corrected before mass production begins. It is much easier to send out 50 "updates" (which in fact are bug fixes) than to rip open hundreds, or even thousands, of shrink-wrapped packages.

PHASE FOUR—EXTERNAL (ACCEPTANCE TEST)

The custom-application Beta test ends with the entry of real data to initiate what could be called the acceptance test. If the system was installed during Beta and loaded with dummy data, it is necessary to cleanse this data, reinitialize the system, and bring it up into an operational mode. In sites where the new application is replacing an existing system (whether manual or automated) it is essential to demand that the existing system be run parallel with the new application during the acceptance test. This is a self-checking process; the new system should agree line-for-line, number-by-number with the old system. Sometimes very subtle logical and/or arithmetical errors can only be uncovered during this parallel processing period.

If the contractual obligations of the developer include training, it should be done during this phase. Whether this training is done in a classroom setting or on a one-to-one basis, the acceptance test period provides an excellent opportunity to integrate the user into the final system.

The term "acceptance test" has excellent psychological impact. At the end of this test the user has accepted the code, paid the developer, and is ready to give the developer more work if necessary or desired. The project ending point is clearly marked by the end of this phase. All of the terms of the contract should be fulfilled at this point, except for any guarantees or warranties which may extend for ninety days or so. The final acceptance document should clearly state that the project is over, the terms have been met, and the code has been accepted. It can be a letter or memo, but should have a space for the client's signature.

In a healthy, ongoing client relationship, there may be any number of projects going on at one time. Acceptance documents aid project management, because the developer can give the client concise status reports on the progress of each project at any time.

In conclusion, remember that you are better off planning not to be perfect. It is extremely professional to include testing as billable time in the project plan. A good testing system, such as the one proposed here, offers the developer a systematic way to catch errors in the development process, and clean them up long before the final system goes on-line at the end-user's site using real data. We also suggest that, when applicable, the project plan should include provisions for parallel operation of the new application and the existing system.

It is the mark of a good developer to deliver code that has been subjected to a rigorous testing system, so that it is bug-free and "idiot-proof" upon delivery.

Chapter 10

Installation, Training, and Support

This phase of a project is usually an afterthought to the task itself. In some cases, the user might already have at least some of the computer equipment that is going to be used to run the new system. In other cases, the user is making the transition from a completely manual system to automation. The spectrum of needs and responsibilities in the installation phase is quite broad, and we will discuss several approaches that are popular for applications developers.

THE INSTALLATION PROCESS

The most common situation facing the developer is that there is no pre-existing computer system. The typical first-time user depends on the developer to help in acquiring the equipment and system software to set up the computer system. The developer might actually provide the hardware, acting as what is known as a Value Added Retailer (VAR). Professional accounting firms often act as middle men in the acquisition of the system upon which to run accounting and/or financial analysis software. The developer can thus be a sole provider, an overseer of a multi-vendor install, or part of a multi-source process.

Whatever the scenario, there is one inescapable fact if the installation must include everything: there is going to be a major period of upheaval in the daily operations of the client. Bringing both the computer and the newly created application to the end-user staff all at once is the worst possible situation. When users must overcome fear and anxiety of the "machines" and the "program," both entities seem to have arrived to muck up their lives.

The developer is often in the middle of the maelstrom. You are responsible for the acquisition of the computers, monitors, disk drives, memory, communications cards, cables, system software and, in some cases, even furniture. As the sole source in such an installation, take great care to make sure that:

- ☐ All components are delivered on time.
- ☐ The CPU, system boards, and peripheral hardware are all in working order, configured properly, and operate as a system.
- ☐ All cables, connectors, and communications ports are correct and working.
- ☐ If possible, "burn in" the system components before delivery.

The developer should also make sure that the operating software is installed, hard disks are formatted, user software is installed, and system menus are constructed. If a Local Area Network is involved, implying that there will be a number of computers in the company connected by cable, the developer must also make sure that the cable is installed, including any amplifiers or hubs. This often requires dealing with electricians or building operations staff. The operative rule is that everything that needs to be in place, must be. If not, the professional developer *cum* installation coordinator wastes time and loses user confidence.

Systems delivered to inexperienced users must also be eased into place psychologically. The users must be made to feel involved in what is going on. Ask users where they want their machines, when is the best time for you to disrupt their office, and so on. Try to minimize the disruption caused by the install. If possible, begin the work after-hours or on weekends.

Multi-user LAN installs should be done like pseudo-military campaigns. For example, we were once involved in an installation of a 16-computer Local Area Network in a hospital. Weeks before the install date, all of the hardware was collected at a "staging area." All of the equipment was uncrated and set up. Boards were stuffed with memory chips and placed in machines. Hard disks were formatted. Everything that was to be in the LAN was burned in. While this burn-in was going on in the staging area, the hospital electricians were laying coaxial cable for the LAN throughout the hospital. Members of the install team oversaw the placement of cable, active- and passive-amplification hub devices, and wall plates for cable ends.

When the day of install came, the process began at the loading dock at 8:30 A.M. Fifteen of the 16 workstation nodes were in operation, with software running, by 11:30 that same morning. The impact to the hospital was minimized by good planning and execution.

If off-site staging and burn-in is not possible, you still should uncrate and bring up the machinery on a table out of the way, and actually bring the system into a client workspace only after it has passed its infant mortality test. Most microcomputer equipment is extremely reliable after it has been burned in for about a day. If the system powers up and lives for a day or so, it is said to have passed the period of infant mortality.

We have never had an IBM PC just die after it has been running for a while. Printers die. Disk drives, both floppy and hard, die. In fact, a rule of thumb worth remembering is that electromechanical devices are far less reliable than electronic devices. Burn-ins, especially if conducted away from client view, will save the developer the embarrassment of hardware failure, as well as minimize the time wasted by disrupting the user's workspace.

Once the equipment is in place, turned on, running, and ready to be "turned over" to the users, the hardware installation phase has ended.

If the application being developed is to be added to an existing computer system, a number of precautions need to be taken. If the application is non-interactive with the rest of the system, the developer can merely install it on its own subdirectory or disk volume and proceed to bring it up. An example of this would be a financial analysis system being added to a company that had been using its microcomputers to do word processing and client database work. In such a case there is no way (unless your application reformats the disk) of the new system causing problems for the existing, working system.

If, however, the new application, is, for example, going to modify files in the accounting system, take great care to test it on a subdirectory containing a copy of the real accounting fields. If there are bugs, the new stuff can only destroy the "play" data, and leave the real information intact. It is a serious sin, not to mention bad form, to damage a production system. Do not put yourself in a position where such an event is even plausible.

The software installation is just beginning. In the case of an accounting system, for example, the user will now have to enter charts of accounts, accounts receivable and accounts payable data, inventory information, and whatever else will be needed to run the system. Hopefully, the developer has made the user aware of whose responsibility system data entry will be. A great source of dispute at this point is that the user might expect the developer to type the actual, live data into the application. This is a nontrivial task for a company with 2000 inventory items, 5000 customers, and 1000 vendors in the accounts payable file. Again, the project task contract would avoid problems, but only if such considerations were included.

Once the data is entered, there is still the issue of training the users to use their new "toys." Training is another area often overlooked in planning the total project. It would be madness to merely install the hardware, bring up the software, load the data, and then "hit the road." However, this is often the way systems are given to unknowing, trusting users. Unless the project plan includes a reasonable fee for either the developer or some other trainer to explain the operation of the system, both from a hardware and software point of view, the project will fail.

BACKUP SYSTEMS

One of the most important issues to emphasize to new and experienced computer users alike is the absolute requirement for a formalized system to produce and store backups. A well-designed hardware system will include some piece of equipment that is capable of storing large amounts of information on some media that can be removed to off-site locales. In the event of catastrophic system failure, this data could then be restored onto new or repaired equipment. This will only work if someone in the end-user community has been responsible enough to keep backups current.

We had a client for whom we designed an application several years ago. As is our custom, we provided him with an external cartridge tape backup system. It was capable of both an image backup, in which every byte on the fixed disk was copied verbatim onto the tape, forming a "mirror image," and a file-by-file operation, in which all of the files, or only those altered since the last backup, were copied to tape. We also set up menu options for each operation and instructed his staff to follow a backup rotation schedule, in which complete image and file-by-file backups were done each Friday afternoon, and daily archival procedures copied each day's altered files to tape. A restore process would then require an image restore, followed by restoring the daily altered files in correct order. This method guarantees that the data loss is limited only to those files that had been worked on since the previous day's backup. Such a system might sound conservative, but has its roots in mainframe operational methods.

Our client and his staff religiously backed up every day, and did the total backups each Friday. For a while. After several months without any problems they began to skip some days. If they had to leave early, they would put off Friday's backups, which could take over an hour, to the next Monday. Eventually they went to a once a week backup, then once a month, after posting the accounting.

Finally, it happened. One November morning, nearly a year later, we got a frantic call from the "responsible" person at the firm. The hard disk wasn't making any noise, and there was a message saying "Error reading drive C: Abort, Retry, Ignore" on the screen. Undaunted, we directed them to bring out the replacement drive provided for under their service contract, and told them that we would be out presently to help them do the restore from their backup tapes. Silence on the other end. The last backup had been done in July. End of story.

TRAINING—FORMAL AND INFORMAL

Training takes two forms, formal and informal. Formal training is exactly what it sounds like. The users are ushered, as a group, into a training area in which some actual hardware has been set up. They are then subjected to classes or training seminars in which they are given a hands on, step-by-step tour of the new hardware and software. These sessions should be based on the conservative philosophical approach we have been recommending—assume nothing.

The "virgin" user group may have never worked on any computer before. If so, they do not really understand concepts like format, path, and logical disk drive. Sessions should start with how to turn on the machine, what are the various system components, how to form-feed the printer, and similar basic topics. The software concepts should not be introduced until the group is comfortable with the hardware. In each user group, designate one or two people as "system managers," and make them responsible for fundamental maintenance procedures like backup and recovery, loading paper into printers, and acting as a first-stage filter for user questions. Many consultants are often frustrated by unsophisticated end-users calling them for every little thing. By making some responsible person at the client company the only person authorized to call for help, this problem is minimized. It also shows a more professional attitude on the part of the consultant, helping the client organization save on consulting fees when they are not really needed.

Formal training, in some cases, can be done by computer stores or software vendors. Such training, usually done at the stores or at a hotel meeting room, would bring your client, along with several other users, into a classroom setting with books, teachers, and sample data sets. Such training is very popular for accounting systems (users go to module-by-module training), database management systems, spreadsheets, and electronic desktop publishing. If new employees are added, or new software packages are brought on-line, users can go to such classes as they become available, which is very often, in most metropolitan areas.

In the case of custom applications, however, only the author organization is capable of doing the training. If such work is to be included in the project plan, remember that it will take some time to develop lesson plans and course materials. As a rule, plan to leave these materials with the client organization, so that they can train new people or offer a periodic refresher course. If the client wants you to do the training again, at some future date, treat that as a new task, usually under a consulting rate.

A technique that we have found valuable under certain circumstances has been the use of video taping equipment to record training sessions on the user application system. The size, complexity, and cost of portable VHS video cameras and portable tape decks has come down to the point where their use, even by a small firm, is feasible. It was once considered too difficult and expensive to produce training tapes, but the new generation of video equipment allows for the creation of acceptable product without the need for video professionals. It is true that these tapes will not be as slick and professional-looking as one produced by an IBM or XEROX training division, but they still serve a very useful purpose. Video tapes of the user training sessions can be left with the client organization, and can be used to train new employees, or provide existing end-users with refresher courses on points they might not have picked up in the original training sessions.

The state of miniaturization in the video market has even made it possible to have lightweight "camcorders," which are cameras with the tape recording electronics and mechanics built right in. Even a one-person training operation should have no difficulty setting such a unit up on a tripod, pointing it in the direction of most of the speaking (preferably near the microcomputer workstation), checking the sound, and then letting it run. The hand-held unit could occasionally be pointed directly at the display screen to record visual data pertinent to the training. After the training, these tapes can be copied so that the developer retains at least one good copy, and then distributes others to the end-user community. Because this approach cuts off the potential of further revenue from follow-up training, some developers charge additionally for the production and distribution of these video tapes. In any event, this is a good method, which gives the client organization more independence from the developer once the system is complete. There will still be new training required in the future each time new enhancements or additions are made to the system.

Typical training fees at the corporate level for services rendered at the client site are about $1000 a day plus expenses. In this method, the teacher brings materials to a conference room or small auditorium at the client's office site. Only the teacher, and assistants, if required, are involved in any travel time. The students can be easily delivered to the class, which can be scheduled either during working hours or not, and the client company can limit the disruption caused. If 10 administrative staff members are given two full days of training in this mode, the cost per student is much lower than if students are to be trained off-site in smaller groups. The off-site training schedules might also be less flexible, because they tend to be set up to serve as many different people at one time as possible. There is also questionable merit in being one of 50 participants in a three-hour introduction to dBASE at a local computer store. We have never heard of any graduates of such sessions being able to sit down and code like a professional. In fact, most of the comments that we have heard about these classes make us believe that they discourage more users than they inspire. Bringing the trainer into the company conference room to teach a small seminar is clearly more efficient, and more successful.

Classes at computer stores cost from $50 to $200 per day, per student. Some major retail chains will include a certain number of days of training in the cost of a system. For example, a client might purchase an accounting system, a Local Area Network, and all of the computers and peripherals from a retail store, which would allow two or three users to attend classes for each of the purchased modules at no extra charge. These rules are not hard and fast; it is often possible to "slip in" extra students. We do warn, however, that it is rare that an unsophisticated, computer-illiterate end-user would be able to return from such general training and go right to work. That is why the second level of training exists. The informal approach, in which the user and a trainer sit together at the workstation and go through the system in a one-to-one manner, is often required. This might seem extravagant, because only one user is being trained at a time, but in the long run, it does lead to a higher level of confidence and competence in the user population.

Informal training is hard to gauge in terms of time and manpower, and should thus be set up as an hourly billing. Some users might only need an hour or two, others might need a whole week. You can often negotiate a special rate for this type of training, especially in custom applications. Do not forget to exclude these charges in the project specification document, lest you find yourself spending two to three non-billable weeks on training.

Informal training should be oriented toward extensive use of on-line help, if available, and the user documentation. Try to develop a self-sufficient user as much as possible. While it is often ego-strengthening to have users "need" you, it can quickly become a problem of major proportions.

SUPPORT

Ongoing support of a computer system is a many-faceted problem. The system is usually a multi-vendor hodge-podge of hardware, canned software, and custom application packages. The developer must plan to offer a continuing support package, and provide an effective set of guarantees to the end-users concerning system maintainability and recovery in the event of catastrophic failures.

Hardware Support

The concept of a service contract lends itself well to the hardware. Users historically have been offered such contracts with other major pieces of office equipment and home appliances. Typical costs are about 1 1/2 percent of the retail price per month. This translates to 18 percent per year, and might seem quite steep to a novice end-user. These contracts are actually insurance policies, and the service provider is betting that the hardware will not fail in a given time.

In the days of minicomputers and mainframes these contracts were expensive and absolutely necessary. To repair a "downed" large computer often took time, expertise, and money. Because the contracts were based on high-cost items, however, the service companies could make a profit. As with insurance companies, the chance that the service company will make money depends on that company having a large number of clients, with the hope that they will not all crash at once.

It is generally a good idea to suggest that an end-user sign on with a very large, reputable service company like TRW or Sorbus.

Buying a five-year contract from "Joe's Computer Place" is not really a good idea. Under no circumstances should a developer consider taking on a service contract. Even if you have provided all of the hardware, and have great faith in it, the statistical nature of insurance implies that it is bad business to bet on low volumes.

If a user calls you at seven in the evening on Saturday, and tells you that the system hard disk has just died, you would have to go to the client's office, fix or replace the dead drive, and restore the system to operating condition. For free! With $10,000 worth of hardware under contract, you might only be receiving $150 per month. If you had to replace an expensive component in the first few months, you would lose money, and, more importantly, time. If you had 100 such clients, and were receiving $15,000 a month in fees, it would be easier to absorb the loss involved in replacement, repair, and labor.

Although the new microcomputers themselves are quite reliable, electromechanical devices such as disk drives, printers, and tape drives are, by their very nature, prone to failure. Do not be seduced by the "easy money" of service contracts. Leave it to the big guys. They can offer 24 hour, on-site, repair or replacement at competitive rates, and it takes the burden off of the application developer.

Some users may choose a "spares" policy rather than a service agreement. In such an approach, they purchase extra hardware, have it configured and tested, and then put it in the closet. If a failure occurs in the main system, they remove the faulty component, pop in the spare, and get the system back up in minimum down-time. The failed unit can then be carried or sent to a repair depot, which is usually much less expensive than on-site work. Once the unit is repaired and returned, it becomes the new spare.

This method makes sense in terms of numbers. If the user is getting 15 computers, three printers, and five hard drives, and puts an extra one of each group in the stock room, the cost, as a percentage of system cost, will be lower than a traditional service contract. The disadvantage is that the user would have to be the service technician, working with boards, cables, and peripherals. In the case of a failed hard disk drive, the user would need to format the replacement, and restore backed-up data to the new drive. Such tasks are nontrivial and should not be dismissed as easy-to-do. Often, the developer would be called in to help with the swap processes in the event of problems.

The choice for support is up to the user, but we do suggest that both options be made clear by the developer. The analysis should show economic comparisons and relative time impacts for each choice. We favor the service contract approach for the hardware.

One approach that should be completely discouraged is not having any plan for hardware support. Things have a way of breaking just when it is most disastrous for them to do so. We often say that hard disks "know" to crash only when there isn't an adequate backup of critical data. Users who simply choose to take their chances are playing Russian Roulette. While this may be a reasonable philosophy for a home or hobby computer system, it is irrational to follow in even a small business. If a user has all financial or accounting data on a microcomputer, and is cut off from it while it is brought (or sent) somewhere to be repaired, there might be real trouble. Imagine the loss of accounts receivable, inventory, and customer information—all at once. If the computer has been in place for a while, old manual systems might be out of date, if they exist at all. Service contracts or spares would prevent such a catastrophe, because the replacement hard disk data files could be restored from the backup data, enabling the user to be back on-line in the shortest amount of time.

"Canned" Software Support

Ongoing support for canned software packages is often available from the manufacturer for a fee. The value of such support is questionable. Phone-in support by the company that produced the software is usually expensive and should only be used after all other avenues are exhausted. Specific questions might be better handled by an advisor, or the application developer. It is usually hard to get through to a major software vendor, and these delays can be frustrating.

A system manager, if one has been designated, should handle such telephone support, only after the question has been researched through the available documentation. Calling the manufacturer and saying, "It broke. I don't know what I did," is worthless. Before telephone support is initiated, make sure that the problem is defined in terms of:

- ☐ What happened.
- ☐ At what point in the program.
- ☐ What error messages appeared.
- ☐ Printouts or print screens that were saved.

This information will help the person on the other end solve the problem. In the case of mass-marketed software packages, it is rare to find a true bug. Most of the problems are user-initiated. Also, telephone support is very often timed, so the more defined the problem, the lower the cost of service.

Some software support contracts guarantee free, or low cost, updates. This is usually a good investment, but needs to be weighed economically. In the case of a C compiler, for example, the user might wish to receive the two or three updates per year that are offered under the software maintenance agreement. A word processor, however, is static, and thus is not updated often. To pay $100 per year to receive free updates of WordStar would be foolish. These static packages are updated very infrequently, and often offer registered users updates at little or no cost.

In these days of software piracy and industry-wide disagreements about copy protection, software support is often linked to proper product registration. Most microcomputer packages are sold on a per-computer license agreement. The developer should advise the users to complete each and every registration card that comes with the system. This should be done regardless of the source. Otherwise, if there are problems, the user will call the developer because Lotus will not respond. Because, as the developer, you are often involved as the system integrator, such details have a habit of falling in your lap.

The developer who provides an application that is to be run on a number of computers at the end-user site should take care to make sure that proper license registrations are made for each package on each CPU. Suppose that the developer writes a series of Lotus templates, and sells the client a copy of Lotus 1-2-3 for each processor that is going to use these templates. This approach would be in complete compliance with the Lotus license agreement. If, however, the client is provided with only one copy of the package, and the client (or someone at that firm) makes copies for the rest of the users' machines, the developer is at risk in any potential legal action unless the end-user has been warned against this behavior in the project or task agreement. Such written communication about the issue might help defend the developer against any wrongful-action suits on behalf of Lotus.

If the client (or an employee) calls Lotus for support, and they find out that illegal copies of 1-2-3 have been made for other machines, the developer might still be implicated in any resulting litigation. Although most large companies are very adamant about software copying, we have found that small firms tend to be lax. Thus, the developer must act as the "policeman" in this issue, just to keep out of trouble.

A number of mass-marketed software programs can be made available using an on-site license or multi-user agreement. In such cases, just make sure that the correct numbers are purchased, and that multi-user terms are met. It is always good business to keep out of harm's way. Several large vendors have taken small users to court over these issues, so be warned.

Custom Software Support

The final area of support is for the custom application itself. This is an extremely grey area because there is a fine line between making the end-user dependent on the developer and meeting the needs of the developer to protect proprietary code. We suggest that the developer retain the source code and deliver only executable code to the user. This means that the user must deal with the developer to fix bugs or upgrade the program. The developer must, therefore, be available to the end-user for such support.

The alternative would be to give the user a limited-use copy of the source. In this case, users could contract with another consulting programmer to make desired changes, or hire programmers of their own. Any changes made in your code should invalidate any guarantees you have given, and this should be made clear in writing. A special limited license and liability-release document should be created to cover these situations.

Some users might ask for access to the source only if the developer goes out of business, dies, or leaves for any other reason. This is a reasonable request, because the user might be extremely reliant on the application for the daily operation of business. It could be disastrous if it became impossible to support at some time in the future.

Most computer program needs are dynamic. As needs change, code changes. If the developer is not willing to make an ongoing commitment to support the application code, be willing to offer viable options. One of the most common arrangements is for the developer to place a copy of the source code in escrow with a bank or a law firm, along with a mutually signed contract governing the exact terms and conditions under which the escrow is to be executed. The expense of the escrow process is normally handled by the client. This method gives the client assurance of access to the source code if the developer can no longer support it.

It would not be unreasonable to charge a contract fee for ongoing support, much like the hardware and software vendors. We suggest, however, that support be divided into two parts. First, the application developer must fix bugs. In most cases, the developer offers a guarantee period, say, 90 days. During this time, there should be no charge for the required work. As a professional promising high-quality work, you should be prepared to stand behind it.

This initial period should also be more than enough time for the end-user to "exercise" the system and uncover any existing bugs that may have slipped through the testing and evaluation process. After the warranty is up, there should be a contractual agreement for an hourly rate to fix code problems. The fees should be defined using task agreements.

The second part of support is the question of enhancements and changes. These should be considered separately and are covered in the next section.

Summarizing, we feel that it is the application developer's responsibility to oversee the installation, training, and support aspects of the final system. The contracted obligation is to deliver a complete, integrated, and working system. Finger-pointing between various vendors, with the end-user in the middle, is hardly a professional impression to leave the end-user with. Satisfied clients lead to more work.

BUILDING AN ONGOING CLIENT BASE

The project is over. Everything is signed off, the hardware is in and running well, the software hums along in a real environment. During the development process, a number of changes might have been requested. If the procedures outlined in this book were followed, these change requests were compiled into a wish list. Because the initial project task agreement outlined all of the work to be done in the earlier task, changes must be handled in subsequent tasks. This is the basis for additional business. The satisfied end-user has a working system, and knows that the application developer can deliver what he said he could. The client should be aware of the cost/performance benefits of the new system. Even if $10,000 was spent on the new application, there should be clear and powerful improvements in doing business.

The developer can take the wish list, estimate the time and charges involved in writing the additional code, and present the client with a new Task Order Request. These are usually little tasks like adding fields to a report, creating new sorts, or changing the width of a data entry field.

THE WISH LIST

The fact that the next task can be so easily constructed stems directly from the project definition itself. As we mentioned, earlier, the project has a definite end, at which point the user accepts the finished product and agrees that the task is over. There is none of the blurring that occurs in the absence of the clear definition of completion. Pity the poor programmer who simply stuffs the wish-list changes onto the end of a project, sometimes at little or no charge. Not only can this be wasted profit, but there is nothing with which to create the next task.

Converting the wish list into a task requires the same care as the definition of the original task. The new Task Order Request needs to be signed, with each function clearly delineated. This second task must also have an end. Then, once again, new requests can be processed in new tasks. This is good business. It tends to build an ongoing user base, with good cash flow and excellent prospects for the growth of the consulting firm.

CREATING NEW TASKS

A second class of new tasks are additions to the system rather than changes to the code already delivered. Such things as new reports and new databases fall under this heading. These should be handled differently than changes, because they may be, in fact, code created from scratch. Do not do these until the wish list task is finished. New modules should be treated exactly as the initial project, including user interviews, design reviews, and an extensive task agreement. Although little changes like adding a totals column at the bottom of a report page are easy to define, code, test, and deliver, the developer should not risk the integrity of a working system by adding new modules that have not been through the full development cycle. We thus suggest that all new functions be combined into yet a third task.

As a good business practice, you should require payments at the beginning and completion of each task. It is reasonable to stop all work on all tasks for a given client if payments are late, as defined in the contract. One of the primary rules of consulting in general, and applications development specifically, is "never work for free!" The threat of suspension of work on a subsequent task like the wish list functions as a good inducement for the client to pay. We suggest that work not even begin until the project agreement is signed and the deposit paid, so the late-payment scenario should be prevented.

WRITTEN COMMUNICATION

Another good rule to follow is to put all promises in writing. Letters, notes, and memos between the developer and the client are a much better way of communicating problems and requests than verbally. These written documents can also make it easier to construct future tasks. In any event, they help to limit the "but you said . . . " dialogue.

This approach of sequential tasks has the potential to give the developer a nice amount of billable work, and has the advantage of being deliverable in blocks that are easier for the client organization to absorb, both economically and structurally. As time goes by, the developer will see the practice growing and stabilizing financially because of the multi-client multi-project base that has been developed. It is very dangerous for the developer to attempt to build a business on one or two clients, because the loss of a client could be catastrophic. Keeping clients happy, and fulfilling your obligations, will keep the cash flow going.

ETHICAL ISSUES

As a final note in this section we would like to mention the possible horizontal and vertical market spread of a custom project. Some applications are so specialized that there is absolutely no way that anyone other than the client would be interested in acquiring a copy. Other applications have the potential, with some recoding, of being used by other companies in the same market (vertical spread) or by similar companies in other markets (horizontal spread). Such spread brings up interesting issues. How should the developer handle proliferation of code? If one of your client's competitors comes to you and offers you twice what the program cost to develop, are you bound, by any ethical reasons, to your original client? Once a client has paid $10,000 for the development of an applications program, is it fair to mass market the program in magazines or by direct mail for $50 a copy? These are volatile issues to say the least.

If the initial project task agreement states clearly that the application developer owns the source code, and all rights attached to it, it is probably legal to do anything that you want to do. Both questions in the preceding paragraph might have affirmative answers legally but still might not be ethically correct. For example, selling to the client's competitor might betray significant confidential information about the way that client does business. In manufacturing for instance, the code might contain algorithms that describe how to calculate retail price from cost of goods, overhead, and labor. Just by buying a copy of the code, which the developer owns, the competitor can acquire information that the client might consider trade secret or proprietary. The client would be justified in initiating litigation to prevent such a sale, or sue for damages after the fact. Therefore, tread very lightly on the vertical market-spread issue. We are often asked to sign an agreement limiting our rights to sell our code to the client's competitors and have done so. In one case, the client gave us a list of companies that we could not offer the program to. We agreed, and this agreement became a part of the initial project agreement. Such limitations are really not restrictive, because they also define all of the companies that you can approach with impunity. In the absence of such agreements, use common sense.

If the developer is planning a vertical market application from the outset, it should be made known to the initial client. It is common practice to lower the fee, because it is expected that research and development, programming, testing, and other costs will be recouped in the mass-marketing phase. For example, if you plan to sell your program for $500 to all companies in a target vertical market, you should not charge the first company $10,000. If you do that, you can bet that you will have an extremely upset former client. There is, of course, the risk that no one else will buy it, in which case you lose. Thus, it might be reasonable to charge $2500 for the project, giving a 75 percent discount from the usual rate. Then, the client wins even if the developer loses. You can also use this argument to soothe your client's nerves after the program has been chosen "Software Product of The Year." We would even offer a refund, if sales are good enough, to the original client, to lower the cost to the current market cost.

Consider a software product that was being sold for $200 for about two years. A reasonable number of people purchased it at that price. Then, the company announced that they had recouped their research and development costs, and were lowering the cost of the same product to under $100. Imagine how the first purchasers felt when they read that announcement. Certainly, those who purchased the product the week before the announcement of the price reduction was made felt some serious resentment. In such a case, a refund policy is self-defeating. The developer was only able to lower the price because the earlier units had cost more. A better choice might have been to pick an initial market price that was lower, then lower the price in increments as sales increased.

In any event, the developer should make sure that the client for whom the programs were initially developed is completely aware of any plans to market them elsewhere. It would be better for everyone to iron out any potential problems before the actual marketing begins.

In conclusion, sound business practices and good project definition pave the way for an ongoing relationship, in which the developer and client benefit from the dynamic evolution of computer applications. The client gets the application wanted, and the developer attains a satisfactory work and cash flow.

Chapter 11

The Interapplication File Interchange Problem

With the proliferation of IBM PC compatible computers and application packages, the problem of data interchange has reached major proportions. It is now estimated that nearly five million PCs exist, and more are being placed each day. Users have acquired many of these devices through non-centralized, non-standard methods, often bypassing the traditional data processing purchasing channels. Thus, it is not unusual to find, in any given site, a number of PCs running a variety of software packages, from word processors, to database managers, to spreadsheets.

THE TOWER OF BABEL

As attempts are made to link the individual workstations into an integrated information processing environment, either by using LANs or by incorporating the PCs into the mainframe or minicomputer system as intelligent terminals, the "Tower of Babel" effect becomes more pronounced. Each user might have data that needed by other users, but this data might not be directly compatible with other packages. A number of methods exist for data interchange, typically based on the use of flat ASCII text or delimited files. These methods require some sophistication on the part of the user to actually accomplish the data interchange, and often the task falls to a programmer in the MIS area. This problem is not difficult, but is also nontrivial. It is a task that is taking more and more time in corporate and institutional data processing areas. It is even more important when a mainframe downloads data into the PC environment and some users want to use the data in dBASE, others in 1-2-3, others in Multimate, and so on. Because the conversion is mechanistic, it should be possible to automate the process.

FILE CONVERSION EXAMPLE

As an illustration of the way in which these file conversions are processed, we will show the migration of a downloaded mainframe file, as shown in Fig. 11-1, into a form which can be used by dBASE III PLUS. The sample file was extracted from an IBM 4341 mainframe using the IBM 3270 Communication Program. The file has the typical garbage, and header and footer information.

This file is a flat ASCII file of the format known as Standard Data Format (SDF) in dBASE. A programmer would need to take a printout of this file, count the locations of each piece of data in

Fig. 11-1. Raw mainframe download data file (INP.TXT).

```
EDIT --- TGJZS.EMPLOYEE.DATA -----------------------------------COLUMNS 001 072
COMMAND ===>                                                   SCROLL ===> CSR
****** ***************************** TOP OF DATA ******************************
000001 100101689ALFRED    STEVENS   MPHDBRIGHTON   098290A12MIS       8002130751
000002 100106105CHARLES   CARAGIANESMBS DEDHAM     035047B06PURCHASING6003171234
000003 100111106MARK      JONES     MAA DEDHAM     045025C12ACCOUNTING8006280009
000004 100119950KATHY     HOUSMAN   FBS REVERE     050875A12PURCHASING8002130751
000005 100126933ROGER     LEVINSON  MBS BRIGHTON   045245B06PURCHASING8002130751
000006 100124440OLGA      PONG      FHS STONEHAM   025340C12ACCOUNTING8002130751
000007 100141875RICH      GARLAND   MAA BRIGHTON   025120C12PURCHASING8002130751
000008 100142166JANE      CRUSOE    FMS WELLESLEY  087645B06PURCHASING8002130751
000009 100143413LOUIS     MERZ      MMS ROXBURY    035047A12MARKETING 8002130751
000010 100155843JOHN      WADSWORTH MBS DORCHESTER 050875C12ACCOUNTING8002130751
000011 100162791MARYLOU   MACTRATH  FAA MILTON     056789D18ACCOUNTING8002130751
000012 100164984MYRA      FRIESEN   FPHDNEWTON     023678A12MARKETING 5908060141
000013 100166514CHARLES   GOTT      MBS BRIGHTON   034678B06ACCOUNTING8107160991
000014 100175025SEYMOUR   MECHLING  MHS SOMERVILLE 073456D18MIS       8092141561
000015 100182121ALFRED    SAVIO     MHS ROXBURY    035047C12ACCOUNTING8002130751
000016 100189299MARSHA    POPPE     FAA NEEDHAM    056789D18PURCHASING8002130751
000017 100196019REBECCA   BAUER     FBS WELLESLEY  029645B06PURCHASING8002130751
000018 100198578BETTYJEANPERRY      FHS WELLESLEY  024456C12MARKETING 8002130751
000019 100108097ARTHUR    REAVES    MHS REVERE     021587C12ACCOUNTING8002130751
****** *************************** BOTTOM OF DATA ****************************
```

Fig. 11-2. Data file structure for INP.TXT.

Fieldname	Start	Width	Type
COMMAND	1	7	C
SSNUMB	8	9	N
FIRSTNAME	17	10	C
LASTNAME	27	10	C
SEX	37	1	C
DEGREE	38	3	C
LOCATION	41	11	C
EMPLOYEENO	52	6	C
MAILSTOP	58	3	C
DEPT	61	10	C
PHONE	71	10	C

the line, and use this information to create a database in dBASE. The starting columns, and name, type, and width of the data fields are determined, and are displayed in Fig. 11-2.

Using this information, the programmer would go into dBASE, and create a database in which to place this data. Figure 11-3 is the captured screen showing the created database structure.

Once this empty database is created the dBASE code shown below brings the SDF data from INP.TXT into the database, INP.DBF. The first three records and the last record in the file are deleted to remove unwanted header and footer information, and then the file is packed.

```
USE INP
APPEND FROM INP.TXT SDF
GOTO TOP
DELETE NEXT 3
GOTO BOTTOM
DELETE
PACK
```

An EDIT command, executed at this point, will display the correctly captured data, as can be seen in Fig. 11-4.

The data field COMMAND is not required in the target file, and the application that is going to use this data requires that the data fields be in a different order. The programmer must thus create or use another database, called INP2.DBF, with the structure shown in Fig. 11-5.

Fig. 11-3. dBASE CREATE screen for INP.DBF.

```
                                                    Bytes remaining:   3920

+----------------+-------------+-------------+---------------------+
| CURSOR  <-- --> |   INSERT    |   DELETE    | Up a field:    ^    |
|  Char:   <- ->  | Char:  Ins  | Char:   Del | Down a field:  v    |
|  Word: Home End | Field: ^N   | Word:   ^Y  | Exit/Save:     ^End |
|  Pan:   ^<- ^-> | Help:  F1   | Field: ^U   | Abort:         Esc  |
+----------------+-------------+-------------+---------------------+

     Field Name  Type      Width  Dec          Field Name  Type      Width Dec
     -------------------------------           -------------------------------
   1 COMMAND     Character    7              9 MAILSTOP    Character    3
   2 SSNUMB      Character    9             10 DEPT        Character   10
   3 FIRSTNAME   Character   10             11 PHONE       Character   10
   4 LASTNAME    Character   10
   5 SEX         Character    1
   6 DEGREE      Character    3
   7 LOCATION    Character   11
   8 EMPLOYEENO  Character    6


CREATE STRUCTURE|<C:>|INP                |Field: 1/11       |      |   Caps
                              Enter the field name.
Field names begin with a letter and may contain letters, digits and underscores

                                                Caps
```

Once INP2 is created, the following dBASE code will move the data into the required form:

```
USE INP2
APPEND FROM INP
```

The final data record can be examined using the EDIT command as in Fig. 11-6.

Once in dBASE, this data can be manipulated from the dot prompt under program control, or exported to other microcomputer applications. If you wanted to send this data to Lotus or WordStar, you could use the dBASE command:

```
COPY TO INP.OUT DELIMITED
```

This would produce the file displayed in Fig. 11-7.

It is thus possible, though tedious, to move data through a

Fig. 11-4. Imported data in EDIT mode.

```
Record No.       1                                  Caps
+------------------+---------------------+--------------+---------------------+
| CURSOR   <-- --> |          UP   DOWN  |    DELETE    | Insert Mode:   Ins  |
|  Char:    <-  -> | Field:    ^     v   | Char:    Del | Exit/Save:    ^End  |
|  Word:  Home End | Page:  PgUp  PgDn   | Field:   ^Y  | Abort:         Esc  |
|                  | Help:   F1          | Record: ^U   | Memo:        ^Home  |
+------------------+---------------------+--------------+---------------------+
COMMAND     000001
SSNUMB      100101689
FIRSTNAME   ALFRED
LASTNAME    STEVENS
SEX         M
DEGREE      PHD
LOCATION    BRIGHTON
EMPLOYEENO  098290
MAILSTOP    A12
DEPT        MIS
PHONE       8002130751
```

Fig. 11-5. MODIFY STRUCTURE for target database (INP2.DBF).

```
                                                    Bytes remaining:   3927
+------------------+-------------+--------------+----------------------+
| CURSOR  <-- --> |   INSERT    |    DELETE    | Up a field:      ^   |
|  Char:    <- -> | Char:   Ins | Char:    Del | Down a field:  v     |
|  Word: Home End | Field: ^N   | Word:   ^Y   | Exit/Save:    ^End   |
|  Pan:  ^<- ^->  | Help:  F1   | Field: ^U    | Abort:         Esc   |
+------------------+-------------+--------------+----------------------+
    Field Name  Type       Width  Dec           Field Name  Type      Width  Dec
    ------------------------------              ------------------------------
  1 FIRSTNAME   Character    10               9 DEPT        Character   10
  2 LASTNAME    Character    10              10 PHONE       Character   10
  3 SSNUMB      Numeric       9    0
  4 SEX         Character     1
  5 DEGREE      Character     3
  6 LOCATION    Character    11
  7 EMPLOYEENO  Character     6
  8 MAILSTOP    Character     3

MODIFY STRUCTURE|<C:>|INP2                   |Field: 1/10        |      |  Caps
                              Enter the field name.
Field names begin with a letter and may contain letters, digits and underscores

                                                         Caps
```

Fig. 11-6. Final database record.

```
Record No.     19                                Caps
+-----------------+--------------------+-------------+--------------------+
| CURSOR  <-- --> |         UP   DOWN  |   DELETE    | Insert Mode:   Ins |
|  Char:    <- -> | Field:   ^     v   | Char:   Del | Exit/Save:    ^End |
|  Word: Home End | Page:  PgUp  PgDn  | Field:  ^Y  | Abort:         Esc |
|                 | Help:  F1          | Record: ^U  | Memo:        ^Home |
+-----------------+--------------------+-------------+--------------------+
FIRSTNAME   ARTHUR
LASTNAME    REAVES
SSNUMB      100108097
SEX         M
DEGREE      HS
LOCATION    REVERE
EMPLOYEENO  021587
MAILSTOP    C12
DEPT        ACCOUNTING
PHONE       8002130751
```

series of file conversions to get nearly any desired file structure. These structures could be used in a variety of application software packages, but the potential complexity of the intermediate processes can discourage even the most enthusiastic system integrator.

THE MULTI-PATH TOPOLOGY

The current state of affairs is that several vendors have created methods by which files can be imported and exported to a number of other major packages. Topologically this is very complex, because different paths probably exist to move a file from any given source to any given application. As in our example, some users import data from an ASCII file into dBASE using the APPEND FROM FILE.TXT SDF (standard data format), then manipulate the file in dBASE (deleting fields and records that are not needed, modifying other fields) and then output the data using COPY TO OUT.TXT DELIMITED so that it could be imported into LOTUS 1-2-3. These tasks can be programmed, using the dBASE procedural language, on a case by case basis, but this is still time consuming and tedious.

The major problem in the direct importing with "on the fly" translation is that the import must take all of the offered data. If, for example, the mainframe "prints" a 17 column report to the hard disk, with headers, column graphics, footers, and page breaks, the import process will pull off a great deal of garbage. If this file is

Fig. 11-7. Delimited data file INP.OUT.

```
"ALFRED","STEVENS",100101689,"M","PHD","BRIGHTON","098290","A12","MIS","8002130751"
"CHARLES","CARAGIANES",100106105,"M","BS","DEDHAM","035047","B06","PURCHASING","6003171234"
"MARK","JONES",100111106,"M","AA","DEDHAM","045025","C12","ACCOUNTING","8006280009"
"KATHY","HOUSMAN",100119950,"F","BS","REVERE","050875","A12","PURCHASING","8002130751"
"ROGER","LEVINSON",100126933,"M","BS","BRIGHTON","045245","B06","PURCHASING","8002130751"
"OLGA","PONG",100124440,"F","HS","STONEHAM","025340","C12","ACCOUNTING","8002130751"
"RICH","GARLAND",100141875,"M","AA","BRIGHTON","025120","C12","PURCHASING","8002130751"
"JANE","CRUSOE",100142166,"F","MS","WELLESLEY","087645","B06","PURCHASING","8002130751"
"LOUIS","MERZ",100143413,"M","MS","ROXBURY","035047","A12","MARKETING","8002130751"
"JOHN","WADSWORTH",100155843,"M","BS","DORCHESTER","050875","C12","ACCOUNTING","8002130751"
"MARYLOU","MACTRATH",100162791,"F","AA","MILTON","056789","D18","ACCOUNTING","8002130751"
"MYRA","FRIESEN",100164984,"F","PHD","NEWTON","023678","A12","MARKETING","5908060141"
"CHARLES","GOTT",100166514,"M","BS","BRIGHTON","034678","B06","ACCOUNTING","8107160991"
"SEYMOUR","MECHLING",100175025,"M","HS","SOMERVILLE","073456","D18","MIS","8092141561"
"ALFRED","SAVIO",100182121,"M","HS","ROXBURY","035047","C12","ACCOUNTING","8002130751"
"MARSHA","POPPE",100189299,"F","AA","NEEDHAM","056789","D18","PURCHASING","8002130751"
"REBECCA","BAUER",100196019,"F","BS","WELLESLEY","029645","B06","PURCHASING","8002130751"
"BETTYJEAN","PERRY",100198578,"F","HS","WELLESLEY","024456","C12","MARKETING","8002130751"
"ARTHUR","REAVES",100108097,"M","HS","REVERE","021587","C12","ACCOUNTING","8002130751"
```

imported into dBASE using the standard data format approach, "dummy" fields must be created to correspond to column delimiters like exclamation points or asterisks. Header, border, and footer information will also be "translated" into the dBASE file, as will form feeds and other potentially dangerous printer control characters. The user must use the MODIFY STRUCTURE command in dBASE to delete the dummy fields, as well as those fields that are not of interest, then BROWSE through the database and mark for deletion all records containing useless header, border, or footer information. The user then must PACK and INDEX the file before it can be used by any dBASE application or exported to another microcomputer program.

As a second example, one of our clients is a large commercial bank. They have a Token-Passing LAN made up of over 40 computers spread over many floors in their Dallas headquarters building. They are also running a 3270 SNA Gateway into their IBM host computers in San Antonio and Houston. The wire transfer department has three PCs and is using a reporting and tracking program written in dBASE III PLUS and compiled using Clipper. Each hour this department uses the gateway feature to sign on to the host, and downloads a file which contains current information on the wire transfer transactions in progress. The gateway system "prints" the file to the LAN's hard disk file server. The file is made up of ASCII characters with a line width of 132 and line termination using carriage returns and line feeds.

Of the 15 fields on each line, the dBASE program only needs the transaction number, the time, the status, and the amount. There are, thus, a number of additional steps required to convert the information from the file to the required form for the dBASE application. If someone else on the network needed access to some of the data in another form, the MIS people would need to either program other conversions, or outline the series of manual steps that are be required. These "little tasks" can, and often do, add up to significant amounts of programming time. Such hidden costs contribute to the negative attitude that most mainframe-oriented data processing managers have toward the "invasion" of microcomputers into the corporate data processing world.

AN AUTOMATED SOLUTION

The automation of these processes is clearly desirable, as many companies have discovered. For each origin and destination structure, individual programs are being written, tested, and put into production. If, for any reason, the host program alters the report structure (even just to add one column to a character field) the interapplication program would need to be changed. A generic approach to the automation of interapplication file interchange processes would be much more desirable.

It might seem that the problems inherent in the automation of such a process are infinite, due to the number of different file structures that can exist. Although it is true that the complexity of the file structures might be high, it is possible to construct a data structure which can offer a fairly complete description of a text file or a delimited file. This structure, which can be called a Text Descriptor File (TDF), can be designed so that it contains enough information for a program to process the data in a text file by referencing the TDF. These programs, called Descriptor File Processors (DFP) can thus be used to perform the automated data interchange.

For this concept to work, the TDF must be complete. A description is complete if it contains enough information to tell a processing program what to do with various components of the source file. This approach borrows liberally from statistical thermodynamics in Physics. Although a gas is much too complicated to understand directly, it is possible to create mathematical descriptions of the behavior of the gas that are complete enough to enable a scientist to make predictions about its future states. Similarly, we propose that a sufficiently complete description of a text file might allow for automated processing into target structures.

The actual information contained in the description is the information that a programmer would need to design code to do the conversion. This includes the number of characters per line, the line termination code, whether or not the file is delimited, and, if so, with what characters. The number of fields, their data types, and starting and ending columns, would also need to be known. The description should include a mechanism to identify which lines are to be ignored, where on a "page" data starts and ends, whether or not there are form feeds, and how special data lines are identified.

Given a standard structure for the text description file, it becomes possible to build a class of programs, such as Descriptor File Processors, that would know exactly where to look in the TDF to find each piece of data that it needs to perform its task. Once someone builds a TDF for a particular file, an end-user who needed to get that data into, say, dBASE would simply run the DFP for dBASE on a microcomputer. This same DFP for dBASE could be used for any source file for which a TDF can be built. Because many downloading and file interchange processes are repetitious (data may be passed in a particular report each day or week), this approach could save considerable time. Also, if the source report is changed in any way, updating the TDF structure guarantees that the file would be delivered correctly to each target application format. In a LAN/Gateway scheme, data files can be brought to the LAN, have a TDF created, and then easily delivered to users requiring that data in dBASE, Lotus 1-2-3, Multimate, WordStar or any other microcomputer application for which a DFP exists on the LAN.

Users can create the TDF by studying the file to be described, using hard copy or screen display, and extracting parameters as required by the TDF. Each user could choose data fields and the order they wish them to appear in the final file. By including information on lines that can be ignored, they can also limit the clean up process in the target file.

Descriptor File Processors can be written for any application, assuming that the TDF is a standard description of the text file. Using the description of the file, the program knows how to set up data fields, extract data, and format it directly into file formats for the target programs. We have written DFPs in BASICA, C, and dBASE III PLUS, compiling them to form the actual executable files. The finished products are fast, efficient, and extremely easy to use.

During the development of a proposed TDF standard, a number of DFPs have been written to test the completeness of the TDF. As of this writing DFPs exist for:

- ☐ dBASE III PLUS and all programs that read .DBF files.
- ☐ Lotus 1-2-3 and all programs that can use .WKS or .WK1 files.
- ☐ Multimate.
- ☐ WordStar/Mailmerge.
- ☐ Standard Data Format (SDF).
- ☐ Delimited Format.

If a user has a library of DFPs, and a TDF exists for a given source file, data can be processed into the required target format knowing only the name of the file. This scenario might be as follows:

- ☐ The MIS Department downloads a data set onto a LAN by "printing" it to the LAN fileserver hard disk. A TDF is then created by the MIS staff, and placed on the disk. The file "TEST.TXT" and its description, "TEST.TDF" are now available to all the users.
- ☐ A user needs the data brought into dBASE. Invoking a program called DFPDBF, the user types in the name of the file, "TEST," and the DFP does the rest. A file called

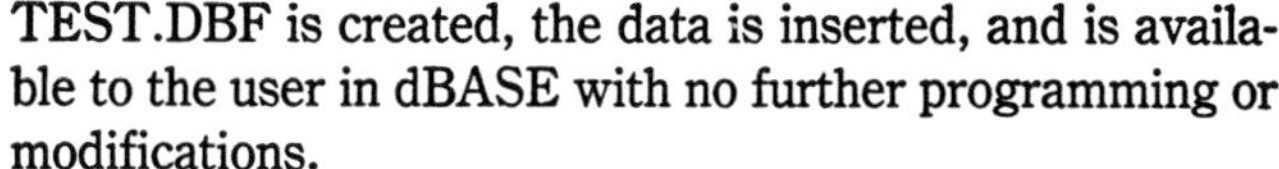

TEST.DBF is created, the data is inserted, and is available to the user in dBASE with no further programming or modifications.

- A second user wishes to do an analysis using Lotus 1-2-3. This user runs DFPLTS, enters the name of the file, "TEST," and has a file named TEST.PRN created. After loading Lotus 1-2-3, the user imports the file. Again, no additional programming or structural modification is required.
- Two different groups wish to perform a mail-merge function using the data. One group has WordStar, the other Multimate. The WordStar group uses DFPWSM, and has both the data and document header file automatically created. The Multimate group uses DFPMMT and has data and document files created in Multimate file format. Once again, this conversion occurs without programming or modification.

The MIS department in the preceding example was not involved at the user conversion level. The only requirement was the creation of the TDF; all other processes were automated. The user applications can also generate files in text or delimited formats, and thus can also create TDFs, giving a method for file interchangeability between applications.

Custom applications software can be designed to automatically create TDFs at the time of report generation, completely removing any need for interim processing. Applications can be written to provide a greater level of integration in a multi-product environment. It unrealistic to try to force users to adopt a single set of application software packages, so this interapplication file interchange system makes considerable sense.

This methodology, in which a standard for Text Descriptor Files is used to process data files into multiple target formats, can offer significant savings in manpower. It can also aid the total integration of PCs and applications into an institutional information processing system.

Chapter 12

Case Study

To illustrate how the issues discussed in the previous chapters actually relate, a typical project will be followed from conception, through birth, infancy, and the middle age of normal operation. We have created a hypothetical company with application requirements that cover a wide range different possibilities. The company and situations presented here do, in fact, stem from reality, but any similarities to people or events in the real world are purely coincidental.

THE CLIENT

ABC Sportswear, Inc., is a company founded in 1956 by three returning Korean War veterans, Albert Kaplan, Bruce Wilson, and Charles Evans, to import and distribute women's sportswear produced in Asia. Through contacts at a number of factories in Hong Kong, Taiwan, and Korea, ABC orders by the shipload, then transports the goods to its warehouses in New Orleans, Seattle, and Philadelphia. Salesmen market the clothing to hundreds of department stores and boutiques throughout the United States. ABC now has over 3000 clients and is doing over thirty million dollars in direct sales. The entire operation is handled by the Houston corporate office, where twelve administrative staff members share space in a downtown office building with 11 salespeople. Albert died in 1970, Bruce retired in 1980, and Charles runs the company now with his daughter, Sue, who is in charge of the accounting division, which is made up of three other clerical people.

Because so much work is done in their Asian factories, ABC relies heavily on Telex messages and facsimile transmitters. Sales orders are phoned in and processed in Houston. One goal is to try to sell shipments even before they arrive at a port warehouse. This results in a complicated inventory system, in which ABC considers items on the ships as actually in stock and available for sale.

There are approximately 40 people employed at the port warehouses. In 1980, after Bruce retired, Sue insisted that ABC sign on with a time-sharing service bureau to have payroll checks and associated paperwork done by computer. This was the first move toward automation, and made people in the company realize that computers could make their lives easier.

ABC retains Kaplan, Goodson and Roberts (KG&R) as an accounting firm. This accounting firm helps ABC do its quarterly and yearly reports, and comes in to help make journal adjustment entries at the end of each month. In 1984, KG&R began to suggest that ABC might do well to purchase a microcomputer-based accounting system, consisting of General Ledger, Accounts Payable, Accounts Receivable, Inventory Control, and Payroll modules. ABC eventually agreed, and in early 1985 purchased an IBM PC/AT with a 20 megabyte disk drive, a series of accounting modules from Open Systems, and an Okidata high-speed dot matrix printer.

The accounting firm had an arrangement with a vendor which provided the system, the software, the installation, and the training. This system cost ABC over $12,000. KG&R then spent nearly two months helping ABC put its data into the accounting system and "bring it up." This added another $10,000to the system cost.

Millie, the bookkeeper who had been with ABC since 1963, resisted changing her ways. She had to be trained, retrained, and nearly fired before she accepted the computer system. Some of the staff picked it up quickly, however. All things considered, it tooknearly six months to get the system up and running with real data.

Once running, a number of problems appeared. First, the quirk of considering inventory in-transit as available to sell could not be accommodated the "off the shelf" version of the Open Systems Accounting System. The accounting firm, and its representative which provided the system, had, on numerous occasions, told both Charles and Sue that this would not be a problem, because the code was easily modifiable. Also, the extensive Report Writer module that they purchased would surely make the special report that was required. This turned out not to be true, and the accountants were in the embarrassing position of playing finger-pointing games with the system vendor.

The second problem was that now all of the information was on the one computer, and the programs were single-user and single-task in philosophy. There was, therefore, no way for the accounts receivable clerk to use the computer while the pay checks were being prepared, and visa versa. Some standard processes, such as posting, took hours to do, which meant that several people were spending a great deal of time waiting for the machine to finish.

Charles and Sue were happy with the system, but disappointed with the problems. Computers are supposed to add efficiency and help management get the information that is needed, whenever it isneeded. Sue also felt that ABC's staff should be able to do things like word processing, budgets, financial analysis, mail-list management, and database management.

The accounting firm's dispute with the system supplier ended in their partnership, and left ABC in an uncomfortable situation. Responding to the lack of comfort, KG&R began to look for a microcomputer consulting group. We had done some application development work for one of their other clients, with success. In October of 1985, we were introduced to the people and computer system at ABC Sportswear.

THE INITIAL MEETING

The purpose of our original meeting was to prepare an assessment of what new software and hardware would be required to accomplish ABC's desires. The first meeting included Charles, Sue, and Kathy, who was KG&R. Kathy introduced us as a consulting group which had helped set up a custom-designed system for one of their other clients. This type of introduction meant that we did not have to do very much selling of to our ability to provide a valuable service to ABC. Some time was spent discussing our experience, credentials, and capabilities. Each person at the meeting was also given a copy of our brochure and rate card.

Once the preliminaries were completed, Charles gave us some history and Sue began to discuss their desires and problems. We had requested, in preparation for this meeting, that documents be provided, including sales orders, invoices, inventory reports and whatever else was relevant to help us understand the data flow in the business. We asked how an order went through the physical system, as well as how it was handled through the computer. We were given a tour of the office, meeting the various employees, and asking them questions about the information flow.

We also were told beforehand exactly what hardware and software they had, so it was not necessary to spend much time looking at the computer system. In a little under two hours, we had learned enough to suggest that our firm could be of assistance, preparing a needs assessment study and providing them with a detailed report, listing their options and the costs of each option. We also explained that this study would be billable at our consulting rate, and gave them an estimate of its cost. We made it clear that our firm would be available to write any custom code that might be required for the special reports Charles and Sue needed, and that such programming would be covered under our standard project contracts and task orders. Charles was offered a blank copy of the agreements so that he could check them with his attorney. Charles and Sue decided at that meeting to retain us for the study, and we were asked to complete our work and return within two weeks.

THE PRELIMINARY STUDY

In order to construct a complete proposal, it was necessary to identify the components of the desired work. We were sure that a multi-user system was required. The work was divided in the manual system into payables, receivables and other accounting tasks, so we felt that a LAN would be helpful. In a LAN, two or three computers could be placed in the accounting office and different tasks could be accomplished simultaneously. The big assumption here was that aaccounting system was available in a version that could support such multi-user functions as record locking. In fact, the Open Systems Accounting is written to allow multiple users with the purchase of an upgraded interpreter.

We knew that the Open Systems package used Business BASIC, instead of IBM PC BASICA. This interpreted language, and the accounting package itself, had actually been scaled down to microcomputers after being developed in a multi-user minicomputer environment. We spoke to the manufacturer of the software, and several local vendors, and felt sure that the multi-user aspect could be handled by the package with an off-the-shelf upgrade. This was much better than if the code would have had to be reworked from single-user to multi-user. Such customization is extensive, and costly, and thus not a very good option. Very few microcomputer accounting packages offermulti-user versions, but we would have suggested conversion rather than customization.

Once satisfied that the accounting system could handle the multi-user requirement, we were still faced with the choice of which LAN to recommend. Being conservative concerning standards, we were leaning toward the newly announced IBM Token Passing

Ring. In our opinion, over the long run, most software will adapt itself to the NETBIOS (the software interface to the network) that IBM has announced. However, inquiries led to the discovery that there was little product availability, a sin often committedin the microcomputer industry. Products are often announced far in advance of their actual ship dates. Although it was our intention to put ABC into IBM PC Token Ring Networks, it was not yet feasible. Another fallout of the lack of product availability was that Open Systems was not ready, either, to offer a version of their multi-user interpreter that could run on the new IBM system. Of the two networks Open Systems did support—Novell and 3Com—we chose what we felt was the less of two evils, 3Com.

As was discussed in Chapter Seven, there are two types of LAN access methodologies, Token Passing and Carrier Sense Multiple Access with Collision Detect (CSMA/CD). Token Passing is deterministic, so that it is possible to calculate a worst-case response time. CSMA/CD is statistical, with no limit on the worst case. For several years we had worked with Token Passing bus systems based on ARCNET protocol. We had experience in such products, and felt uncomfortable proposing 3Com's Ethernet-type architecture. Still, there was already in place a running accounting system, with trained users, that could easily be upgraded to multi-user operation using this 3Com LAN. We decided to put aside our reservations, rationalizing that this system would never grow to the size or activity level that would cause the collision rate to significantly impair throughput. 3Com is a large and reputable company, and several local vendors offered to supply product, install the software, and train the users. One vendor specialized in placing the multi-user Business BASIC Interpreter for Open Systems on 3Com networks. We solicited and received bids for the network hardware, installation, cable installation, and training. Although 3Com was not the least expensive LAN to implement, we had arrived at our choice, and felt that a strong technical case had been made.

Because the original machine was an IBM PC/AT with a 20 Megabyte fixed disk drive and 512K of RAM, we decided that it needed to be upgraded somewhat for use as a file server in the network. To add memory, we was suggested that an AST Advantage Card with 128K be purchased. This brought the AT up to the 640K limit addressed by the current DOS (3.1). Although the 80286 chip is capable of addressing much more memory, none of the current applications make use of this extra memory. This AST card fulfilled our needs at the time, and also offered considerable expansion whenever future applications grew to demand more memory.

We also felt that the 20 megabyte disk would be inadequate

as the only drive on the network, but here the solution was more complex. We could have added a second drive to the AT with up to 40 megabytes. However, this would have given the LAN much more storage at risk, in the event of a catastrophic failure of the file server. We like to design LANs to be fault-tolerant to the point where there is more than one hard disk in the network. This allows for high-speed network backup of crucial data files and programs, so if the main file server disk dies, the data is available to the system from another source. With this in mind, we suggested that a 30 megabyte fixed disk be placed in one of the new network machines. For these workstations, we chose IBM PC clones, with 8088-2 processors running at what are called "turbo" speeds. Many of these products have 640K RAM on their motherboards, built-in serial ports, and other features that are actually better than the original PC. Because the LAN provides "network" time stamping, it was unnecessary to provide clocks in each of the workstations. Two clones were recommended, each having monochrome displays, 640K, and one floppy drive at a cost of less than $800 each. We also specified that a 30 megabyte half-height fixed disk be installed in one of the clones.

This three-machine LAN would become the accounting "departmental" system that could easily be expanded as other parts of the company wanted "on the network." To that end, we also separately priced a complete additional LAN workstation; basically a floppy-based clone with a LAN card in it. Thus ABC could, between the time of the proposal and the contract, choose the actual number of nodes to be initially installed in the network. ABC would also have an idea of future upgrade costs, although if the past is any indication, such costs will be lower.

A number of license issues were also addressed in the study and in the proposal. Some software packages are licensed based on the number of central processing units (CPUs). Charles and Sue were told that they would need to specify how many people would be using, say, Lotus 1-2-3 at the same time. If only one person would be using the spreadsheet on one machine at any given time, it would be legal to buy only one copy of the package. This is, in fact, what ABC's plans were, so one copy of Lotus 1-2-3 and Micropro's WordStar Professional were suggested. We found two vendors: a local systems house specializing in accounting packages, and a local discount warehouse. In the case of such products most customers opt for the lowest price. This makes sense, because these are reputable products with considerable support available from their manufacturers. We know of no reason for our clients to pay list price for such equipment.

We also suggested a number of utility programs, like Sidekick, Superkey, and Fixed Disk Organizer. Again, multi-vendor pricing was provided.

A second printer was suggested, a Texas Instruments 855.This printer has a dot matrix, capable of near letter-quality output that could double as a second report or check writing device. It could also be used as a word processing printer.

The shopping list was rounded out by the addition of various standard features: an auto-dial internal modem, an uninterruptable power supply, stands to allow the CPUs to be placed on the floor, extension cables for the monitors and keyboards, line surge protectors, monitor stands, and a complete assortment of cables.

This, of course, just represented the "gross system structure." We still had to face the issue of getting Charles and Sue their "special" reports that were not possible in the "off the shelf" version of Open Systems Accounting. For this fine tuning, we took two approaches.

We were aware that over the years a number of companies had developed and were marketing "standard customizations" of Open Systems Modules. One such firm, Colossus, has hundreds of such modifications that are inexpensive, debugged, easy to install, and approved by Open Systems headquarters. A number of ABC's requirements, such as longer, more detailed histories, and higher numeric precision in inventory control, were met exactly by the purchase of a few Colossus modifications that cost between $150 and $300.There are a great many advantages to this approach, the main one being that it is cheaper than us doing our own modifications. It is also safer, because Colossus has tested their code changes in the total system with many end-users. If we had chosen to modify the Business BASIC code ourselves, we could have damaged the entire system, and invalidated ABC's support position with the manufacturers. Therefore, we listed a number of recommended modifications from Colossus and included several pages of additional modifications that might be of interest to ABC.

Although most of the user requirements could be handled by "off the shelf" solutions, there still remained crucial areas that could only be resolved by custom applications development. ABC wanted reports that could only be produced by linking several databases that existed within the accounting system. Open Systems offers an extensive Report Writer, but the linkages desired were simply not possible within the accounting system itself. This is not an unusual state of affairs; management often discovers the need for more and more reports as a company becomes more automated. Here, ABC was requiring database functionality from a canned software package that had been written for a vertical application, accounting. We were faced with two choices: to write a custom program in Business BASIC to fulfill ABC's current needs, or to develop a solution which would be inherently more flexible and could thus handle future needs.

We decided to develop a dBASE III application with access to the data contained in the accounting system, and the ability to link the databases in any form required to give ABC the desired reports. The major problem was that the data files within Business BASIC were binary, and thus incompatible with dBASE. We had to develop a system that could export the data in an ASCII format, so it could be imported by our dBASE application. The only way Open Systems could export data into files was by using the Report Writer. The programming component of the task thus had three parts.

First, using the Open Systems Report Writer, we needed to create data report files containing the information from Inventory, Purchase Order, and Sales Orders that we would ultimately need in our dBASE application. Next, we needed to write conversion programs for each of the data files from Open Systems, putting them into a form in which they could be imported into the dBASE application. Finally, we needed to create a complete dBASE application that could use the imported data and produce the necessary linked database reports. This program was also to allow for the manual addition of data, the editing of imported or input data, sorting, and the creation of various standard reporting modules.

We estimated 20 hours to create the report files using Open Systems Report Writer, 20 hours to write the conversion programs, and 60 hours to develop the main dBASE application. In keeping with our style, we would be doing the development in dBASE, C, and BASICA, and providing the client with only compiled executable code.

As a part of our preliminary study, we interviewed Charles, Sue, and several of the clerical people to get a better idea of what they did and how they wanted the new system to help them. Charles and Sue met with us to design the actual linked database report formats. These were laid out, data-field-by-data-field, until we were all very clear on exactly what they would look like. From these designs, the data field list was formulated. The list was created to identify each piece of required information, where it was to come from, where it would be used, how wide it was, and what type of data it contained. We also added to this list data that we felt should be brought to the application in order to give greater future flexibility. From our discussions with the sales staff we decided to add a significant amount of detail from the customer files, so that sales analysis by customer might be possible, using the database.

From this key variable list, we designed four databases. They were Inventory, Purchase Orders, Sales Order Headers, and Sales Order Items. There would also be one "synthetic" database created for linking data. Taking proposed structure of each database, the report forms we had designed with Charles and Sue, the estimates for our programming time, the hardware and software proposal, and an invoice for our time (20 hours) spent in preparing the preliminary study and proposal, we met with Charles and Sue once again.

At this meeting we presented our proposal, a project contract, and a task sheet for the 100 hours of programming, with the starting and ending dates of the first task. During the two-hour meeting, a number of modifications were made to the proposed database structure. For example, Sue wanted to add up to 10 possible freight companies, and their rates to the database. All of this definition and design was done prior to the commencement of any code writing. A change at this point is as easy as using a red pen. Figure 12-1 is the dBASE III PLUS printout of the structure of the databases approved by ABC for the project.

Fig. 12-1. Database structure for ABC Sportswear, Inc.

```
Structure for database: C:INVENTORY.dbf
Number of data records:       6
Date of last update    : 01/20/86
Field  Field Name  Type       Width    Dec
    1  CATEGORY    Character      2
    2  INVENUMBER  Character     12
    3  FIGURENUMB  Character     25
    4  QTYONHAND   Numeric        4
    5  QTYONORDER  Numeric        4
    6  QTYSOLD     Numeric        4
    7  AVAILTOSEL  Numeric        4
    8  TARGET      Numeric        4
    9  LASTCOST    Numeric       11      2
   10  AVGCOST     Numeric       11      2
   11  DISCOUNT    Numeric        6      4
   12  LISTPRICE   Numeric       11      2
   13  ITEMWEIGHT  Numeric        7      2
   14  CUBICFEET   Numeric        7      2
** Total **                     113


Structure for database: C:SALESORDER.dbf
```

Number of data records: 8
Date of last update : 01/23/86

Field	Field Name	Type	Width	Dec
1	ORDERNO	Character	8	
2	ORDERDATE	Date	8	
3	CONAME	Character	30	
4	ADDRESS	Character	25	
5	CITY	Character	15	
6	STATE	Character	2	
7	ZIP	Character	5	
8	QUOTE	Character	1	
9	SHIPNAME	Character	25	
10	SHIPADDRES	Character	25	
11	SHIPCITY	Character	15	
12	SHIPSTATE	Character	2	
13	SHIPZIP	Character	5	
14	CUSTORDER	Character	10	
15	CUSTTAG	Character	10	
16	REQSHIPDTE	Date	8	
17	SALESMAN	Character	3	
18	RATE	Numeric	7	2
19	TERRITORY	Character	3	
20	TERMS	Character	12	
21	CREDIT	Character	12	
22	SHIPVIA	Character	15	
23	FOB	Character	5	
24	FREIGHTTOT	Numeric	11	2
25	ARCHIVE	Character	1	
26	MISCCHARGE	Numeric	11	2
27	MODVENDOR1	Character	15	
28	MODPO1	Numeric	8	
29	MODVENDOR2	Character	15	
30	MODPO2	Numeric	8	
31	MODVENDOR3	Character	15	
32	MODPO3	Numeric	8	
33	FREIGHT1	Numeric	7	2
34	FREIGHT2	Numeric	7	2
35	FREIGHT3	Numeric	7	2
36	FREIGHT4	Numeric	7	2
37	FREIGHT5	Numeric	7	2
38	FREIGHT6	Numeric	7	2
39	FREIGHT7	Numeric	7	2
40	FREIGHT8	Numeric	7	2
41	FREIGHT9	Numeric	7	2

```
   42  FREIGHT10   Numeric        7      2
** Total **                     414

Structure for database: C:PURORDER.dbf
Number of data records:       3
Date of last update    : 01/23/86
Field  Field Name  Type       Width    Dec
    1  FACTORDNO   Character      5
    2  CATEGORY    Character      2
    3  INVENUMBER  Character     12
    4  DESCRIPT    Character     20
    5  FIGURENUMB  Character     25
    6  GLNUMBER    Character     12
    7  QTYORDERED  Numeric        4
    8  ETA         Date           8
    9  QTYSOLD     Numeric        4
   10  AVAILTOSEL  Numeric        4
   11  NUMBSALES   Numeric        4
   12  FORSALESOR  Numeric        8
** Total **                     109

Structure for database: C:ITEMS.dbf
Number of data records:      22
Date of last update    : 01/23/86
Field  Field Name  Type       Width    Dec
    1  ORDERNO     Character      8
    2  QTY         Numeric        4
    3  QTYA        Numeric        4
    4  SOURCEA     Character      5
    5  QTYB        Numeric        4
    6  SOURCEB     Character      5
    7  QTYC        Numeric        4
    8  MAKEORDER   Numeric        5
    9  QTYD        Numeric        4
   10  FACTORDNO   Character      5
   11  GLNUMBER    Character     12
   12  CATEGORY    Character      2
   13  INVENUMBER  Character     12
   14  FIGURENUMB  Character     25
   15  DESCR       Character     25
   16  DISCOUNT    Numeric        6      4
   17  AVGCOST     Numeric       11      2
   18  UNITPRICE   Numeric       11      2
   19  AMOUNT      Numeric       11      2
```

```
   20  ARCHIVE     Character      1
   21  MEASURE     Character      2
   22  LINE        Numeric        2
   23  LTOT        Numeric        2
   24  ORDERDATE   Date           8
   25  CONAME      Character     30
** Total **                     209

Structure for database: C:BACKSALES.dbf
Number of data records:       12
Date of last update     : 01/23/86
Field  Field Name  Type        Width    Dec
    1  FACTORDNO   Character      5
    2  ORDERNO     Character      8
    3  INVENUMBER  Character     12
    4  QTYTAGGED   Numeric        4
** Total **                      30
```

Once all of the definitions and designs were agreed upon, Charles signed them off. Everyone now knew exactly what our project was expected to do, how much it would cost, and when it would be completed. Figure 12-2 shows the Project Agreement between our two firms.

Fig. 12-2. ABC project agreement.

PROJECT AGREEMENT

AGREEMENT made and entered into this 1st day of January 1986, by and between Bodner, Hutchins & Associates, Inc. a Texas Corporation with principal offices at 2300 Old Spanish Trail #2105, Houston, Texas, 77054, hereinafter referred to as "BHA": and ABC Sportswear, Inc., a Texas Corporation with principal office at 2222 Fanin, Houston, Texas 77009, hereinafter referred to as "Client".

WITNESSETH that in consideration of the mutual covenants and conditions herein contained, the parties do hereby agree as follows:

1. During the period of this Project Agreement, BHA will perform systems analysis, programming, and consultation services ("Project Work"). At the option of BHA, the Client agrees to delineate on a Project Order to be furnished by BHA, the precise tasks to be performed. These services will be performed between January 1st, 1986 and December 31st, 1986. This schedule is predicated upon normal

working conditions and is subject to adjustment at any time in the event of intervening factors beyond the control of BHA. In any event, the time schedule for tasks to be performed pursuant to this Project Agreement may be extended by written agreement between the Client and BHA.

2. BHA shall submit an invoice upon execution of this Agreement for one half of the estimated project total. Said invoice must be paid or satisfactory arrangements made with a BHA officer prior to the Commencement of Project Work. The remaining balance will be invoiced at the end of the Agreement and is due and payable within 15 days after date of invoice. Interest may be charged at the maximum non-usurious rate, but in no event to exceed twenty-five percent (25%) on amounts over forty-five (45) days old. The estimated cost for the project outlined above is $7,500.00. If it becomes apparent during the performance of this Agreement that the cost for completion of the Project will exceed the amount stated above by more than ten percent (10%), BHA shall advise Client as far in advance as reasonably possible so that consideration may be given to other arrangements (e.g., change in task requirements, increase in allowable expenditure).

3. BHA retains all rights to inventions, discoveries, improvements, modifications, changes, and developments arising from projects covered under this Project Agreement. End-user and site licenses for any BHA products may be made available at BHA's sole option to the Client by mutual agreement under separate distribution or license agreements.

All programs, specifications, applications, routines, subroutines, techniques, and ideas (BHA Proprietary Information) for Formulae are and shall remain the sole property of BHA. BHA Proprietary Information shall not be disseminated in any means to any person or firm without the prior express written consent of BHA.

4. All statistical, financial, accounting, and personnel data relating to Client's business, which are confidential and clearly designated as such will be kept in strictest confidence by BHA and its employees. BHA is not obligated to keep confidential any techniques relating to electronic data processing that may be developed either solely by BHA or jointly with the Client during the term of this Project Agreement.

5. Client shall reimburse BHA for reasonable and necessary travel and living expenses incurred by personnel of BHA in connection with

work provided that Client has given its approval to said travel.

6. Client shall reimburse BHA for all reasonable disbursements including, but not limited to, long distance telephone calls, supplies, and shipping charges incurred by BHA in performing work for Client.

7. Client shall have the right to cancel without advance notice any Project by advising BHA in writing of such cancellation. BHA shall be entitled to payment under the provisions of paragraphs 2, 5, and 6 above with respect to charges and expenses earned or incurred up to the time of said cancellation. In the event of cancellation, any unused prepaid funds will be refunded to the Client.

8. BHA's liability to the Client for any losses or damages, direct or indirect, arising out of this Project Agreement shall not exceed the total amount billed or billable to the Client for the performance of the particular task which gave rise to the loss or damage. BHA shall not be liable for consequential damages in any event. This clause shall supersede any other clause of this contract that may be deemed inconsistent with it.

BHA EXPRESSLY DISCLAIMS ANY WARRANTY, INCLUDING BUT NOT LIMITED TO EXPRESS OR IMPLIED WARRANTIES OF MERCHANTIBILITY OR FITNESS FOR A PARTICULAR PURPOSE.

9. Services performed under this Project Agreement shall be considered to have been accepted by Client unless written proof of Claim is made to BHA no later than six (6) months after the last day that services were performed pursuant to the project order.

10. No Liability is assumed by BHA for the accuracy of any processed data, except for the corrections of BHA's work.

11. This Project Agreement shall be construed in accordance with the laws of the State of Texas.

12. BHA shall not be liable for the loss, destruction, or damage of Client - supplied materials unless such loss was proximately caused by the negligence of BHA. BHA's liability shall be limited to restoring the lost, destroyed or damaged materials if Client furnishes all source data necessary for such restoration.

13. It is expressly agreed that this Project Agreement embodies the entire contractual agreement of the parties in relation to the subject matter hereof, and that no other agreement or understanding, verbal or otherwise, exists between the parties except as herein expressly set forth. This Project Agreement shall not be amended except by written agreement signed by both parties.

14. BHA reserves the right to subcontract to qualified third persons any part of the services described in any project order hereunder.

15. BHA shall have the right to decline the acceptance of any project order requested of it by Client in the event that such order may come into conflict with another previously scheduled activity of BHA of for any other good and sufficient reason. In such case, BHA shall give Client notice that it declines to accept any such project order within two weeks of receipt of said project order, but in any case not after the date on which the contemplated order was to begin.

16. Each paragraph and provision of this Contract is severable from the Contract and if one provision or part thereof is declared invalid, the remaining provisions shall nevertheless remain in full force and effect.

17. The prevailing party to any action in State or Federal court, at law or in equity to enforce the provisions of this Project Agreement shall be entitled to court costs and reasonable attorney's fees.

18. Client shall not assign this Project Agreement without the written consent of BHA.

Accepted:

ABC SPORTSWEAR, INC.	BODNER, HUTCHINS & ASSOC. INC.
By: ______________________	By: ______________________
MR. CHARLES EVANS	
Title: ____________	Title: ______________
Date of Acceptance: ___________	Date Submitted: ____________

In addition to the Project Agreement, the Task Order Request shown in Fig. 12-3 was signed.

At this point, we were given a check ($2000) for the preparation of the study and proposal, and a second check, ($3750) for half

Fig. 12-3. ABC task order.

TASK ORDER REQUEST

This Project Order/Task Order Request shall be governed by all terms and conditions signed by Bodner, Hutchins & Associates, Inc. and ABC Sportswear, Inc. January 1st, 1986 in the Project Agreement and will remain in full force and effect.

PROJECT NAME: SALES & INVENTORY ANALYSIS SYSTEM
PROJECT NUMBER:
TASK NUMBER: 01
DATE OF ORDER: January 1, 1986
REQUESTED START DATE: January 10, 1986
ASSIGNED START DATE: January 10, 1986
ESTIMATED DUE DATE: March 1,1986

COMPANY REQUESTING TASK: ABC Sportswear, Inc.
CONTACT: Mr. Charles Evans
ADDRESS: 2222 Fannin
CITY,STATE,ZIP: Houston, TX 77009

RATE: $75.00 PER PERSON HOUR
ESTIMATED NUMBER OF HOURS: 100

PROJECT DESCRIPTION (IN DETAIL):

A database management system will be designed and implemented to achieve a method for the real time tracking of inventory items to include items on order in the number available to be sold. The system will be written in the dBase III programming language and compiled using the Nantucket Clipper package. This phase of development includes file interchangeability with the Open Systems Accounting system. As has been discussed, the new system will not require duplicate entry as data from Open Systems will be used. The data in the data base system will, however, lend itself more readily to the reporting requirements outlined by the users, as well as allow easy implementation of additional reporting schemes in the future.

Bodner, Hutchins & Associates, Inc. has completed a preliminary analysis of the project and estimates that the task will require about one hundred hours of programming. Enclosed are preliminary data base structures and data, as well as an outline of the system structure. BHA will create a menu driven interface for the entry of data into the databases, all editing and reporting, as well as on line help. Once the database structures are approved by ABC Sportswear, Inc., the task can be completed within two to three weeks. We understand the priority of this project and will do everything possible to expedite its completion.

This task shall commence immediately on the signing of the standard project agreement and the payment of the contracted fees.

System Outline

As a result of our preliminary study we suggest a database management system made up of at least the following databases ;

1. Inventory
2. Sales Orders
3. Sales Order Line Items
4. Backorders
5. Backorder Line Items (committed to Sales)

The inventory database should match the Open Systems Inventory file but will allow for the calculation of the amount available for sales. The sales Order database will contain the header information for each sales order, and the sales order line items database will contain information about each line item. Backorders will hold information such as total ordered, ETA, number committed, and number available, while the line item file will contain information as to specific commitments.

The major report will be that required by the sales staff as outlined by Mr. Evans.

Additionally, the three reports requested by Sue will be included. Reports, forms and desired information need to be defined in the early part of the project, but these at least are guaranteed in the time estimate given.

Any requests not defined in the initial project will be

considered in future tasks.

EQUIPMENT (PROJECT SPECIFIC):
IBM PC AT

ESTIMATED TRAVEL (LIST DESTINATIONS,DATES,AND APPROX. LENGTHS OF STAY):
N/A

SOFTWARE PACKAGES REQUIRED: N/A

DBASE III	___	
LOTUS 1-2-3	___	
SYMPHONY	___	
FRAMEWORK	___	
COMMUNICATIONS	___	NAME ______________
WORD PROCESSING	___	NAME ______________
OTHER	___	NAME ______________
		NAME ______________

ADDITIONAL PROJECT EXPENSES:
N/A

SUBMITTED BY: ______________ MR. CHARLES EVANS	ACCEPTED BY: ______________
COMPANY: ABC SPORTSWEAR, INC.	BODNER HUTCHINS & ASSOC. INC.
TITLE: ______________	TITLE: ______________
DATE: ______________	DATE: ______________

of the cost of the first Task Order.

ABC now began to acquire the various hardware and software products chosen from our proposal, and we began to write the application code.

PROGRAM DEVELOPMENT

The information flow for the ABC system is a sequential set

of processes, developed in their natural order. Before any code could be written, we needed to go into the Open Systems Accounting Report Writer and construct the format for each of the data file reports that we needed to export. For this phase, it was necessary to go onto the user's site and actually run the program on their computer. To minimize time impact on ABC's daily operation, we arranged with Sue to have access after normal business hours. Open Systems has good documentation, and we had little difficulty setting up our "Print Report Instructions."Figure 12-4 shows the data screen we built for the Sales Order items.

Fig. 12-4. Open systems report writer screen.

```
01/12/86                    ABC SPORTSWEAR                         PAGE 1
                      PRINT REPORT INSTRUCTIONS

                 SALES ORDER PROCESSING - OPEN ORDERS

P r i n t   I n s t r u c t i o n s
H e a d i n g s   a n d   O u t p u t   A p p e a r a n c e
- - - - - - - - - - - - - - - - - - - - - - - - - - - - - - -
 1.0                     2.0



XXXXXXXX                 999999.000-
999999-                  $999999.00-
XX                       9999999.00-
XXXXXXXXXXXX             MM/DD/YY
XXXXXXXXXXXXXXXXXXXXXXXXX XXXXXXXXXXXXXXXXXXXXXXXXXXXXXXXX
- - - - - - - - - - - - - - - - - - - - - - - - - - - - - - -
D a t a   N a m e s
- - - - - - - - - - - - - - - - - - - - - - - - - - - - - - - - - - - - - -
  1.0                     2.0
 OUR ORDER NO            AVERAGE COST
 QTY ORDERED             UNIT PRICE
 CATEGORY                EXT PRICE
 INV NO                  OUR ORDER DATE
 DESC                    NAME
- - - - - - - - - - - - - - - - - - - - - - - - - - - - - - - - - - - - - -
S o r t   I n s t r u c t i o n s
* *   N o n e   * *
- - - - - - - - - - - - - - - - - - - - - - - - - - - - - - - - - - - - - -
P i c k   I n s t r u c t i o n s
* *   N o n e   * *
- - - - - - - - - - - - - - - - - - - - - - - - - - - - - - - - - - - - - -
```

```
O u t p u t   I n s t r u c t i o n s
- - - - - - - - - - - - - - - - - - - - - - - - - - - - - - - - - - -
    PRINT TO
      1 SCREEN                    FILE NAME   ITEMS
      2 PRINTER                   CONVERSION  ASCII
      3 FILE                      PRINT AUDIT ?      NO
      3

    PAGE FORMAT
      1 LEFT                      DOUBLE SPACE?            NO
      2 CENTERED                  PRINT DETAIL?            YES
      1                           PRINT TOTALS?            NO
                                  PRINT PAGE HEADINGS?     NO
                                  PRINT COLUMN HEADINGS?   NO
                                  PRINT PAGE SKIPS?        NO
- - - - - - - - - - - - - - - - - - - - - - - - - - - - - - - - - - -
G r a p h   I n s t r u c t i o n s
* *   N o n e   * *
- - - - - - - - - - - - - - - - - - - - - - - - - - - - - - - - - - -
```

Using the database definition for items, we selected the corresponding field names in Open Systems, and arranged display formats and field widths. We told Open Systems to print the report to an ASCII format file called ITEMS. Report Writer puts the data out in an intermediate format which must finally be converted to the ASCII Text structure desired by running a program called CONVERT. The output file is called ITEMS.OUT and part of it is listed in Fig. 12-5.

With a little deciphering, you can identify the variables shown in Fig. 12-6.

To pass this file to dBASE requires some intermediate processing. Several of the fields are variable in width and are delimited in a number of ways. We chose to write a family of intermediate file conversion processors that would read the .OUT files produced by Open Systems and put the data into a form more easily digestible by dBASE. This type of a task could be well handled by BA-

Fig. 12-5. Sample record from ITEMS.OUT.

```
"1601"12.000
4$29.7000
"70"110.80
"00110348AT"12/20/85
"103 3/4"""P.V.F. MIDWEST"
```

Fig. 12-6. ITEMS.OUT variables.

```
OUR ORDER NO = 1601
AVERAGE COST = $12.00
QTY ORDERED = 4
UNIT PRICE = $29.70
CATEGORY = 70
EXTENDED PRICE = $110.80
INV NO = 0010348AT
OUR ORDER DATE = 12/20/85
DESC = 103 3/4"
NAME = P.V.F. MIDWEST
```

SIC, and could be made into a fast executable module using the IBM BASIC Compiler. By writing and debugging in interpreted BASICA, and compiling only when we felt ready to test the executable file, the development process was much more efficient. The BASIC program for the ITEMS file processing is listed in Fig. 12-7.

Fig. 12-7. BASIC listing for ITEM.BAS.

```
10 REM * -----------------------------------------------------------------
20 REM *
30 REM * Program:            ITEM.BAS
40 REM * System:             ABC Sportswear International
50 REM * Programmer:         Michael Simon Bodner
60 REM * Written:            01/20/86
70 REM * Revised By:         Michael Simon Bodner
80 REM * Revision Date:      04/14/86
90 REM *
100 REM * -----------------------------------------------------------------
110 REM *
120 REM * Comments:      OPEN SYSTEMS SALES ORDER ITEMS TO DBASE III SDF FILE
130 REM *
140 REM * -----------------------------------------------------------------
150 REM *
160 REM * Calls:         NONE
170 REM *
180 REM * -----------------------------------------------------------------
190 REM *******************************************************************
200 REM *                                                                 *
210 REM *  COPYRIGHT 1986, BODNER, HUTCHINS & ASSOCIATES, INC. HOUSTON, TX *
220 REM *                                                                 *
230 REM *******************************************************************
240 COLOR 10,1:COUNT=0
```

```
250 REM **************************************************
260 REM *  SET UP SCREEN INFORMATION DISPLAY              *
270 REM **************************************************
280 LOCATE 11,16:PRINT"Converting Open System ITEMS to dBase III format"
290 LOCATE 17,16:PRINT"Copyright 1986, Bodner, Hutchins & Assoc., Inc. "
300 LOCATE 13,12:PRINT"+---------------+--------------+-------------------+"
310 LOCATE 14,12:PRINT"| Order #       |Date          |Company            |"
320 LOCATE 15,12:PRINT"+---------------+--------------+-------------------+"
330 WIDTH "LPT1:",132
340 REM **************************************************
350 REM * OPEN FILES, INITIALIZE VARIABLES                *
360 REM **************************************************
370 OPEN "O",#2,"ITM.APP"
380 DIM A$(13),B$(13),M$(13),O$(13)
390 M$(1)="ORDERNO    "
400 M$(2)="QTY        "
410 M$(3)="CATEGORY   "
420 M$(4)="INVENUMBER "
430 M$(5)="FIGURENUMB "
440 M$(6)="AVGCOST    "
450 M$(7)="UNITPRICE  "
460 M$(8)="AMOUNT     "
470 M$(9)="ORDERDATE  "
480 M$(10)="CONAME     "
490 OPEN "I",#1,"ITEMS.OUT"
500 IF EOF(1) THEN CLOSE #1:CLOSE #2:END
510 REM **************************************************
520 REM *  GET DATA FROM INPUT FILE ITEMS.OUT UNTIL EOF   *
530 REM **************************************************
540 FOR I=1 TO 5
550 LINE INPUT #1,A$(I)
560 NEXT
570 REM **************************************************
580 REM *  DECIPHER AND MANIPULATE DATA FIELDS            *
590 REM **************************************************
600 FOR I=2 TO LEN(A$(1))
610 IF MID$(A$(1),I,1)=CHR$(34) THEN N=I:GOTO 630
620 NEXT:N=I
630 B$(1)=MID$(A$(1),2,N-1)
640 IF LEN(A$(1))>6 THEN B$(2)=MID$(A$(1),N+1,LEN(A$(1))-N) :GOTO 660
650 B$(2)=A$(1)
660 B$(3)=A$(2)
670 B$(4)=MID$(A$(3),2,2)
680 IF LEN(A$(3))<=4 THEN A$(3)=LEFT$(A$(3)+"      ",5)
```

```
690 B$(5)=RIGHT$(A$(3),LEN(A$(3))-4)
700 FOR I=2 TO LEN(A$(4))
710 IF MID$(A$(4),I,1)=CHR$(34) THEN N=I:GOTO 730
720 NEXT:N=I
730 B$(6)=MID$(A$(4),2,N-2)
740 B$(7)=RIGHT$(A$(4),8)
750 FOR I=LEN(A$(5)) TO 1 STEP -1
760 IF MID$(A$(5),I,1)=CHR$(34) THEN M=I:GOTO 780
770 NEXT:M=I
780 A$(5)=LEFT$(A$(5),M):FOR I=M-1 TO 1 STEP -1
790 IF MID$(A$(5),I,1)=CHR$(34) THEN N=I:GOTO 810
800 NEXT:N=I
810 B$(8)=RIGHT$(A$(5),M-N)
820 B$(8)=LEFT$(B$(8),LEN(B$(8))-1)
830 B$(9)=LEFT$(A$(5),LEN(A$(5))-LEN(B$(8))+4)
840 B$(9)=RIGHT$(B$(9),LEN(B$(9))-1)
850 IF LEN(B$(9))<=7 THEN B$(9)=LEFT$(B$(9)+"        ",8)
860 B$(9)=LEFT$(B$(9),LEN(B$(9))-7)
870 FOR I=1 TO LEN(B$(3))
880 IF MID$(B$(3),I,1)="$" THEN N=I:GOTO 900
890 NEXT:N=I
900 B$(10)=MID$(B$(3),1,N-1)
910 IF LEN(B$(3))=0 THEN 930
920 B$(3)=MID$(B$(3),N+1,LEN(B$(3))-N)
930 O$(1) =B$(1)
940 O$(6) =B$(2)
950 O$(7) =B$(3)
960 O$(3) =B$(4)
970 O$(8) =B$(5)
980 O$(4) =B$(6)
990 O$(9) =B$(7)
1000 O$(10)=B$(8)
1010 O$(5)= B$(9)
1020 O$(2)= B$(10)
1030 B1=VAL(O$(1))
1040 O$(1)=STR$(B1)
1050 B$(1) =LEFT$(O$(1)+"            ",8)
1060 B$(2) =LEFT$(O$(2)+"            ",4)
1070 B$(3) =LEFT$(O$(3)+"   ",2)
1080 B$(4) =LEFT$(O$(4)+"            ",12)
1090 B$(5) =LEFT$(O$(5)+"                         ",25)
1100 B$(6) =LEFT$(O$(6)+"            ",11)
1110 B$(7) =LEFT$(O$(7)+"            ",11)
1120 B$(8)=LEFT$(O$(8)+"           ",11)
```

```
1130 B$(9)= LEFT$(O$(9)+"        ",8)
1140 B$(10)= LEFT$(O$(10)+"                              ",30)
1150 REM ***************************************************
1160 REM *  IGNORE INVALID DATA FIELDS                     *
1170 REM ***************************************************
1180 IF LEFT$(B$(5),4)="CUST" OR LEFT$(B$(5),4)="    " THEN 500
1190 REM ***************************************************
1200 REM *  CREATE OUTPUT STRING FOR TARGET FILE           *
1210 REM ***************************************************
1220 LN$=B$(1)+B$(2)+B$(3)+B$(4)+B$(5)+B$(6)+B$(7)+B$(8)+B$(9)+B$(10)
1230 REM ***************************************************
1240 REM *  UPDATE SCREEN INFORMATION DISPLAY              *
1250 REM ***************************************************
1260 LOCATE 19,39:COUNT=COUNT+1:PRINT COUNT
1270 LOCATE 14,22:PRINT LEFT$(B$(1),7):LOCATE 14,35:PRINT B$(9)
1275 LOCATE 14,54:PRINT LEFT$(B$(10),14)
1280 REM ***************************************************
1290 REM *  PRINT DATA TO OUTPUT FILE ITM.APP              *
1300 REM ***************************************************
1310 PRINT #2,LN$
1320 GOTO 500
```

To write the BASICA program, we used the IBM Personal Editor 2 (PE2) as a text editor, ran the program in BASICA, then went back to PE2 for more editing. Note the internal documentation used in the program. Similar programs were written for each of the four output files from Open Systems. The BASICA programs were compiled into executable modules of about 58K, and were thus callable from within dBASE III PLUS using the RUN command.

The ITEM.EXE program takes the data in ITEMS.OUT and converts that data into the format shown in the listing of ITEM.APP, which is in Fig. 12-8.

This data is now in the format called Standard Data Format

Fig. 12-8. Data file listing of ITEM.APP.

```
 1681 2 700010148AT 101  3/4"    18.441  28.620  57.24  12/20/85 P.V.F. MIDWEST
 1681 4 7000101A8AT 101  1"      25.600  34.560 138.24  12/20/85 P.V.F. MIDWEST
 1681 4 7000101B8AT 101  1 1/4"  41.960  47.520 190.08  12/20/85 P.V.F. MIDWEST
 1681 4 7000101C8AT 101  1 1/2"  41.960  69.660 278.64  12/20/85 P.V.F. MIDWEST
 1681 2 7000101E8AT 101  2"      84.218  82.620 165.24  12/20/85 P.V.F. MIDWEST
 1681 8 700010338AT 103  1/2"    10.330  28.350 226.80  12/20/85 P.V.F. MIDWEST
*1681 4 700010348AT 103  3/4"    12.000  29.700 118.80  12/20/85 P.V.F. MIDWEST
 1681 9 7000103A8AT 103  1"      20.934  39.150 469.80  12/20/85 P.V.F. MIDWEST
```

(SDF) by dBASE III PLUS. Each of the intermediate data file processors created files of this type, and this ended the development of the second software component. Now the accounting clerks could run the reports in Open Systems, and create the cryptic data files that would eventually be processed into SDF files for inclusion in our dBASE application.

We were now ready to begin to write our main application. There were a number of ways to proceed. We might have used one of the application generators described in Chapter Six, or a "screen painter" to build all of the screens and then add the code ourselves. Because we needed more report formats and file interrelationships than could be offered by any of the application generators that we had access to, we chose a novel approach.

We loaded the Dan Bricklin Demo Program and, using its excellent screen editor, with direct graphics, we proceeded to construct the various menus and data entry forms that were required. We "printed" these screens to a text file, using options to directly save the line graphics, then loaded these files into Personal Editor

Fig. 12-9. Bricklin screen capture file.

```
07/17/86                                                          Rev 3.5
+-----------------------------------------------------------------------+
| ABC Sportswear,Inc Database Management System - Main System Menu     |
+------------------+----------------------------------------------------+
|  Option Code     |     Available System Options                       |
+------------------+----------------------------------------------------+
|                  |                                                    |
|      <1>         |  o  Inventory Maintenance                          |
|                  |                                                    |
|      <2>         |  o  Sales Order System                             |
|                  |                                                    |
|      <3>         |  o  Purchase Order System                          |
|                  |                                                    |
|      <4>         |  o  Purchase Order/Sales Order Linked File         |
|                  |                                                    |
|      <5>         |  o  Report Subsystem                               |
|                  |                                                    |
+------------------+----------------------------------------------------+
|      <Q>         |  o  Completely EXIT from System                    |
+------------------+----------------------------------------------------+
|  F1 = Help       |  Please enter number of desired option             |
+------------------+----------------------------------------------------+
Thursday                                                         11:25:59
< Copyright 1986 by Bodner, Hutchins & Associates, Inc., Houston,TX >
```

and began to write dBASE code around them. Figure 12-9 is the raw screen file from the Bricklin Program.

Figure 12-10 is the main menu program for the ABC application, showing how we built @SAYs and @GETs into the screen mask to build a program.

Fig. 12-10. Main menu program for ABC Sportswear.

```
* ----------------------------------------------------------------------------
*
* Program:            MENU.PRG
* System:             ABC Sportswear Database
* Programmer:         Michael Simon Bodner
* Written:            01/20/86
* Revised By:         Michael Simon Bodner
* Revision Date:      04/14/86
*
* ----------------------------------------------------------------------------
*
* Comments:           This is the main program for the entire system
*
* ----------------------------------------------------------------------------
*
* Calls:              INV.PRG,SOR.PRG,POR.PRG
*
* ----------------------------------------------------------------------------
CLOSE DATABASES
RELEASE ALL
SET BELL OFF
SET TALK ON
CLEAR
SET SAFETY OFF
SET TALK OFF
SET DEVICE TO SCREEN
SET UNIQUE OFF
SET SCORE OFF
PUBLIC MREV,CALL_PRG,HLPFLG,CLIPPER,BA1,BA2,BA3,ML1,ML2,ML3,ML4,ML5,ML6
PUBLIC DATABASE,NDX,FLDNAME,FLDSZE,FS,RCDS,TPMN,XNAME
IF CLIPPER
EXTERNAL ISCOLOR,ISPRINTER
IF ISCOLOR() .AND. CLIPPER
   SET COLOR to GR+/B,R+/
ELSE
   SET COLOR to W/ , /W
ENDIF ISCOLOR
```

```
ENDIF CLIPPER
IF ISCOLOR()
 SET COLOR to W/ , /W
 CLEAR
 SET COLOR to GR+/B,R+/
ELSE
 CLEAR
ENDIF
@ 10,10 SAY '+------------------------------------------------------+'
@ 11,10 SAY '¦    Initializing System Databases.................    ¦'
@ 12,10 SAY '+------------------------------------------------------+'
ML1='+------------------------------------------------------+'
ML2='¦       ABC Sportswear Database Management System      ¦'
ML3='+------------------------------------------------------+'
ML4='+------------------------------------------------------+'
ML5='¦   Please enter the code for your desired option      ¦'
ML6='+------------------------------------------------------+'
BA1='+---------------------------------------------------------------------+
BA2='¦  ABC Sportswear Inventory and Sales Database Management System       ¦
BA3='+---------------------------------------------------------------------+
IF .NOT. CLIPPER
  STORE file('SOR.NTX') TO MQDX
  IF MQDX
   !ERASE *.NTX
  ENDIF
ELSE
  STORE file('SOR.NDX') TO MQDX
  IF MQDX
   !ERASE *.NDX
  ENDIF
ENDIF
   IF .NOT. CLIPPER
     STORE file('SOR.NDX') TO MQDX
   ELSE
     STORE file('SOR.NTX') TO MQDX
   ENDIF
   IF .NOT. MQDX
      SELECT 1
      USE SALESORDER
      @ 23,10 SAY 'Sales Order Database is now being indexed......         '
      DO SORGO
      CLEAR
   ENDIF
   IF .NOT. CLIPPER
```

```
      STORE file('INV.NDX') TO MQDX
    ELSE
      STORE file('INV.NTX') TO MQDX
    ENDIF
IF .NOT. MQDX
    SELECT 1
    USE INVENTORY
    @ 23,10 SAY 'Inventory Database is now being indexed......
    DO INVGO
    CLEAR
ENDIF
IF .NOT. CLIPPER
  STORE file('CA.NDX') TO MQDX
ELSE
  STORE file('CA.NTX') TO MQDX
ENDIF
IF .NOT. MQDX
    SELECT 1
    USE INVENTORY
    @ 23,10 SAY 'Inventory Database is now being indexed......
    DO INVGO
    CLEAR
ENDIF
IF .NOT. CLIPPER
  STORE file('POR.NDX') TO MQDX
ELSE
  STORE file('POR.NTX') TO MQDX
ENDIF
IF .NOT. MQDX
  SELECT 1
  USE PURORDER
    @ 23,10 SAY 'Purchase Order Database is now being indexed......
    DO PORGO
    CLEAR
ENDIF
IF .NOT. CLIPPER
  STORE file('SOR2.NDX') TO MQDX
ELSE
  STORE file('SOR2.NTX') TO MQDX
ENDIF
IF .NOT. MQDX
    SELECT 1
    USE ITEMS
    @ 23,10 SAY 'Sales Order Items Database is now being indexed..
```

```
   DO SOR2GO
   CLEAR
ENDIF
IF .NOT. CLIPPER
  STORE file('FAC2.NDX') TO MQDX
ELSE
  STORE file('FAC2.NTX') TO MQDX
ENDIF
IF .NOT. MQDX
   SELECT 1
   USE BACKSALES
   @ 23,10 SAY 'Back Order Database is now being indexed......
   INDEX ON FACTORDNO TO FAC2
   CLEAR
ENDIF
   IF .NOT. CLIPPER
     STORE file('FAC.NDX') TO MQDX
   ELSE
     STORE file('FAC.NTX') TO MQDX
   ENDIF
   IF .NOT. MQDX
      SELECT 1
      USE BACKSALES
      @ 23,10 SAY 'Back Order Database is now being indexed......          '
      INDEX ON INVENUMBER TO FAC
      CLEAR
   ENDIF
HLPFLG=0
STORE 'Rev 3.5' TO MREV
CLOSE DATABASES
SELECT 1
USE INVENTORY INDEX INV,CA
SELECT 2
USE SALESORDER INDEX SOR
SELECT 3
USE ITEMS INDEX SOR2
SELECT 4
USE PURORDER INDEX POR,PINV
SELECT 5
USE BACKSALES INDEX FAC,FAC2
MDAYNAME=CDOW(DATE())
IF ISCOLOR()
 SET COLOR to W/ , /W
 CLEAR
```

```
 SET COLOR to GR+/B,R+/
ELSE
 CLEAR
ENDIF
STORE .T. TO MQU
DO WHILE MQU
  IF HLPFLG=0
    MM1="+------------------------------------------------------------------+"
    MM2="¦   ABC Sportswear Database Management System - Main System Menu   ¦"
    MM3="+----------------+-------------------------------------------------+"
    IF ISCOLOR()
      @ 2,6 SAY MM1
      @ 3,6 SAY MM2
      @ 4,6 SAY MM3
    ELSE
      @ 2,6 GET MM1
      @ 3,6 GET MM2
      @ 4,6 GET MM3
    ENDIF
    @ 5,6 SAY "¦ Option Code  ¦   Available System Options                      ¦"
    @ 6,6 SAY "+--------------+-------------------------------------------------+"
    @ 7,6 SAY "¦              ¦                                                 ¦"
    @ 8,6 SAY "¦      <1>     ¦ o  Inventory Maintenance                        ¦"
    @ 9,6 SAY "¦              ¦                                                 ¦"
    @10,6 SAY "¦      <2>     ¦ o  Sales Order System                           ¦"
    @11,6 SAY "¦              ¦                                                 ¦"
   @ 12,6 SAY "¦      <3>     ¦ o  Purchase Order System                        ¦"
   @ 13,6 SAY "¦              ¦                                                 ¦"
   @ 14,6 SAY "¦      <4>     ¦ o  Purchase Order/Sales Order Linked File       ¦"
   @ 15,6 SAY "¦              ¦                                                 ¦"
   @ 16,6 SAY "¦      <5>     ¦ o  Report Subsystem                             ¦"
   @ 17,6 SAY "¦              ¦                                                 ¦"
   @ 18,6 SAY "+--------------+-------------------------------------------------+"
   @ 19,6 SAY "¦      <Q>     ¦ o  Completely EXIT from System                  ¦"
   @ 20,6 SAY "+--------------+-------------------------------------------------+"
   @ 21,6 SAY "¦    F1 = Help ¦ Please enter number of desired option           ¦"
   @ 22,6 SAY "+--------------+-------------------------------------------------+"
   IF ISCOLOR()
    SET COLOR to GR+/
   ENDIF
   @ 1,68 SAY MREV
   @ 1,6 SAY DATE()
   @ 23,67 SAY TIME()
   @ 23,6 SAY MDAYNAME
```

```
IF ISCOLOR()
 SET COLOR to GR+/B,R+/
ENDIF
C01='< Copyright 1986 by Bodner, Hutchins & Associates, Inc., Houston,TX >'
@ 24,6 GET C01
CLEAR GETS
ELSE
 HLPFLG=0
ENDIF
CALL_PRG='MENU'
HLPFLG=0
STORE ' ' TO MQ
  DO WHILE MQ =' '
   @ 21,70 GET MQ
   READ
  ENDDO
HLPFLG=0
IF UPPER(MQ) = 'H'
   DO HELP
   IF ISCOLOR()
    SET COLOR to W/ , /W
    CLEAR
    SET COLOR to GR+/B,R+/
   ELSE
    CLEAR
   ENDIF
ELSE
IF UPPER(MQ) = '1'
   DO INV
   IF ISCOLOR()
    SET COLOR to W/ , /W
    CLEAR
    SET COLOR to GR+/B,R+/
   ELSE
    CLEAR
   ENDIF
ELSE
IF UPPER(MQ) = '2'
   ??CHR(7)
   TT="¦      <2>      ¦ o  Sales Order Headers or Items (H/I)?
   @10,6 GET TT
   CLEAR GETS
   STORE ' ' TO MQS
   DO WHILE MQS =' ' .AND. MQS<>'H'.AND. MQS<>'I'
```

```
    @ 21,70 GET MQS
    READ
    MQS=UPPER(MQS)
    ENDDO
    IF MQS='H'
      DO SOR
    ENDIF
    IF MQS='I'
      DO SOR2
    ENDIF
    RELEASE MQS
    IF ISCOLOR()
     SET COLOR to W/ , /W
     CLEAR
     SET COLOR to GR+/B,R+/
    ELSE
     CLEAR
    ENDIF
ELSE
IF UPPER(MQ) = '3'
    DO POR
    IF ISCOLOR()
     SET COLOR to W/ , /W
     CLEAR
     SET COLOR to GR+/B,R+/
    ELSE
     CLEAR
    ENDIF
ELSE
IF UPPER(MQ) = '5'
    DO RPT
    HLPFLG=0
    IF ISCOLOR()
     SET COLOR to W/ , /W
     CLEAR
     SET COLOR to GR+/B,R+/
    ELSE
     CLEAR
    ENDIF
ELSE
IF UPPER(MQ) = 'M'
    SET COLOR to W/ , /W
    CLEAR
ELSE
```

```
IF UPPER(MQ) = 'C'
   SET COLOR to GR+/B,R+/
   IF ISCOLOR()
    SET COLOR to W/ , /W
    CLEAR
    SET COLOR to GR+/B,R+/
   ELSE
    CLEAR
   ENDIF
ELSE
IF UPPER(MQ) = '4'
   DO BKS
   IF ISCOLOR()
    SET COLOR to W/ , /W
    CLEAR
    SET COLOR to GR+/B,R+/
   ELSE
    CLEAR
   ENDIF
ELSE
IF UPPER(MQ) = 'D'
   CLOSE DATABASES
   RELEASE ALL
   IF ISCOLOR()
    SET COLOR to W/ , /W
    CLEAR
    SET COLOR to GR+/B,R+/
   ELSE
    CLEAR
   ENDIF
   CANCEL
ELSE
IF UPPER(MQ) = 'I'
  CLOSE DATABASES
  USE INVENTORY
  @ 23,15 SAY 'Inventory Database is now being indexed......      '
  INDEX ON INVENUMBER TO INV
  INDEX ON CATEGORY TO CA
  USE SALESORDER
  @ 23,15 SAY 'Sales Order Database is now being indexed......   '
  INDEX ON ORDERNO TO SOR
  USE ITEMS
  @ 23,15 SAY 'Sales Order Items Database is now being indexed.. '
  INDEX ON ORDERNO TO SOR2
```

```
      USE PURORDER
      @ 23,15 SAY 'Purchase Order Database is now being indexed..... '
      INDEX ON FACTORDNO TO POR
      INDEX ON INVENUMBER TO PINV
      USE BACKSALES
      @ 23,15 SAY 'Back Order Database is now being indexed......    '
      INDEX ON INVENUMBER TO FAC
      INDEX ON FACTORDNO TO FAC2
      CLOSE DATABASES
      @ 23,15 SAY '                                                  '
      SELECT 1
      USE INVENTORY INDEX INV,CA
      SELECT 2
      USE SALESORDER INDEX SOR
      SELECT 3
      USE ITEMS INDEX SOR2
      SELECT 4
      USE PURORDER INDEX POR,PINV
      SELECT 5
      USE BACKSALES INDEX FAC,FAC2
    ELSE
    IF UPPER(MQ) = 'Q'
      CLEAR
      QUIT
    ENDIF 1
    ENDIF 2
    ENDIF 3
    ENDIF 4
    ENDIF 5
    ENDIF Q
    ENDIF D
    ENDIF H
    ENDIF M
    ENDIF C
    ENDIF I
ENDDO  MQU
RETURN
```

Figure 12-11 is the input/output screen constructed from another screen mask.

As can be seen from the menus, we offered all of the usual modules such as ADD, GET, EDIT, and REPORT for each of the databases. Additionally, the option that would import the data from the accounting system was placed on the main menu. This option runs

Fig. 12-11. ABC Sportswear input/output screen.

```
07/17/86      Thursday           Inventory Database System        GET   Rev 3.5
+-------------------+----------------------------------------------------------+
| Category : 30     | Inventory Number : 0005049NJ                             |
+-------------------+----------------------------------------------------------+
| Figure Number : CS050  3/4"    304  NPT                                      |
+------------------------+-------------------------+--------------------------+
| Quantity on Hand :   0 | Quantity on Order :   0 | Quantity Sold :   0      |
+------------------------+--+-------------------+---+-------------------------+
| Available to Sell :   0    | Target :    0       | List Price $        0.00  |
+-------------------------+-+-------------------+--------+-------------------+
| Last Cost $         5.99 |  Average Cost $         5.99 | Discount : 0.0000 |
+-------------------------+-------------------------+-----+-------------------+
| Item Weight (in pounds) :    0.00                     | Cubic Feet :    0.00 |
+-------------------------------------------------------+----------------------+
|     ABC Sportswear, Inc. - Inventory and Sales Database Management System   |
+------------------------------------------------------------------------------+


 ENTER (N)ext, (P)revious, (S)earch, (M)ore Commands, RETURN to EXIT
```

the programs like ITEM.EXE, then moves the imported data into the dBASE files, as shown in the code fragment in Fig. 12-12.

As a result of this import process, the current data from the Open Systems Accounting Program is made available for the data-

Fig. 12-12. Code fragment showing import module.

```
IF CLIPPER
   CALL _scrsave WITH SCREEN1
   SAVE SCREEN
ENDIF
DO CASE
   CASE UPPER(MCMD)='I'
   SELECT INVENTORY
   IL1='+--------------------------------------------------+'
   IL2='|  Are you really sure that you want to do this (Y/N)?  |'
   IL3='+--------------------------------------------------+'
   @ 12,12 GET IL1
   @ 13,12 GET IL2
   @ 14,12 GET IL3
   CLEAR GETS
   MANS=' '
   DO WHILE MANS<>'Y' .AND. MANS<>'N'
     @ 13,67 GET MANS
```

```
  READ
  MANS=UPPER(MANS)
ENDDO MANS
IF MANS='Y'
   IL2='¦  Now importing Inventory files - DO NOT DISTURB !!!!   ¦'
   @ 12,12 GET IL1
   @ 13,12 GET IL2
   @ 14,12 GET IL3
   CLEAR GETS
   IF CLIPPER
      SAVE SCREEN
   ENDIF
   ! INV
   IF CLIPPER
      RESTORE SCREEN
   ENDIF
   SELECT INVENTORY
   ZAP
   IL2='¦  Now restructuring Inventory   - DO NOT DISTURB !!!!   ¦'
   @ 12,12 GET IL1
   @ 13,12 GET IL2
   @ 14,12 GET IL3
   CLEAR GETS
   APPEND FROM INV.APP SDF
   IL2='¦  Now REINDEXING Inventory files - DO NOT DISTURB !!!!  ¦'
   @ 13,12 GET IL2
   CLEAR GETS
   SELECT INVENTORY
   INDEX ON INVENUMBER TO INV
   INDEX ON CATEGORY TO CA
   SELECT 1
   USE INVENTORY INDEX INV,CA
ENDIF MANS
IF CLIPPER
  CALL _scrrest WITH SCREEN1
ELSE
  CLEAR
ENDIF
RELEASE IL1,IL2,IL3,MANS
LOOP
```

base operations. The primary result is that complex linking of the data can be done, to produce the reports defined and required by the Task Order Request. Figure 12-13 shows the main report, in which inventory purchase orders and sales order information have

Fig. 12-13. ABC inventory status report (with linkages).

```
                              ABC Sportswear, Inc. Database Management System

                                    Sales Daily Inventory Status Report

07/24/86                                                                                            00:24:42
==============================================================================================================
Ca Inventory Figure Number          Qnty  Qnty  Qnty  Qnty  Purch  Qnty  ETA    Total        Quantity   Qnty   Target
                                     on    on         Avail Order   on           On          on Hand    Avail
                                    Hand  Order Sold To Sell        Order        Order       Available  To Sell
==============================================================================================================
10 01503G2DA  1503  3"    XU  S/40     3     0     0     3
                                                 ==========
                   Purchase Order Totals -->>      0     0                                       3         3       0
--------------------------------------------------------------------------------------------------------------
10 01512E1AA  1512  2"    X           57    80    12   125
                                                   0    68   537     68 02/28/86    68
                                                  12     0   537     12 02/28/86    80
                                                 ==========
                   Purchase Order Totals -->>     12    68                                      57       125     150
--------------------------------------------------------------------------------------------------------------
10 01512E2AA  1512  2"    XU          49     0     0    49
                                                 ==========
                   Purchase Order Totals -->>      0     0                                      49        49       0
--------------------------------------------------------------------------------------------------------------
10 01512E4AA  1512  2"    L            7     0     0     7
                                                 ==========
                   Purchase Order Totals -->>      0     0                                       7         7       6
--------------------------------------------------------------------------------------------------------------
10 01512F1AA  1512  2 1/2" X          15    12     2    25
```

```
                                       0    2   537     2 02/28/86     2
                                       0   10   563    10 03/29/86    12
                                     ============
              Purchase Order Totals -->>   0   12                                          13      25      25
--------------------------------------------------------------------------------------------------------------
10 01512G1AA  1512  3"     X          131   71  13  189
                                       0   10   537    10 02/28/86    10
                                       0   58   539    58 02/03/86    68
                                       0    3   566     3 04/04/86    71
                                     ============
              Purchase Order Totals -->>   0   71                                         118     189     230
--------------------------------------------------------------------------------------------------------------
10 01512G2AA  1512  3"     XU           3    0   0    3
                                     ============
              Purchase Order Totals -->>   0    0                                           3       3       0
--------------------------------------------------------------------------------------------------------------
10 01512G4AA  1512  3"     L            2   11   0   13
                                       0   11   546    11 02/28/86    11
                                     ============
              Purchase Order Totals -->>   0   11                                           2      13      17
--------------------------------------------------------------------------------------------------------------
10 01512H1AA  1512  4"     X           78  109  30  157
                                       0   36   537    36 02/28/86    36
                                       0   16   537    16 02/28/86    52
                                       0   57   563    57 03/29/86   109
                                     ============
              Purchase Order Totals -->>   0  109                                          48     157     150
==============================================================================================================
                                    Page Number      1
==============================================================================================================
```

been correlated to show that items on order, but not yet in stock, are available to sell. It also shows what sales orders are holding which items from each purchase order. This is the report Charles and Sue wanted all along, because it represents the way they do business. Using this report, salespeople can see how much is actually available to sell from a given shipment, and can then sell it, "tag" it, and serve their customers more efficiently.

The richness of the dBASE III PLUS procedural language is illustrated in the code fragment from the report program shown in Fig. 12-14. This listing was produced using the dFlow documentation product mentioned in Chapter Six, and thus includes line numbering, logical indentation, variable and module concordance, and formatting of the code so that it can be printed on an 80 column display. These screen displays were captured by the Capture memory-resident program from Dan Bricklin's Demo Program, and then printed to a file for use here.

This code demonstrates how, using multiple databases, a report can be constructed with field data from each database. The report code also illustrates how to do page counting and pagination.

Fig. 12-14. ABC Sportswear report program under dFlow.

```
- Module ABCRPT
* --------------------------------------------------------------------------;
----
*
* Program:             ABCRPT.PRG
* System:              ABC Sportswear Database
* Programmer:          Michael Simon Bodner
* Written:             01/20/86
* Revised By:          Michael Simon Bodner
* Revision Date:       04/14/86
*
* --------------------------------------------------------------------------;
----
*
* Comments:            This is the SALES INV program for the RPT system
*
* --------------------------------------------------------------------------;
----
*
* Calls:
*
* --------------------------------------------------------------------------;
----
```

```
SELECT 1
USE INVENTORY INDEX CA,INV
SELECT 4
USE PURORDER INDEX PINV,POR
SELECT 1
SET RELATION TO INVENUMBER INTO PURORDER
GOTO TOP
MCLINE=0
MPAGE=0
TVAR=SPACE(39)
HD=SUBSTR(ML2,2,55)
? SPACE((140-LEN(HD))/2)+HD
?
?'                                                          Sales Daily';
+ ' Inventory Status Report'
?
?DTOC(DATE())+'                                                         ';
+ '                                                              '+TIME()
?;
'=====================================================================';
+ '=========================================================='
?'Ca Inventory Figure Number            Qnty  Qnty  Qnty  Qnty   Purch';
+ '  Qnty   ETA   Total              Quantity    Qnty    Target'
?'                                       on    on          Avail  Order';
+ '   on          On               on Hand    Avail  '
?'                                      Hand  Order Sold To Sell      ';
+ '  Order       Order             Available  To Sell '
?;
'=====================================================================';
+ '=========================================================='
DO WHILE .NOT. EOF()
W    TQTYS=0
W    TSEL=0
W    IF QTYONHAND+QTYONORDER+QTYSOLD+AVAILTOSEL>0
W   T    IF MCLINE<>0
W   T   T    ?'-----------------------------------------------------------';
W   T   T    + '---------------------------------------------------------';
W   T   T    + '-----------------'
W   T    ENDIF
W   T    ? CATEGORY+' '+SUBSTR(INVENUMBER,1,11)+FIGURENUMB+STR(QTYONHAND,;
W   T    5,0)+STR(QTYONORDER,6,0)+STR(QTYSOLD,6,0)+STR(AVAILTOSEL,6,0)
W   T    TVAR=SPACE(39)
W   T    MCLINE=MCLINE+2
W   T    MORD=0
```

```
W   T     MINV=INVENUMBER
W   T     MFIG=FIGURENUMB
W   T     SELE 4
W   T     FIND &MINV
W   T     DO WHILE INVENUMBER=MINV
W   T   W     ?    ? TVAR+'          '+STR(QTYSOLD,6,0)+STR(AVAILTOSEL,6,;
W   T   W     0) +'    '+FACTORDNO+STR(QTYORDERED,5,0)+' '+ETA
W   T   W     TVAR=SPACE(39)
W   T   W     MORD=MORD+QTYORDERED
W   T   W     TQTYS=TQTYS+QTYSOLD
W   T   W     TSEL=TSEL+AVAILTOSEL
W   T   W     ??STR(MORD,7,0)
W   T   W     MCLINE=MCLINE+1
W   T   W     SKIP
W   T   W     IF MCLINE>45
W   T   W   T     MCLINE=0
W   T   W   T     MPAGE=MPAGE+1
W   T   W   T     ?;
W   T   W   T     '========================================================';
W   T   W   T     + '======================================================';
W   T   W   T     + '========================'
W   T   W   T     ?'                                                    Page';
W   T   W   T     + ' Number  '+STR(MPAGE,5,0)
W   T   W   T     ?;
W   T   W   T     '========================================================';
W   T   W   T     + '======================================================';
W   T   W   T     + '========================'
W   T   W   T     ? CHR(12)
W   T   W   T     ? SPACE((140-LEN(HD))/2)+HD
W   T   W   T     ?
W   T   W   T     ?'                                                       ';
W   T   W   T     + ' Sales Daily Inventory Status Report'
W   T   W   T     ?
W   T   W   T     ?DTOC(DATE())+'                                          ';
W   T   W   T     + '                                                      ';
W   T   W   T     + '                         '+TIME()
W   T   W   T     ?;
W   T   W   T     '========================================================';
W   T   W   T     + '======================================================';
W   T   W   T     + '========================'
W   T   W   T     ?'Ca Inventory Figure Number              Qnty  Qnty ';
W   T   W   T     + ' Qnty  Qnty   Purch  Qnty   ETA   Total             ';
W   T   W   T     + '   Quantity    Qnty    Target'
W   T   W   T     ?'                                         on    on   ';
```

```
W   T   W   T    + '     Avail  Order   on          On                 ';
W   T   W   T    + '  on Hand    Avail  '
W   T   W   T    ?'                                         Hand  Order';
W   T   W   T    + ' Sold To Sell        Order        Order                ';
W   T   W   T    + '    Available  To Sell '
W   T   W   T    ?;
W   T   W   T    '=====================================================';
W   T   W   T    + '===================================================';
W   T   W   T    + '========================'
W   T   W   T    TVAR=CATEGORY+' '+SUBSTR(MINV,1,11)+MFIG
W   T   W   ENDIF MCLINE
W   T   ENDDO
W   T   SELE 1
W   T   ? TVAR+'               ============ '
W   T   ? '                         Purchase Order Totals -->> '+STR(TQTYS,;
W   T   6,0)+STR(TSEL,6,0)+'                                                ';
W   T   + ' '+STR(AVAILTOSEL-TSEL,6,0)+'    '+STR(AVAILTOSEL,6,0)+;
W   T   STR(TARGET,9,0)
W   T   TVAR=SPACE(39)
W   T   MCLINE=MCLINE+2
W   T   IF MCLINE>45
W   T   T   MCLINE=0
W   T   T   MPAGE=MPAGE+1
W   T   T   ?;
W   T   T   '=========================================================';
W   T   T   + '=======================================================';
W   T   T   + '================'
W   T   T   ?'                                                   Page';
W   T   T   + ' Number  '+STR(MPAGE,5,0)
W   T   T   ?;
W   T   T   '=========================================================';
W   T   T   + '=======================================================';
W   T   T   + '================'
W   T   T   ? CHR(12)
W   T   T   ? SPACE((140-LEN(HD))/2)+HD
W   T   T   ?
W   T   T   ?'                                                 ';
W   T   T   + ' Sales Daily Inventory Status Report'
W   T   T   ?
W   T   T   ?DTOC(DATE())+'                                             ';
W   T   T   + '                                                         ';
W   T   T   + '                 '+TIME()
W   T   T   ?;
W   T   T   '=========================================================';
```

```
101 W   T   T    + '============================================================';
101 W   T   T    + '================'
102 W   T   T    ?'Ca Inventory Figure Number               Qnty  Qnty  Qnty ';
102 W   T   T    + ' Qnty   Purch  Qnty   ETA   Total              ';
102 W   T   T    + ' Quantity    Qnty    Target'
103 W   T   T    ?'                                          on     on        ';
103 W   T   T    + ' Avail  Order   on         On                   on';
103 W   T   T    + ' Hand    Avail  '
104 W   T   T    ?'                                         Hand  Order Sold';
104 W   T   T    + ' To Sell        Order        Order              ';
104 W   T   T    + ' Available  To Sell '
105 W   T   T    ?;
105 W   T   T    '=============================================================';
105 W   T   T    + '============================================================';
105 W   T   T    + '================'
106 W   T   T    TVAR=CATEGORY+' '+SUBSTR(MINV,1,11)+MFIG
107 W   T    ENDIF MCLINE
108 W    ENDIF QTY>0
109 W    SKIP
110 ENDDO
111 ??;
111 '============================================================================';
111 + '================================================================'
112 ?'                                                    Page Number  '+;
112 STR(MPAGE,5,0)
113 ?;
113 '============================================================================';
113 + '================================================================'
114 ? CHR(12)
115 SELECT 4
116 USE PURORDER INDEX POR,PINV
117 SELECT 1
118 USE INVENTORY INDEX INV,CA
119 RETURN
              ++ End of program ++  dFLOW found   0 errors.


         VARIABLES: LOCAL CONCORDANCE FOR ABCRPT

Variable    Line number in listing
--------    ----------------------
AVAILTOSEL:   43   47   56   60   86
CATEGORY:     47   81  106
ETA:          56
```

```
FACTORDNO:    56
FIGURENUMB:   47  52
HD:           29  30  71  96
INVENUMBER:   24  47  51  55
MCLINE:       26  44  49  62  64  65  88  89  90
MFIG:         52  81 106
MINV:         51  54  55  81 106
ML2:          29
MORD:         50  58  61
MPAGE:        27  66  68  91  93 112
QTYONHAND:    43  47
QTYONORDER:   43  47
QTYORDERED:   56  58
QTYSOLD:      43  47  56  59
TARGET:       86
TQTYS:        41  59  86
ETA:          56
FACTORDNO:    56
FIGURENUMB:   47  52
HD:           29  30  71  96
INVENUMBER:   24  47  51  55
MCLINE:       26  44  49  62  64  65  88  89  90
MFIG:         52  81 106
MINV:         51  54  55  81 106
ML2:          29
MORD:         50  58  61
MPAGE:        27  66  68  91  93 112
QTYONHAND:    43  47
QTYONORDER:   43  47
QTYORDERED:   56  58
QTYSOLD:      43  47  56  59
TARGET:       86
TQTYS:        41  59  86
TSEL:         42  60  86
TVAR:         28  48  56  57  81  85  87 106
TSEL:         42  60  86
TVAR:         28  48  56  57  81  85  87 106
-------------------------------------------------------------------------------
                VARIABLES: GLOBAL CONCORDANCE

Variable occurs in Modules
--------           -------
AVAILTOSEL         ABCRPT
CATEGORY           ABCRPT
```

```
ETA                 ABCRPT
FACTORDNO           ABCRPT
FIGURENUMB          ABCRPT
HD                  ABCRPT
INVENUMBER          ABCRPT
MCLINE              ABCRPT
MFIG                ABCRPT
MINV                ABCRPT
ML2                 ABCRPT
MORD                ABCRPT
MPAGE               ABCRPT
QTYONHAND           ABCRPT
QTYONORDER          ABCRPT
QTYORDERED          ABCRPT
QTYSOLD             ABCRPT
INVENUMBER          ABCRPT
MCLINE              ABCRPT
MFIG                ABCRPT
MINV                ABCRPT
ML2                 ABCRPT
MORD                ABCRPT
MPAGE               ABCRPT
QTYONHAND           ABCRPT
QTYONORDER          ABCRPT
QTYORDERED          ABCRPT
QTYSOLD             ABCRPT
TARGET              ABCRPT
TQTYS               ABCRPT
TSEL                ABCRPT
TVAR                ABCRPT

Recursion check: No recursions
```

These programs were written, as has already been mentioned, in the dBASE III PLUS procedural language. Personal Editor 2 was linked into dBASE by setting up the field TEDIT = PE2 in the file CONFIG.DB. In this development environment, the split screen and block-move capabilities of PE2 really prove to be valuable. Using windowing, it is possible to lift entire blocks of working code from one module to another, then customize the target module. For example, once the INVADD program was written to add items to the inventory database, it was easy to move most of the code to the PORADD module, which adds data to the purchase order database. This cuts development time and increases efficiency. A good editor is not only recommended, but is essential in large development projects such as this one.

The code was executed in the interpreted mode, edited, re-executed and so on until it was, supposedly, ready to compile. Before the compilation, however, the code was once again run through the dFlow system, to do an error checking test of all of the modules. dFlow found a number of small errors, like unclosed DO WHILEs and IF-THENs, as well as a few syntax and typing errors. It even warned that a LOOP command after a RETURN or CANCEL would never be executed. While this is technically an error, we still chose to use good structured programming techniques and leave each LOOP closed.

After another round of testing the code under the interpreter, re-editing, and re-testing, the code was run through dFlow for one final check. This time dFlow returned a clean slate, which meant that the code was almost ready to compile.

Note that there are some differences between the available functions in Clipper and dBASE. When we write code we initialize a PUBLIC variable called CLIPPER, which is set false in dBASE and true if running compiled code. Using this as the basis of a logical test, you can write code that will run under the dBASE interpreter and then run in a slightly different manner under Clipper. This becomes important is in the use of User Defined Functions (UDFs). These are modules written in C or assembly language, separately compiled or assembled, and declared in Clipper syntax as EXTERNALs. For example, a UDF called ISPRINTER( ) exists in an extended library called EXTENDA.OBJ. Note that these are actual programs written by Tom Rettig and supplied with Clipper. This function tests to see if the printer is on-line, to prevent going to a print function and getting the dreaded "printer not ready; Abort,Retry,Ignore" DOS message. Because the function ISPRINTER( ) is not in dBASE the following "trick," shown in Fig. 12-15, is required. In the dBASE mode this test will not be executed; the code will just go to the printer and, hopefully, the user has indeed set it up. In the Clipper mode, the loop asking for the user to set up the printer will execute until the printer is ready and ISPRINTER( ) returns "true."

Because we make extensive use of UDFs which cannot be tested under the dBASE interpreter, we wrote a few small code fragments, compiled and tested them, and then included them in the main program body. The Clipper compiler will run through the dBASE code and call each program it finds. If the code is not on the directory in its .PRG form, Clipper assumes it to be external, and expects that an .OBJ version will be included at linking time.

Fig. 12-15. Multi-environment code fragment.

```
PUBLIC CLIPPER
IF CLIPPER
     EXTERNAL ISPRINTER()
ENDIF
*
*        OTHER CODE
*
* TEST IF PRINTER IS READY
IF CLIPPER
     DO WHILE .NOT. ISPRINTER()
       @10,10 SAY "PLEASE SET UP PRINTER, THEN PRESS RETURN"
       WAIT
     ENDDO
ELSE
       @10,10 SAY "WAIT"
ENDIF
PRINT ROUTINE
```

Thus, the libraries containing the UDFs, and any other modules to link, must be included in the link statement.

For example, we often use our own Pro Search Window (PSRCH) program in client applications. This program opens a window on the screen that allows the user to scan up and down through a database using a key fragment to initiate a search. Because the program has been separately developed, programmed, debugged and compiled, it merely needs to be LINKed with the client application. Thus, we might have a link command (using the PLINK86 linker supplied with Clipper) of:

PLINK86 FI MENU FI PSRCH FI EXTENDA .

FI means file, MENU is the object file produced by Clipper for ABC's application, PSRCH is the Pro Search Window object file, and EXTENDA is the name of the Clipper extended library that contains the UDF ISPRINTER( ).

After the compile generates an executable module, the pre-Alpha test phase can begin. Going to the first option of the main menu, each choice was exercised. Each time a noncritical bug (one that did not cause a crash) was found, it was recorded using a screen print. Critical errors, that cause crashes, sent us back to the source code, to fix the fatal errors as well as eradicate the nonfatal ones from the printed screen pile. This process has a number of cyclic iterations, but eventually we got through the program without any errors. All of the reports were printed at this time, to make sure that the columns were lined up and that the logical and arithmetical functions were working.

Because the early phase of program development occurred at ABC's office on their Open Systems Report Writer, the data files that were used for testing were, in fact, real data. This guaranteed that the system would not produce any surprises when it was installed.

The Clipper compiler allows the developer to build context-specific on-line help by using the F1 key and a number of parameters. Therefore, pre-Alpha testing included a procedure that checked the help screens at every level in the code. The help screen invoked by pressing the F1 function key from the main system menu is shown in Fig. 12-16.

Next, the code was ready for Alpha testing. The program was given to the person who would conduct the test. The programmer helped install it, explained it somewhat, demonstrated how to get help, and left.

The main purpose of the Alpha test is to catch syntax errors,

Fig. 12-16. Sample on-line help screen.

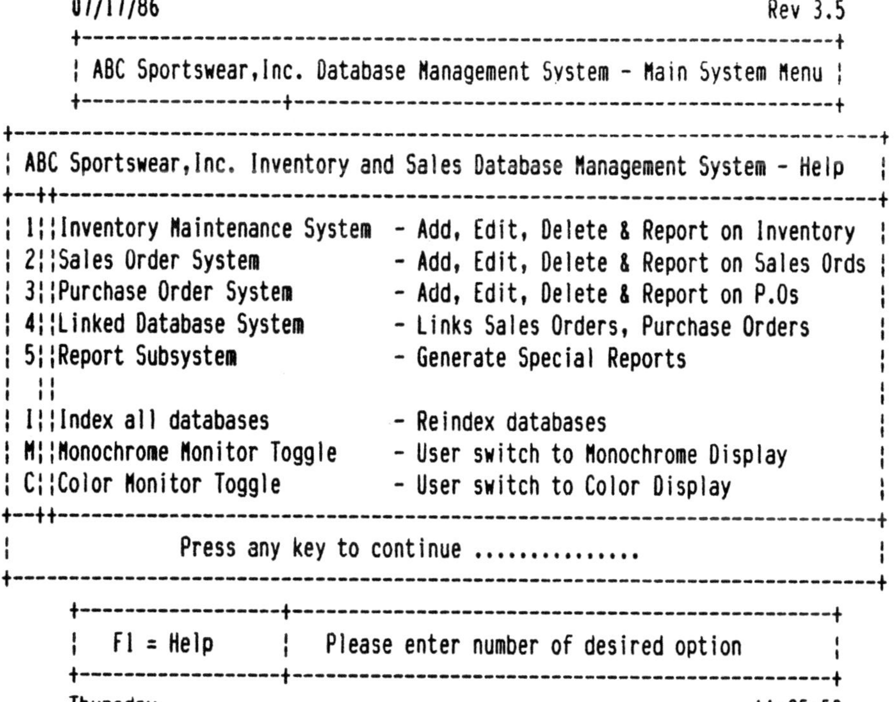

```
     07/17/86                                                      Rev 3.5
     +-----------------------------------------------------------------+
     | ABC Sportswear,Inc. Database Management System - Main System Menu |
     +----------------+------------------------------------------------+
+------------------------------------------------------------------------+
| ABC Sportswear,Inc. Inventory and Sales Database Management System - Help  |
+--++--------------------------------------------------------------------+
| 1||Inventory Maintenance System  - Add, Edit, Delete & Report on Inventory  |
| 2||Sales Order System            - Add, Edit, Delete & Report on Sales Ords |
| 3||Purchase Order System         - Add, Edit, Delete & Report on P.Os       |
| 4||Linked Database System        - Links Sales Orders, Purchase Orders      |
| 5||Report Subsystem              - Generate Special Reports                 |
|  ||                                                                       |
| I||Index all databases           - Reindex databases                        |
| M||Monochrome Monitor Toggle     - User switch to Monochrome Display        |
| C||Color Monitor Toggle          - User switch to Color Display             |
+--++--------------------------------------------------------------------+
|              Press any key to continue ..............                   |
+------------------------------------------------------------------------+
     +----------------+------------------------------------------------+
     |   F1 = Help    |  Please enter number of desired option         |
     +----------------+------------------------------------------------+
     Thursday                                                     11:25:59
```

spelling errors and other cosmetic flaws, and to test "data entry flow." This term refers to the way in which the data entry fields are arranged during user interface. The cursor should flow naturally, either across a line or down a column of data. It should not jump around in an arbitrary fashion. The order should also make sense logically, so that the user can operate the system relying on common sense. The person writing the code is never as brutal or crafty as the Alpha tester should be. The code was returned to us, and after several more hours spent repairing problems from the first Alpha test, and then testing the repairs, the code was sent back to Alpha testing. This time it passed, and was ready to be Beta tested on the ABC's system.

INSTALLATION AND INTEGRATION

The proposal to ABC included a number of choices concerning the source and costs of the various hardware components of the system. We left it up to them to make the final purchasing decisions. They chose several vendors, basing their decision completely on cost. During the time spent developing ABC's application, ABC purchased the remaining hardware and software required for a multi-user LAN system. Based on price, they decided to purchase two IBM PC clones with one floppy drive, 640K RAM and monochrome displays for each workstation. They also bought a 30 megabyte half-height hard disk drive to put in one of the clones. These items were bought from a "cash and carry" discount house, and consequently were sold with no installation or support beyond the manufacturers' warrantees. Thus, ABC expected us to configure and install these machines, an option which we offered to them in our original proposal, quoting an hourly billable rate.

For the LAN itself, ABC took a more traditional approach. They chose a vendor that specialized in Open Systems on 3Com LANs. They arranged to purchase the LAN hardware, Open Systems upgrade, installation, and LAN training from this vendor. Our firm was to act only as an overseer in this part of the installation, still billing at an hourly rate. When all of the hardware and accounting software was up and running, we were to complete our installation of the custom application, after which the final acceptance test on the final hardware configuration would be executed.

Although this multi-source, multi-vendor arrangement might sound straightforward, Murphy's Law guarantees complexities will develop. They did. When the clones were unpacked, it was discovered that 640K RAM meant 256K RAM installed and the rest in antistatic tubes. The clone documentation was terrible, and nearly four hours were spent inserting chips, setting switches, and discovering one dead keyboard. When the hard drive was installed in Clone "A," there was a low-level format error requiring several phone calls to the dealer. After the low-level format procedure, a high-level DOS format was performed.

To complete the testing of the newly configured equipment, several software packages were installed on the drive, and the system was turned over to Sue with instructions to exercise it. We gave her our "infant mortality" speech, and then went away for what we thought was going to be two or three days.

In keeping with their agreement, ABC told the LAN vendor that we had completed the configuration of the hardware and that the system was now ready for the LAN install. During the period between the proposal and this call, the vendor had sold its inventory of LAN interface cards. They also mentioned that there was a temporary back-order, causing a delay of three to four weeks. This threw the entire schedule off, because we had intended to implement and test the database application on the LAN, which was to be the final system configuration.

Charles and Sue met with us to discuss a "Plan B." We suggested that, while waiting for the LAN to be delivered, we could bring our new application up on the IBM AT, giving us the opportunity to "shake out the bugs," train the users, and refine the reports. When the LAN was completely up and running, we would move our application from the AT fixed disk to the fixed disk in the computer that would reside on Sue's desk, and implement security so that the files could only be available at her workstation under password control. Although this would require two complete installs of our application software, we decided not to bill for the additional time. There are times when business interests are best served by not charging for services, and this was one of them. We were thus able to turn the negative of unexpected delay into the positive of free additional testing. Arrangements were made for the application software to be installed the next Monday morning.

The actual installation of the software was fairly straightforward. The application files were copied onto the hard disk from floppy disks that had been prepared and tested at our facility. As a precaution, two complete copies of these diskettes were brought to the user site to ensure that no "gremlins" have popped into a sector. Experience teaches that Murphy's Law creeps in and messes up your only copy of the "must have" files. Better safe than sorry.

After a successful copy process, the application was installed on the Fixed Disk Organizer menu, with options to run the application and to back up critical data files to diskettes. Once the LAN was on-line, an option was also added to back up these files over the network to a subdirectory on the AT fixed disk. Sue and her accounting clerks were then given an initial orientation on the new system.

Each task was explained in detail to the group. We demonstrated "exporting" data to the interim file format, showing them how to execute reports to the named files using the Open Systems Report Writer. This process took several hours, during which scheduling issues and operational procedures were discussed. We went through the process keystroke-by-keystroke, stopping at each step to answer each question, and to explain what was about to happen. In the final integrated system, Borland's Superkey program was used to record all of the keystrokes for all of the export processes so that they could be executed by pressing ALT-F10. The process could then be initiated at day's end and be complete before morning, causing little operational impact to the company. Special care was taken to make the clerks aware that there were certain accounting processes, such as posting, that needed to be done in a very specific order to guarantee that the exported data was correct and up-to-date. As a group, we created a checklist for these procedures. The clerks had to initial each step, including the time and date, to make sure that all accounting tasks had been done before pressing ALT-F10. During this orientation and training session, a number of general questions about the operation of the computer, backing up, and formatting floppies were covered. The group was informed that the LAN was coming, and that they would have more training to help them deal with that system when it went on-line.

With the accounting group trained in the data exporting process, it was now time to meet with the employees who would be responsible for running the custom application. This phase of the installation was part of what we call the acceptance test, which is really a Beta test. Starting with the main system menu, the users were guided menu-option-by-menu-option through the system. One of the key issues was the import process, in which the interim files produced by the Open Systems Report Writer were brought into the database format required by the application. A major component of the test was that the form and content of the reports met with Charles' and Sue's approval. These reports were the reason for the development itself, so they needed to be perfect. Along the way, the users were trained to FIND, EDIT, DELETE, and otherwise manipulate the data in the system. Some time was spent demonstrating how to invoke help and explaining each help item.

During these sessions several observations were made, some of which were classified as current changes required by the project definition and others that were considered items for the "wish list." Sue felt that the data entry flow on one of the screens was not in the correct order. The program was filling in some information horizontally, and Sue wanted it to move vertically. Because this was merely a cosmetic variation in a gray definition area, we agreed to make this alteration as a part of the current project. Sue also asked if the main system report could have some additional data information. This was a change of a specific feature of the report, so it was agreed that it be considered a future task.

With the ABC people watching, the import procedure was activated, showing that the data had, indeed, arrived in the application. They were also shown the Search Window operation to find various items in the database, and how to run the reports. We then sat back and let Sue and her people run the system while we watched, making notes on any problems that arose. By the end of the day, they could run both the export process and the new database system. We explained that the users needed to make notes of any problems (we never say "bug" or "anomaly" to our clients) so that they could be reproduced and repaired. Over the next few days, three operational problems arose, which were corrected and installed by Friday of that week.

During this time the wish list was growing. The next Friday, we returned to ABC, and presented Charles with a new Task Order for 20 hours to accomplish the additional items requested. Charles signed an acceptance form for the custom application software, at which point payment was made for the second half of the first task, as well as the first half of the new task. Our client had a working system, we had more work, and we had been paid. The only untied end was in the hands of the systems house that was to bring up the LAN and the multi-user module implementation of the accounting software. Because this was not our direct responsibility, we were not involved in the heat that ABC was generating due to the delays, which stretched from the promised three weeks to well over six weeks. Our only involvement in this was to oversee the eventual LAN installation and move our system on to the second fixed disk.

By the time the LAN was ready to be installed, the second task was completed and arrangements were made to have the user acceptance test done on the AT before the network was installed. This task simply added a number of reporting options, so testing was limited to determining if the reports worked. They did. During the three weeks that passed in the interim, a number of other changes were requested, including the ability to communicate with the warehouses to send certain reports by modem each night. We suggested that these developments be delayed until the systems house had finished its work, so there would be a fully operational multi-user accounting system on the LAN. Charles and Sue agreed, and we became ABC's consulting "overseers" during the LAN install.

The systems house, XYZ Corporation, brought a set of 3Com Network Interface cards, the network software (also from 3Com), the Business BASIC software that allows the Open Systems Accounting System to run in a multi-user mode (from 3-10 users), and the necessary cables to connect the computers together. They arrived at about 9:00 in the morning and announced that the entire 20 megabyte hard disk on the AT would need to be reformatted as part of the network install. This meant that all of the programs and data on the disk needed to be backed up to floppy disks, and then reinstalled later. This is a tedious procedure in the case of the copy protected software, like Lotus 1-2-3, dBASE III, Open Systems and some of the utility packages. XYZ said that they would not do the backup or the restore, because it was not part of their normal installation charge. Although they had been informed that they were installing a LAN onto an existing system, they claimed that it was ABC's responsibility to do this backup and restore and make the disk available for their technician to format. This is the dreaded finger-pointing that we warned about in the case of multi-source, multi-vendor deals.

Because we were there, and billing for "overseeing," we decided to propose that we do the backup, including the "de-installing" of the copy protected software. XYZ's technician could set up the hard disk so that 3Com's software would treat it as a network file server, and then we would re-install the software programs and data files. Because this process would take several hours, so the installer was directed to begin work on the two clones first. Each one had to be opened up, the network interface card installed, and then closed up again. Also, cable needed to be strung up into the ceiling, then dropped down inside the drywall so that it could be pulled out and mounted on a faceplate using a standard BNC-type connector. This job took more than enough time to allow us to back up the AT drive. The entire process was very disruptive to the client, which is why it is suggested that such work be done very early or after business hours. By the time the cards were installed in each clone, and the wiring for the LAN was complete, with its continuity tested, it was "quitting time" for the XYZ technician. The AT drive had been backed up and formatted, blocking ABC from its normal accounting practices for one complete day, and now they were being told that they would not be able to run their reports that evening!

In their proposal, XYZ had represented that their install would be completed in one business day. This had not been true, but there was little either we or our client could do about it except complain to XYZ, which we did. It didn't help. We comforted our clients, told them that things like this sometime happen, and everyone went home.

The next day went well. By 11:00 in the morning the XYZ technician announced that the LAN was up and running. The technician partitioned the AT hard disk so that the Open Systems Accounting resided on a "logical" drive designated as "drive D:" to DOS, while Lotus 1-2-3 was to run in a partition called "drive E:," with WordStar and other utilities on "drive F:." As we had instructed, the hard disk drive on the clone that was placed on Sue's desk would be the home of the custom application, and this drive was not made a network resource.

Only Sue would have access to programs and data on this drive which her system saw as a real, fixed disk "drive C:." The network software allowed her to mount applications like accounting or word processing on "logical" drives D: through F:. Once mounted, she could use simple DOS COPY commands to move files to and from her hard disk. The custom application installed on her drive was told to look for the interim data files from Open Systems and Drive D:. Thus, it was possible for her to run exported data from any machine on the network. The Open Systems software was available to her in a "shared" multi-user mode. In fact, in order to save time, she could do three different "exports" at once, using the three available PCs. In keeping with the design, however, the only machine allowed to import the data was her own. It was only on her workstation that anyone could have access to the database application, or generate any of its reports.

The various user security levels were protected by menu passwords from the Fixed Disk Organizer package, as well as network passwords. Thus, each workstation had a completely "personalized" menu, giving its user specific access rights and capabilities. It took much of the second day to complete this software reinstallation and system integration. By 2:00 in the afternoon, the accounting people were allowed back on the AT, at which time they entered the backlog of work that had developed.

The XYZ technician spent the rest of the day setting up the print-spooling software and a few networking niceties. By the end of the second day, the technician was finished and gone.

As part of XYZ's task, they had agreed to train the users on how to work in a multi-user mode with the accounting software on the LAN. This training began on the next day and ran for two days. The trainer was very good, and, because ABC had been using the software for some time, there were few problems in the upgrade itself. One of the major operational changes when a company installs a LAN is that they must designate a responsible person to act as the network manager. This is an important job, including keeping track of passwords, backups, system maintenance, and so on. This is often the point at which some poor soul has to act as a data processing department manager as well as do another job. The XYZ trainer spent a good amount of time describing the duties and responsibilities of this system manager, and ABC decided that Sue would be the one.

ABC was given the names and telephone numbers of the XYZ support people who would be available to answer any questions that came up about the accounting software, or the LAN itself. After the LAN training had ended, there was one more session to show Sue how to run the system from her menu on her workstation. The goals were finally met. The client had the system that we had designed and contracted to deliver.

SUPPORT AND MAINTENANCE

Once the system was completely operational, we spent some time helping ABC choose a service company that would support the hardware after the initial 30 or 90 day warrantees had expired. In keeping with our philosophy, we suggested one of the national chains, although several less-expensive local organizations were discussed. Charles was convinced that it would be false economy to go with an independent, which might not be able to offer the quality of service or the availability of spare or replacement parts that could be offered by the nationally-affiliated organization. We helped him negotiate a fairly standard service contract which provided four-hour response time, on-site repairs, and a field replacement policy that would, hopefully, guarantee minimum down time for ABC.

XYZ offered a software support agreement with a fixed number of telephone support hours at a fixed yearly price, and a rate schedule for hours above that limit. Their support package was $600 per year with up to 15 hours of support, with additional hours billed at $60 per hour. This included questions concerning the accounting and the LAN software, and was actually quite reasonable. For a comparison, another vendor was contacted. Their plan for "non-contract" support was $2.95 per minute for the first five minutes, with each additional minute billed at $3.50. There was also a minimum charge of $15.00 per call. A yearly contract with unlimited phone support was $300 per module, which in the case of ABC's system would have been $2100 per year.

Our suggestion to Charles was that he not sign a software service contract. The accounting software was available at a noncontract rate which, although high, might not need to be used too often, and the LAN support could be handled by XYZ on an hourly service method. There was, therefore, little perceived value in long-term maintenance agreements. We were also fairly confident that the accounting people at ABC were well trained in the software, because they had been using it for a while before the LAN arrived. Any LAN-related changes could be easily handled by XYZ, and we could act as backup problem solvers.

SUBSEQUENT TASKS

As was mentioned earlier, the system was well received, operated as promised, and showed Charles, Sue, and the employees at ABC that computers could help them become more productive.

ABC eventually purchased PC clones, printers, Hayes-compatible modems, and Transporter, a file-transfer software system from Microstuff, to set up remote report print-stations at each of the warehouses. Transporter allows for unattended file transfers over dial modems. Each warehouse has a 10 megabyte hard disk, and is set up to run Transporter in the "receive" mode each night. At ABC's main office, Transporter is set up to dial each warehouse, send the file images of the desired reports, and hang up. In the morning, at the warehouse, a user selects a menu item that activates a batch file, to spool all of the recently received text files to the print spooler supplied with DOS.

We now hear from ABC occasionally. Sometimes there are questions, sometimes requests for new tasks. They consider us a technical resource, and have been very helpful in referring us to their friends and colleagues.

This case study has shown how it is possible for an applications developer/consultant to perform a wide range of services for a client. These processes rarely run as planned, and we have endeavored to show that the consultant must be flexible and act in the best interest of the client. Clear task definitions help minimize confusion and potential misunderstanding, and help move the project along to a successful conclusion. Although each case is, by definition, unique, we hope that the features included in this one give a global overview of our general approach, and help coalesce the concepts in our book into a working philosophy.

Chapter 13

The View From Here

The microcomputer industry is now in its second decade. Few can argue that the influence of these electronic marvels will continue to grow, until they permeate every aspect of life. In this chapter, we would like to enjoy the luxury of conjecture, and propose our opinions on the fate of the industry in the next few years.

THE DISTINCTIONS BLUR

In the very near future, it will become very difficult to define the difference between microcomputers and minicomputers. The current labels trace their roots to the days when the number of bits a processor could handle at one time defined its "species." Thus, microcomputers are defined as eight-bit to 16-bit processors, built using Very Large Scale Integration (VLSI) microchip technologies, and oriented toward single-user tasks. Minicomputers are larger devices, capable of handling 32-bit and words, and designed with small, multi-user, multi-tasking operating systems. Mainframes handle even larger words (64-bit and more), have very large memories, can allow simultaneous access to a large number of users running many different tasks, and do it all at very high speeds. Using this definition, the IBM PC is a classic microcomputer, and PC-DOS is the very epitome of a single-user, single-task operating system.

The IBM PC/AT and it clones, however, are the first of a new generation of microcomputers that begin to blur the distinction between microcomputers and minicomputers. The microprocessor chip around which these machines are designed, the Intel 80286, can, in fact, handle 32-bit operations, address large memories, and support multi-user, multi-tasking operating systems. The current versions of DOS, designed to run on both the older 8088s and these new chips, by severely underutilizes the power of the 80286. Microsoft will soon release a new version of DOS, reputed to be called DOS 5.0, which will finally unleash the capabilities of the 80286, but will, therefore, not run on the 8088-based machines.

This will produce the second major schism in the microcomputer market; the first occurred when the 16-bit PC-DOS world grew from the previously homogeneous eight-bit CP/M market. Now we will see a 32-bit universe develop, with its own versions of application software and attendant peripherals. This does not mean that the approximately five million 8088 machines will disappear, just that there will be two distinct markets in the future. Application developers should pay special attention to this issue, because they will need a separate set of hardware and software tools to address the needs of both markets at the same time. We hope, and expect, that the major software companies will offer versions of their products that run in both environments, with enough similarities to minimize the need for programmers and developers to learn entirely new systems. Thus, dBASE IV (if that is what it will be called) will hopefully just be a bigger, faster version of dBASE III PLUS, with the multi-user, multi-tasking features of the new DOS operating environments merged in as native features.

This new machine environment will soon have its own successor to deal with—the Intel 80386. The term used to describe the power of this chip is "supermicro," because it will outperform a majority of minicomputers in the marketplace today. Supermicros will open a myriad of new vertical markets to developers, due to this raw power. Graphics applications on these new microchips will rival the quality of dedicated CAD/CAM systems. New high-resolution graphics cards are being released to use this power. The IBM high-resolution standard, defined by its Enhanced Graphics Adapter (EGA), has already been cloned massively, resulting in lower prices and more applications software for the new cards. This is the economic cycle that we discussed in Chapter One. Dozens of clones of the AT exist, and offer significant price/performance benefits to the end-user. IBM's market penetration in the AT market has been much lower than its performance in the PC market several years ago, primarily due to this fact.

Targeting the ultra high-resolution graphics market, IBM has developed a Professional Graphics Adapter (PGA), which is destined to become a standard in that area. Using 80286, 80386, or other superchips, graphics applications that once required extremely expensive dedicated workstations will be done on microcomputers. These powerful graphics workstations will be coupled with even higher resolution, full-color laser printers, to offer desktop publishing a quality rivalling the best processes available today, at a fraction of the cost. Architecture, advertising, construction, and design will all be areas begging for application development expertise.

High-power graphics should also finally result in an icon-based operating environment as a defacto user interface standard. Many people believe that the winner in this area will be Microsoft's Windows, and we must agree. These icon-based operating systems will make powerful computers more accessible to more users by making them easier to use.

Another area in which more powerful processors will be of great value is in the LAN systems market. Supermicros are ideally suited to act as network file servers, communication servers, and print servers. Their speed, memory addressability, and multi-tasking design will allow for the construction of larger, faster, and more efficient networks. These networks will often make use of the older PCs as workstations, thus extending the useful life of these machines well into the next decade. Using a 640K PC as an intelligent workstation, with access to a large fixed disk and other network resources, will still make more economic sense than giving each node in the LAN its own supermicrocomputer. Many word processing, database, and spreadsheet applications do not require the power of the more advanced machines, and their use in such situations would be economic and technical overkill.

The direction, in the area of magnetic media, has been to push the information density to nearly molecular limits. In a fixed disk that held 10 megabytes just a few years ago, it is not unusual to see 40, 60, 80, and even 100 megabyte capacities today. Manufacturers have begun, using the new 3 1/2 inch hard disks, to provide peripheral cards holding the drive and all of its electronics. Such devices exist today in 10, 20, and 30 megabyte sizes. The maximum density for magnetic media has yet to be defined, but its limit is coming.

Users seem to need more and more on-line storage. In the case of LANs, it is not unusual to see massive disks, such as the 300 megabyte Data Tower from Priam, linked to an AT-type machine which is acting as the network file server. Because many networks are, or will soon be, capable of supporting multiple file servers we expect to see multi-user PC-based networks with gigabytes (billions) of magnetic storage. These systems will be difficult to distinguish from mainframe multi-user systems, and will probably be able to outperform many such mainframes.

THE OPTICAL REVOLUTION

The hunger for storage and access speeds has already driven the research and development groups of several major corporations investige entirely new technologies. One very promising area is optical disk technology. For several years, video equipment capable of playing a digitized laser-encoded disk has been available. The amount of data that could be recorded using this technology is in the multi-gigabyte range per disk. Recently, compact versions of these laser disks have become quite popular in the high-fidelity stereo market. Several groups in the computer industry are seeking to incorporate these new technologies into storage systems.

Laser Disk Technologies

The main problem with the current technology is that the information is burned into a laser disk-hole by-hole, corresponding to each bit of binary data. Once a hole is burned, it cannot be "unburned" or erased. The technology is thus known as Write Once Read Many (WORM). This is not necessarily bad.

Microsoft is attempting to establish a set of standards for a class of products known as CD which use the same technology as stereo compact disks (CDs). Onto these disks could be placed entire encyclopedias, huge databases, or any large reference libraries that you could imagine. These disks could be manufactured, or published, like a music CD, thus keeping the cost down. CD ROM readers already exist, with DOS device drivers that allow users to access the data on these CD ROMs directly into their applications. With over five gigabytes to a disk, the possibilities are endless. There should be considerable activity in this area over the next few years, as the reader standard develops and more media becomes available. Perhaps dBASE IV will need to be able to address files as big as five gigabytes? We would bet on it.

Although CD ROMs hold great promise for Read Only applications, the read-write problem must be addressed before optical technology can be considered a serious contender to magnetic methods. Currently several very clever methods are being proposed. One of the most interesting approach involves mimicking the read-write functionality using software device drivers.

This method uses a WORM system, with software that modifies the disk directory. Each time you update a file, you make a new copy of the data on an unused section of the optical disk. The old file can be marked as archival, producing instantly available on-line backup automatically, or it can be "erased," by having holes burned everywhere. This is plausible because there is so much storage: five to 10 gigabytes on a 5 1/4 inch form factor, or up to 30 gigabytes on a disk the size of the home-video laser disks.

A user would merely use a disk until it is full, then move all of the most recent, active data onto a new disk, placing the old disk in a holder as archival storage. The disks themselves are fairly impervious to harm and should last for years, which cannot be said about floppy disks or tape. Unless some major breakthrough in read-write optical technology occurs in the near future, this method will become the industry standard.

Fiber Optics for Data Transmission

Another major area in which optics will play an important part will be data transmission. Fiber optic cables are currently being used to replace copper in many long-distance voice and data communication systems. Although the cable itself is more expensive than its copper counterpart, there is a pressing reason for its adoption—it is not effected by electromagnetic interference, or noise, the way copper is.

The defense industry and the military, particularly, are interested in this attribute, because they discovered that a high-altitude thermonuclear explosion would cause an electromagnetic pulse (EMP) which would knock out electronics and interfere with communications over thousands of miles. Fiber optics would not be swamped by the noise produced by the EMP. Thus, assuming that the electronics themselves could be "hardened," our country would be able to communicate during the first few hours of a thermonuclear war. There is even a hardening standard for computers and other electronic devices, called "Tempest."

We mention this interest on the part of the defense establishment to support our belief that considerable research and development into fiber optic communication and optical electronic devices will exist. We also believe that this funding will lead to rapid development of this technology.

The major non-defense related benefit will be that fiber optic systems will allow ultra high-speed data communication with very low error rates. There are current laboratory-based fiber optic Token Passing rings that are said to operated at speeds of 400 megabits per second, roughly 40 times faster than copper based

LANs. Thus, we can look forward to the day when the processors themselves are slower than the communication system, removing the LAN bottleneck problem forever.

PRINTER TECHNOLOGY

Modern printer technology is mostly electromechanical in concept. The majority of computer printing devices in existence today are of the dot matrix or wholly formed character type, in which electromagnets drive hammers or wires into ribbons to produce documents. Although these devices are the current standard, their inherent limitations of resolution and duty cycle make it unlikely for them to remain the primary printing technologies.

The major contender for dominance in this area has already been invented—the laser printer. This device is basically a copy machine, in which the image of the original is electronically created from a bit-mapped graphic array. A laser printer can produce documents of near typeset quality at very high speeds. High resolution and excellent character quality make it the perfect choice for both graphics and character-oriented applications. The current desktop models are slow, producing only eight pages per minute. It is almost certain that the next few years will bring breakthroughs in price, speed, resolution, and duty cycles, to the point where they will become the standard for almost every user application.

The other major new printer technology is the ink-jet device. These printers are small, quiet, and fast. One unit, by Diconix, weighs just a few pounds and can run from batteries. Ink-jets of this type will probably take over the niche of portable computer applications. As the lap-top microcomputer market develops, ink-jets will be there.

PORTABLE MICROCOMPUTERS

Speaking of lap-tops, we believe that they will become as inexpensive and ubiquitous as calculators, and that the breakthrough product has not yet arrived. You will know when it does.

The recently announced IBM Convertible has not caused the market reaction that was expected. The Toshiba 1100, which is a low power CMOS version of the 8088, seems to be much closer to the type of machine that users would like to have as a portable. A lap-top should be small, light, able to run on batteries for about eight hours, and be completely compatible with the machine back at the office. Such devices will arrive within the next few years. By then, the 3 1/2 inch floppy disk standard should be far enough along to help with the machine's acceptance. Look for a great deal of competition in this market.

SOFTWARE

As the operating systems and machines become more powerful, we should see the development of microcomputer application packages that address the strengths of the new environments. The major differences will probably be in the areas of multi-user implementations.

Accounting, word processing, and database management systems will run on microcomputers much in the same way as they currently do on minicomputers and mainframes. LANs will eventually win out over time-sharing multi-user systems, because users will demand the type of performance possible by the intelligent workstation, not the dumb terminal. It is also to be expected that more transparent integration between applications and systems will develop, so that users will not be bothered with interapplication and intersystem maintenance tasks. A user will not know, or care, if a file that is being accessed is from the company mainframe in Dallas, or down the hall. Icon-oriented user interfaces will become standard, giving a wider class of end-users access to the corporate computing facilities.

We also expect that Artificial Intelligence will finally arrive, and that fourth generation languages will exist to help even non-sophisticated users develop complex applications. This might seem to be bad news for application developers, but we still see the need for computer professionals' broad levels of expertise in the area of problem definition, design, and execution.

CONCLUSION

The future for our industry looks bright. Ours is an enterprise forged from innovation and creativity. Programmers, consultants, and application developers will continue to create new uses for the technologies as they develop, and increase the demand for the invention of even greater wonders. Our function will be, as it has always been, to bridge the gap between technology and utility for the general population.

Appendix

Appendix

Vendor Information

This appendix contains the names, addresses and phone numbers of the vendors referenced in the main body of the book. In some cases the cited vendors manufacture many more products than those listed, but only those mentioned or discussed in the text are noted here. The manufacturers or their representatives may be contacted directly for more information.

3Com Corporation
1365 Shorebird Way, Box 7390
Mountain View, CA 94039
(415) 961-9602
Product(s) : *3Com+, ETHERSHARE, and ETHERPRINT.*

American Planning Corporation
4600 Duke St., Suite 423
Alexandria, VA 22304
(703) 751-2574
Product(s) : *MegaBASIC*

ANSA Software
1301 Shoreway Road
Belmont, CA 94002
(415) 595-4469
Product(s) : *Paradox*

Apple Computer, Inc.
20525 Mariani Ave.
Cupertino, CA 95014
(408) 996-1010
Product(s) : *Apple II and Macintosh*

Ashton-Tate
10150 W. Jefferson Blvd.
Culver City, CA 90230
(213) 204-5570
Product(s) : *dBASE II, dBASE III PLUS, and Multimate*

AST Research, Inc.
2121 Alton Ave.
Irvine, CA 92714
(714) 863-1333
Product(s) : *Six Pack PLUS*

ATARI
1196 Vorregas
Sunnyvale, CA 94086
(408) 745-2000
Product(s) : *Microcomputer Products*

AT&T Bell Labs
Crawford's Corner Road
Holmdel, NJ 07733
(201) 949-3000
Product(s) : *UNIX and C*

BASIS, Inc.
5700 Harper Drive N.E. #290
Albuquerque, NM 87109
(505) 821-4407
Product(s) : *Business BASIC Extended*

Bodner, Hutchins & Associates, Inc.
2300 Old Spanish Trail, # 2105
Houston, TX 77054
(713) 797-0007
Product(s) : *Pro Search Window*

Borland International, Inc.
4585 Scotts Valley Drive
Scotts Valley, CA 95066
(408) 438-8400
Product(s) : *Superkey, Turbo Pascal, and Sidekick*

BPI Systems, Inc.
3001 Bee Cave Road
Austin, TX 78746
(512) 328-5434
Product(s) : *Accounting Software*

BYTEL Corporation
1029D Solano Ave.
Berkeley, CA 94706
(800) 631-2229
Product(s) : *Genifer*

Computer Innovations, Inc.
980 Shrewsbury Ave.
Tinton Falls, NJ 07724
(201) 542-5920
Product(s) : *C86*

DAC Software, Inc.
5580 Peterson, Suite 13330
Dallas, TX 75240
(214) 458-0038
Product(s) : *DAC-Easy*

Data Access Corporation
8525 Southwest 129th Terrace
Miami, FL 33156
(305) 238-0012
Product(s) : *Dataflex*

Data Based Solutions, Inc.
1975 Fifth Ave., Suite 105
San Diego, CA 92101
(619) 236-1182
Product(s) : *Data Based Advisor*

Diconix, Inc.
3100 Research Blvd.
Dayton, OH 45420
(513) 259-3100
Product(s) : *Portable Ink-Jet Printer*

Digital Communications Associates, Inc.
1000 Alderman Drive
Alpharetta, GA 30201
(404) 442-4000
Product(s) : *IRMA*

Digital Research, Inc.
60 Garden Court
Monterey, CA 93942
(408) 649-3896
Product(s) : *CP/M*

EPSON America, Inc.
23600 Telo St.
Torrance, CA 90505
(213) 534-4500
Product(s) : *Dot Matrix Printers*

Fox &Geller, Inc.
604 Market St.
Elmwood Park, NJ 07407
(201) 794-8883
Product(s) : *Quickcode, Quickindex, and Quickreport*

Gimpel Software
3207 Hogarth Lane
Collegeville, PA 19426
(215) 584-4261
Product(s) : *C-Terp*

Greenleaf Software, Inc.
1411 Lemay Drive, Suite 101
Carrollton, TX 75006
(214) 446-8641
Product(s) : *C Libraries*

Ibis Research Labs, Inc.
2656 Bridgeway, Suite C
Sausalito, CA 94965
(415) 331-6451
Product(s) : *Colossus Software Modifications*

INTEL Corporation
3065 Bowers Ave.
Santa Clara, CA 95051
(408) 987-8080
Product(s) : *80×86 Microprocessor Chips*

International Business Machines Corporation
1133 Westchester Ave.
White Plains, NY 10604
(914) 765-1900
Product(s) : *IBM, IBM-PC/XT/AT, PC-DOS, BASICA, TOP-VIEW, IBM BASIC COMPILER, and DISPLAYWRITE*

Lattice, Inc.
22 W. 600 Butterfield Road
Glen Ellyn, IL 60137
(312) 858-7950
Product(s) : *Lattice C and SideTalk*

Lotus Development Corporation
55 Cambridge Parkway
Cambridge, MA 02142
(617) 577-8500
Product(s) : *Lotus 1-2-3*

Micro Data Base Systems, Inc.
P.O. Box 248
Laffayette, IN 47902
(317) 463-2581
Product(s) : *KnowledgeMan*

Micropro International Corporation
33 San Pablo Ave.
San Rafael, CA 94903
(415) 499-1200
Product(s) : *WordStar*

Microrim, Inc.
3380 146th Place
Bellevue, WA 98007
(206) 641-6619
Product(s) : *R:base 5000*

Microscience International, Inc.
575 E. Middlefield Road
Mountain View, CA 94043
(415) 961-2212
Product(s) : *Hard Disk Drives*

Microsoft Corporation
10700 Northrup Way
Bellevue, WA 98009
(800) 426-9400
Product(s) : *MS-DOS, Windows, MS-WORD, GWBASIC, QUICKBASIC, Microsoft C, and Multiplan*

Microstuff, Inc.
1000 Holcomb Woods Parkway
Roswell, GA 30076
(404) 998-3998
Product(s) : *CrossTalk and Transporter*

Morgan Computing Company, Inc.
2520 Tarpley Road, Suite 500
Carrollton, TX 75006
(214) 245-4763
Product(s) : *Professional BASIC*

Nantucket, Inc.
5995 S. Sepulveda Blvd., # 300
Culver City, CA 90230
(213) 390-7923
Product(s) : *Clipper*

North Edge Software Corporation
P.O. Box 286
Hamilton, MA 01936
(617) 468-7358
Product(s) : *Timeslips*

NOVELL, Inc.
1170 N. Industrial Park Drive
Orem, UT 84057
(801) 226-8202
Product(s) : *Netware and Advanced Netware*

OKIDATA
532 Fellowship Road
Mt. Laurel, NJ 08054
(609) 235-2600
Product(s) : *Dot Matrix Printers*

Open Systems, Inc.
6477 City West Parkway
Eden Prairie, MN 55344
(612) 829-0011
Product(s) : *Business BASIC and Open Systems*

Peter Norton Computing Company
2210 Wilshire Blvd.
Santa Monica, CA 90403
(213) 399-3948
Product(s) : *Norton Utilities*

Priam Corporation
20 W. Montague Expressway
San Jose, CA 95154
(408) 946-4600
Product(s) : *Datatower*

Radio Shack/Tandy Corporation
1800 One Tandy Center
Fort Worth, TX 76102
(817) 390-3921
Product(s) : *Microcomputer Products*

Realworld Corporation
Dover Road, Willow Hill Building
Chichester, NH 03623
(603) 798-5700
Product(s) : *M.B.S.I Accounting*

Softech, Inc.
16875 W. Bernardino Drive
San Diego, CA 92127
(619) 451-1230
Product(s) : *UCSD Pascal*

Software Garden, Inc.
P.O. Box 238
West Newton, MA 02165
(617) 332-2240
Product(s) : *Dan Bricklin's Demo Program*

Software Publishing Corporation
1901 Landings Drive
Mountain View, CA 94043
(415) 962-8910
Product(s) : *PFS:File and PFS:Write*

Software Solutions, Inc.
12 Cambridge Drive
Trumbull, CT 06611
(203) 374-8000
Product(s) : *DataEase*

Sorbus (A Bell Atlantic Company)
50 E. Swedesford Road
Frazer, PA 19355
(215) 296-6000
Product(s) : *Computer Service and Repairs*

Summit Software Technology, Inc.
40 Grove St.
Wellesley, MA 02181
(800) 225-5800
Product(s) : *Better BASIC*

Tecmar, Inc.
6225 Cochran Road
Solon, OH 44139
(216) 349-0600
Product(s) : *Microcomputer Peripheral Products*

Texas Instruments, Inc.
P.O. Box 225012
Dallas, TX 75265
(800) 527-3500
Product(s) : *Dot Matrix Printers*

The Software Bottling Company of NY, Inc.
6600 Long Island Expressway #308
Maspeth, NY 11378
(718) 458-3700
Product(s) : *Flash-Up and Flashcode*

Tiara Computer Systems, Inc.
2685 Marine Way
Mountain View, CA 94043
(415) 965-1700
Product(s) : *Tiara Multilink*

Toshiba America, Inc.
2441 Michelle Drive
Tustin, CA 92680
(714) 730-5000
Product(s) : *Lap-Top Microcomputers*

True BASIC, Inc.
39 S. Main St.
Hanover, NH 03755
(603) 643-3882
Product(s) : *True BASIC*

TRW
15 Law Drive
Fairfield, NJ 07006
(800) 257-7464
Product(s) : *Computer Service and Repairs*

Versasoft Corporation
723 Seawood Way
San Jose, CA 95120
(408) 268-6033
Product(s) : *DB-Man*

Wallsoft Systems, Inc.
233 Broadway, Suite 869
New York, NY 10279
(800) 233-3569
Product(s) : *dFlow*

Watcom Products, Inc.
415 Phillip St., Waterloo
Ontario, Canada, N2 L3X2
(519)886-3700
Product(s) : *Watcom BASIC*

Wordtech Systems, Inc.
P.O. Box 1747
Orinda, CA 94563
(415) 254-0900
Product(s) : *DBIII Compiler and DBXL*

Writing Consultants, a Division of Microlytics
Techniplex, 300 Main St.
East Rochester, NY 14445
(716) 248-9150
Product(s) : *Wordfinder*

Index

Index

Edited by Marianne Krcma